Faith and Frenzy

Kev Richardson

A Wings ePress, Inc.
Historical Novel

Wings ePress, Inc.

Edited by: Karen Babcock
Copy Edited by: Jeanne Smith
Senior Editor: Pat Evans
Executive Editor: Marilyn Kapp
Cover Artist: Trisha FitzGerald

All rights reserved

Names, characters and incidents depicted in this book are products of the author's imagination or are used fictitiously. Any resemblance to actual events, locales, organizations, or persons, living or dead, is entirely coincidental and beyond the intent of the author or the publisher.

No part of this book may be reproduced or transmitted in any form or by any means, electronic or mechanical, including photocopying, recording, or by any information storage and retrieval system, without permission in writing from the publisher.

Wings ePress Books
www.wingsepress.com

Copyright © 2013 by Kevin Richardson
ISBN-13: 978-1-61309-876-9
ISBN-10: 1-61309-876-6

Published In the United States Of America

Wings ePress Inc.
3000 N. Rock Road
Newton, KS 67114

What They Are Saying About Faith and Frenzy

In **Faith and Frenzy**, Kev Richardson, proven storyteller, transports you into the middle ages, into hearts and minds of bewildered innocents as their world erupts. Hadn't Englanders had enough of invaders, the Vikings, Normans, Picts and Scots without their world now erupting in religious mayhem and civil war?

Richardson paints anguish, ordeal and dolour as families opt for different sides. Can either win?

Another fine work from this writer's canny sense of perception.

Libby Abbott,
Aussie e-Book Reviews

5+ Stars!

Multi-published historical writer, **Kev Richardson**'s slant on 17th Century history comes across as very personally realistic, as factions of the ruling classes fight to maintain a hold on religious beliefs. In **Faith And Frenzy** he introduces Richard Bray, wife, Beatrix and their extensive family who live through and survive England's bloody Civil War.

If you like to live the history you're reading, this book is extremely well presented. I highly recommend it.

JoEllen, Conger
CongerBook Reviews, USA

Dedication

My thanks to sister Valerie Greenhalgh and cousin Desolie Lady Hurley for not only encouragement but help in assembling known remnants of these histories.

Also to Francis Howcutt of London (Brixworth Historian, Bray Family), *Lynn Shumway of Cumbria* (Burgess One-Name Society), *Linda Huntingdon of Lancaster* (Fothergill and Adamthwait Families), *Caroline Morris of Cumbria* (Ravenstonedale Parish History Group) *and Dr. David Parsons FSA,* Emeritus Reader in Church Archaeology, University of Leicester *(on* All Saints, *Brixworth).*

Also to The Fothergills of Ravenstonedale: their Lives and Letters *by Catherine Thornton and Frances McLaughlin; Wm.Heinemann, London 1905*

* * *

Preface

During the sixteenth and seventeenth centuries, England's people had two calamitous barriers to hurdle, decisions to tear at the heart of every man and woman. They threatened to divide parents from children, sibling from sibling, village and town from village and town.

Faith: During the early 1500s, the young Henry VIII took as bride Katherine of Aragon, daughter of the very Catholic King Ferdinand of Spain's Aragon. Henry then, in the name of Holy Rome, triumphed over Scotland. The Church held England in such high regard that the Pope proclaimed Henry "Defender of the Faith."

On the European Continent, however, factions were breaking away from Roman doctrine. The voice of Protestant Luther was being loudly hailed. Henry, basking in papal glory, would have none of it. Lutheran missionaries arriving in England were burned at the stake as heretics.

Yet Henry was to then suffer the trauma of seeing all four precious male heirs Katherine bore either miscarried, stillborn, or dying within days. Distraught, he beseeched the Pope to annul his marriage so he might take a more fertile wife. Yet after considerable delay during which the impatient Henry fumed, even siring a bastard son to a mistress, the Pope said, "No." Henry then requested the Pope legitimise his bastard son, but the Pope again declined.

Henry needed a legitimate heir so badly, in order that the Tudor name continue, that this feted paragon of Rome's vestal priesthood turned his back on the Church. He proclaimed henceforth Protestant, not only himself but, in that Tudor dogma held that sovereignty was God-given power, his entire kingdom—with himself the spiritual head of his new Church of England. All English people were overnight declared no longer Roman Catholics but Anglicans.

"And God help any who fail to conform," Henry further proclaimed.

He then annulled his marriage and took a new bride.

The edict drove broad wedges into Christian breasts, for two monumental problems of faith then faced every English soul.

In a world where all had harboured unqualified support for the faith Rome dictated, spiritually uniting all, the all-powerful King of England demanded reform. He decreed that every man, woman, and child in his realm deny it and adopt a faith denying papal support. Most, however, had yet to discover the new faith's very disposition.

When the clergy objected, royal guards responded with slashing swords and flailing axes. Catholic priests and nuns were in the instant guilty of treason, which meant being burned as heretics. Nor did the dissolution of Catholicism stop at foul murder of the clergy. Papist trappings of churches and cathedrals throughout the land were vandalised.

Henry then waged successful war on Catholic France, adding much of that land to his local triumphs. Could any soul not but believe that outrage and terrible retribution would befall the entire nation? That the Pope would call down frenzies from heaven on the English 'heretics'?

And no less kind for Henry's slight against a Spanish royal daughter was the King of Spain. The super-power of the then-Christian world declared Henry and his realm number one enemy of both Spain and Catholicism.

Frenzy: Changing religion divided more than common families; it divided Henry's heirs. This led to questions of royal power dividing people and districts into those supporting rule by royal decree and those favouring parliamentary power. Royalty lost considerable popularity amongst the power-mongers, and with the bickering over religion, many people became political converts—or even dissented from religion of any kind. Such divisions led to a series of frenzied wars: England's war with Spain, insurgence in Ireland and Scotland, and two civil wars between Anglican factions in England. Different families in different communities found themselves at odds with their normal world in many forms.

This tale illustrates how two such families found themselves on different sides of the same problems.

~ * ~

Seven miles north of Northampton City lies the Parish of Brixworth, its church in the times already unique in two respects. Not only was its Abbot recording baptisms, nuptials and burials more than a century prior to English law making it compulsory, but its very ironstone rocks and mortar were unique. All Saints Brixworth was, and remains, a Saxon gem.

When Vikings were raiding England's northern counties during the ninth and tenth centuries, All Saints was already old. This architectural pearl of history built in AD 680 is not only the world's largest surviving Anglo-Saxon building, but also the best-preserved. It is indeed large. Its tower, a lookout to warn of Viking raiders, was for several centuries the midland's tallest structure. It dominates its Brixworth hilltop and after one thousand three hundred years still services the village devout.

Its earliest year of surviving records includes the baptism of daughter Agnes to a William Bray on 12 June 1568. And Bray was a significant name in Brixworth in the troublesome time of choosing between Catholic and Protestant on the one hand, and Royal or Parliamentary decree on the other. The Bray family's experience of the Civil War years was indeed representative of how the war affected all English families supporting Parliament.

Brixworth Parish was, in coincidental fact, site of the final battlefield in England's First Civil War.

The events and time of England's faith and frenzy all had immense influence on the life of Richard Bray.

~ * ~

In England's far north, in the then county of Westmorland, life was considerably rural and population small. The largely Nordic descendants from Viking days in its Eden Valley were far less influenced by politics than brethren south. Royal decree was the only path the people were used to, so most cared little for the 'new' thing called Parliament. More than any other area of England, those of the far north not only readily accepted conversion to the Protestant faith simply because the King demanded it but, come the Civil Wars, remained steadfastly Royal.

With so much of its population of Nordic descent, family names developed from Nordic language. From *fodder* (animal feed) and *ghyll* (deep ravine), came the common Westmorland name of Fothergill. From *thwait* (ship), came Adamthwait (sometimes with an 'e'). From *bus* (carriage) and *feld* (field), came Busfeld in a variety of spellings.

Whilst the Fothergill, Adamthwait, and Busfeld families in this tale had less interest in England's politics than their countrymen farther south, they however had another highly disruptive influence in their lives.

The Eden Valley, for the same reason that it is today's major highway between England and Scotland, was then the route taken by invading Scots. It is the only valley between the rugged Cumbrian Highlands and the impossible Pennines. Scots envied the food and livestock grown on Westmorland farms, and the savagery of their invasions over centuries caused unbelievable horror and panic amongst the people, not to mention the incessant dread of waiting, wondering when the next would befall them.

Come the Civil Wars, they again found their valley a highway for opposing armies appropriating not only food, livestock and shelter along their path, but every man of an age to wield cutlass, pike, longbow or musket. The result each time was, in a war over politics and religion, frenzied bloodshed and mayhem.

~ * ~

Brixworth...

Willie Bray was, in the 1530s but a babe in arms when King Henry died after a succession of five wives had, between them, given him an only son. Willie was only vaguely aware, as he grew, that the sickly Prince Edward held the throne under a Regent. He was also conscious of his parents' interest in William Caxton's timely invention of the printing press from which Cranmer's translation for the new *English Prayer Book* was widely circulated, quickly followed by the *English Bible*. Both became required texts for religious services in the realm. The boy King, prompted by his advisors, adopted a ruthlessly anti-Catholic stance. He declared Latin liturgies illegal on punishment of death. Young William Bray's family reacted to these decrees with some reservation.

"We can but assume that whatever many of the populace want to believe, it is behove on us to accede to Royal Decree," declared his father. "Surely, faith aside, we must accede even if only for the security of life and family."

The fear complex was such a common philosophy that the law took advantage of it.

Leaders maintained the pressure for change by torture and terrible death.

History records that in the times, whipping of errant wives and children was commonplace. Each village had its whipping post, and justices of the peace were assigned to every village to ensure adherents of the old faith were publicly punished for denying the new. Town stocks were common—sometimes stocks to hold the head captive, others to trap only the ankles. A favourite punishment for errant women was the water-chair in which the woman was confined, then hoisted above the village pond and 'dunked' for various numbers of seconds or minutes, for a varying number of times, subject to her sentence.

Treason called for the culprit to be hanged, drawn and quartered—killed by hanging, then the body stretched tightly on the rack whilst chopped into four quarters to be dragged behind horses to unmarked common graves. The head was retained for mounting on a pike in the town square for everyone to gawk at.

Recalcitrant clerics suffered harsher torture. They were burned to death.

It was into such an emotionally distressed environment that every family's children were being raised, their perceptions of life influenced by it.

When Willie Bray married at Brixworth's All Saints and named his first son Henry, it publicly declared his family King's adherents.

Then when in 1553, the fifteen-year-old King Edward died of consumption, those close to the court, having warning of the inevitable end for more than a year, had plans for succession already made. The throne was willed to Lady Jane Grey, the boy King's cousin. Bypassed in the young King's testament were both half-sisters—highly likely because Mary was Catholic and Elizabeth Protestant. Choosing one could well have delivered the nation into civil war on religious grounds. Mary Queen of Scots, daughter of the late King James V of Scotland, another Catholic, was a third unsuccessful contender.

Lady Jane was, like the deceased King, still a minor, so must also rule under the late Edward's Protector of the Realm, the Duke of Northumberland.

Yet the succession was not to eventuate.

Twenty-eight-year-old Willie Bray would have scratched his head.

"Mary Tudor will nae accept being bypassed, Mother," he informed his wife.

Since his son Henry's birth, he had taken to calling his wife, again large with another child, Mother. She quite accepted her wifely duty of bearing her man's children, raising the daughters and presiding over his table when entertaining, all the while outwardly accepting his opinions, whether believing them valid or not. When out of his hearing, however, she would ensure her daughters grew up conscious of her private opinions. At the same time, of course, their brothers were being influenced by their father's beliefs. So families became divided.

"The cryer claims, Mother, that Mary Tudor doth promise, if given the throne, religious tolerance. People may practise their chosen faith. He claims that in London and the eastern counties, she hath strong support, particularly being the first-born of Henry Tudor."

Mary assembled an army and marched on London, demanding a hearing. She had enough supporters to back her claim that a Lady Jane Grey appointment would lead to civil war. Her voice was heard by Parliament, and on the basis of her promises Mary was crowned Queen of England, a title embodying her England's religious head.

She promptly despatched the complaining Lady Jane Grey to the Tower of London—the 'prison of no return.' And when Mary then sent Protestant Archbishop Cranmer along with many of his bishops to the Tower, a rebellious Protestant mob marched from the archbishop's See of Canterbury. It was ruthlessly crushed by Mary, who then had Lady Jane Grey beheaded. This put paid to hopes of a further claim. And to make doubly sure, Mary had her Protestant half-sister Elizabeth placed under house detention in the palace at Woodstock.

"Would anyone dare question," William Bray quietly asked, "that Mary Tudor may have misled the people when promising religious tolerance?"

So was even William Bray becoming somewhat disenamoured of Royal Decree?

Within a year, in June 1554, Spain's King Philip arrived and married Queen Mary, cementing England even closer, again, to Rome.

"Will England now be partly ruled by Spain?" William likely asked of trusted friends.

In London, Protestant Englanders, in turn, rose in a clamour, with much sabre-rattling in the name of God.

"Hath there not been enough of our country's virile men, sons and brothers, slain during Henry's forever wars in Scotland and Normandy in the name of God? And enough bishops and adherents of either religion already burned or beheaded?"

"And what now of succession? Any heir will be Catholic," mooted William's neighbour James Burgess, another Anglican supporter and William Bray's confidant.

"The pendulum of Christian England is simply swinging again, James. Messengers from London tell me thousands of moneyed Protestants are fleeing to Lutheran Saxony, Protestant Holland or Switzerland."

"Convenient it is for the wealthy to flee, William, but what about the penniless? Nor can we of the land simply walk off farms that are our livelihood."

Simmering divisions in every village began to boil. In most parishes, one faith or the other found itself dominant and in those where Catholicism held sway, Protestants watched their village church stripped of its revered trappings, to be adorned with Catholic, and accordingly rededicated. They no longer had a church in which to pray; nor have newborns received by God into their chosen faith. It brought considerable disharmony.

"All Saints fortunately remains untouched. But for how long, I wonder?"

"Just think, now, how many births and marriages cannot be openly celebrated, let alone recorded. Nor burials. I have great fears for our future."

~ * ~

However that changed when, in November 1554, England was officially received back into the Papal bosom. Parliament in London won the concession that England retain its landed rights to Church properties that Henry VIII had wrested from Rome, which at least held the Christian real estate in English hands, yet Roman priests were now appointed to every parish. Protestant churches were no longer tolerated.

Those who raised objections, including Archbishop Cranmer, were burned at the stake "that their heretical souls be destroyed along with their flesh."

"This be how Bloody Mary fulfils her promise of religious tolerance," was whispered between Bray and Burgess ears, along with countless thousands of others throughout the land.

In January 1558, Calais, England's last outpost on the continent, was under attack from the French. A combined English-Spanish force held the port; when the French attacked, Philip of Spain, the very husband of England's Queen, withdrew his forces. Impossibly outnumbered, the English were routed, and Calais, England's gateway to European markets, was lost to Catholic France.

Sick and dispirited, with most of her people by now ranged against her, Mary died, and her half-sister, the Protestant Elizabeth, succeeded to the throne.

Burnings ceased, and the country began, yet again, a reversal of religious doctrine.

The people again faced the 'as you were' direction. After initial heated arguments, factions in villages gradually, as Elizabeth established a thirty-year peace amongst the nobility, regained their own domestic peace. The varying religions began to learn to live together. And with the wealth derived from her proceeds of privateer seamen and her brazen stance against the threat of war with Spain, the country prospered. England progressively achieved mastery of the seas, and the people enjoyed the benefits of prosperity and plenty.

"Good Queen Bess!" resounded throughout the, at last, mostly united land.

It was to be a long, successful reign by Elizabeth. Yet time was to illustrate it was the Anglican religion that was proving the more popular, because it was proving the least restrictive religious regimen. And because it was now the Royal preference.

~ * ~

In 1580, the people heard of the adventurer Sir Francis Drake returning from the wild scheme he had embarked on to "prove the world is round." The stupid fellow had reckoned that, by sailing ever westward, he would arrive back in England from its east.

"A madness," the people proclaimed, enjoying their heartiest laugh in years.

"Madman incarnate," he was dubbed.

One can imagine the Brays and Burgesses of Brixworth, as well as the Fothergills, Adamthwaits and Busfelds of little Ravenstonedale in Westmorland, would bandy such chatter amongst themselves. Villagers across the land ridiculed the absurdity of such a suggestion and here, there and everywhere, turned back to the meaningful tasks of tilling land and nurturing children. Then, when Drake came home, arriving from the east as prophesised, he became the darling of England. Yet we might imagine that for a long time, many would be shaking heads over it being true, when all had expected he could never be heard of again.

Of course what today's world still fails to realize is that Drake did not discover how the sun sets in the west. The sun never moves. What he saw each evening was earth's horizons rising!

Yet on the downside of this happy period in England, the buoyant times of Good Queen Bess, it was gradually realised that prices of the few commodities rural people needed coin to buy were escalating. It was a thing called 'inflation,' the usurers told them, though few could grasp the concept. It seemed that Spain was reaping so much gold and so many gemstones from its colonies in the Americas, a place so remote that few knew of it, that this 'inflation' had spread throughout Europe and had then reached England. Many believed it a phenomenon like the black plague that had similarly spread from Europe to England in a previous lifetime.

Yet the bubble of prosperity gradually reached bursting point, and the poor suffered most, for they had then to forego the few luxuries their few pennies could once buy. But when at the same time Sir Walter Raleigh introduced tobacco, many began taking a little more interest in this America place. Traders then ventured to the western coast of South America, returning with not only tomatoes but potatoes in great variety, both offering taste sensations to greatly enhance boring English fare.

"If only we had the pennies to buy them," people wailed.

However, adventurous farmers began buying and planting them.

Then joy was expressed by some and cautious fear by others when Good Queen Bess had her cousin, the Catholic Mary Queen of Scots, who had been held captive for several years, beheaded for treason. Mary had been plotting with Spain against her cousin. And well might the more aware Englishmen have trembled when the outraged King Philip of Spain, already piqued at Elizabeth's support of privateer sea captains 'pirating' his galleons on the high seas and plundering cargoes of gold and gems, vowed vengeance.

He called for extra effort to have his armada built the quicker that he could invade heretic England. Spain would colonise that rogue state and return it to the yolk of Rome.

England was in mortal danger of not only losing its liberty, but the people would again be forced to choose between Catholicism or burning at the stake.

BOOK ONE:

Fear Rules Faith

One

Brixworth, Northamptonshire, 1586

"My father was named Henry after the infamous King. Your father's name means nowt. When did England ever have a King James?"

"Never. But why did your father name you Richard and not Henry?"

"Richard was the name of my mother's father. However, 'tis likely my father shall name his next son Henry. Besides, I like the sound of my name. Richard Bray has a pleasing ring to it."

"And Henry Bray doesn't?"

"That is by the way. Why did your father name you Leyton and not James?"

"I don't know. But as first born, I shall certainly inherit Burgess Manor."

"And I shall as certainly inherit Bray House."

We were ensconced in the Bray tree house, built in a fork of a centuries-old oak by my grandparents or even earlier. Whilst we had outgrown it, it remained the only safe haven from my sisters. Lettice at eight and Agnes at three were quite without sense. They simply failed as companions. Leyton had the same problem, so despite lack of leg room, the tree house remained our only refuge.

We had been bosom buddies since playing with wooden swords and both realised by then, that with each due to inherit our homes, we would remain neighbours for the rest of our lives. *We quite felt akin to brothers.*

By springtime, it was clear Philip of Spain was building a fleet to invade England, and we were agog at the looming adventure.

"I am unsure about invasion," declared Leyton. "Invasion is one country crossing the border of its neighbour, killing all who resist. Yet Spain and England share no border, do they now?"

I sighed in frustration. "Leyton, dear friend, this be why King Philip builds so many ships. He must ship cannon and horses as well as soldiers. They need be so large that my father calls them galleons."

Neither of us had seen a ship other than in paintings. Ships and vast oceans left as many questions in our minds as did politics.

"I wonder why King Philip hates England so."

"Leyton, ye remain so naïve for a ten-year-old. Thank the heavens I am older, which makes me wiser!"

I tried stretching my legs, yet the far wall resisted. I instead drew up my knees, clasping arms about them. I noticed a small hole in my left stocking spreading towards the knee but ignored it. I was beginning to feel even more superior. The extra year I had on Leyton was an undeniable advantage.

"I know all about it, Leyton. I knew ye would have questions, so just ask away. Anything."

"Well the Queen has been a long time on the throne, Richard. Why only now does King Philip decide on war?"

"Oh, dear Leyton, know ye nowt? We've been already at war with Spain a twelve-month."

Leyton shrugged. I certainly had the advantage.

"It has until now, however, been a naval war. Each side builds more ships as old ones sink. Spain builds big ships to carry so much gold and jewels from the Americas. England builds small ships which are more manoeuvrable. Our cannon fire can be much closer to the water-line of big ships."

"How do ye know all this?"

"My father tells me."

"How does he know?"

"He goes to Lodge meetings where they talk about such things."

"Did he tell why King Philip so hates the English?"

"Of course. He tells me everything."

"Then why?"

"Because the Queen's father changed our religion."

"Yes, but her sister Mary changed it back."

"Mary died. Then Queen Elizabeth changed it back again."

"All that was so long ago. Everyone should have forgotten it by now."

"Well they haven't. And there's another reason."

"What? The treasure Spain steals from the Americas?"

I had to think about that. I daren't lose the height I'd gained.

"The Spaniards say they do not steal it. They claim America belongs to Spain."

"Did the people just give it to them?"

"I think not. Spain won them in a war, so they don't call it stealing."

"What, then, do they think stealing is?"

"They call Sir Francis Drake a pirate, that he steals their gold."

"Well, he does."

"Yes, but he's not a pirate."

"What is he, then?"

"A privateer."

"What's the difference?"

Fragments of such a conversation over the Bray House dinner table sprang to my mind.

"Sir Francis Drake's ships do not fly the English flag. He owns his ships and calls himself a privateer. He doesn't take prisoners or rape women."

Oh, I just hope Leyton doesn't question me on that last bit. It just slipped out.

Leyton didn't. "My father says Queen Elizabeth helps Sir Francis with money and ships because he gives her much of the Spanish gold."

"How does your father know that?"

"Because he goes to Lodge with your father."

We put our arms around each other.

"We already know fathers tell us only half things. Maybe your father tells you one half and mine tells me the other. We must keep in careful touch."

We each felt somewhat defeated, so shook hands on it and climbed down to stretch our legs.

Two

"Bloody hell!"

Rainold Fothergill swore often. An intolerant man, his temper was always on a short fuse.

Life in Westmorland during the sixteenth century had not been easy, even for gentry, and he liked to consider himself gentry. Physical conditions were harsh. The terrain was mountainous and winters bitterly cold. Even livestock must be housed indoors twenty-four hours a day when outdoors was invariably deep in snow.

Ravenstonedale, an isolated village in the Eden Valley, where it was at least possible to farm cattle, snuggled into a fold of the Pennine Fells. The River Eden lay not too far distant, yet the village had no road, save cart-tracks, to anywhere. West towards the Irish Sea, the Lakes District was so mountainous and rocky that roads were not even possible. Nor was agriculture possible. And eastwards, at Ravenstonedale's back, the Pennine Range was an impassable rocky barrier.

The village was vulnerable, however, to the only pathway north to Scotland on the western side of the Pennines. Marauding Scots, during summer months when travel was possible, satisfied their envy of the pastures by pillaging. Even murder was their habit.

Yet in the moment, it was not invading Scots who incurred Rainold's displeasure; it was his younger son.

"Hain't a man peril enough in life without playthings left where 'e can stumble on 'em, just to climb bloody steps to 'is own bloody house?"

He bellowed for the maid whose job it was to supervise the twins.

His wife Isabell, daughter of the miller Fawcett, had quickly after their marriage delivered him, much to his satisfaction, two sons, Nicolas and Steven. Then just two years ago, twins—daughter and son. It was this third son whose toy, a wooden horse and dray, had caused his stumble.

Nicolas had died an infant, so Steven filled Rainold's need of knowing a son was coming along to one day fill working shoes as help on the farm. Also to inherit Tarn House, a village landmark that had been in the family for centuries.

Whilst daughter Issaybell was a joy for Rainold to behold, as were all only daughters, it was her twin, Maythew, who became the apple of his father's eye.

A wee bit o' coddlin' and cuddlin' o' a boy gi'es a man a sense o' indulgence rather than power, his alter-ego insisted.

It be like candy on the tongue—that's what it be like, he invariably replied to those who remarked on it.

Servant girl Anny scurried down the steps from the cookhouse and patiently listened to his chastisement. She was by now used to her master needing to get blathering and bustling off his chest in times of trauma.

Then, after having massaged his barked shin, he stomped past her up the three gentle steps to the cookhouse door.

Anny stooped and gathered up the offending toy.

"It be normal for a two-year-old deserting what was last minute's interest, when some-it else grabs 'is eye," she muttered to herself. She had no idea what the some-it may have been on this occasion, nor even where the boy had now got to...

"But the dogs won't never leave 'im," she said to the lad's mother, who came to the door from inside, dusting floured hands on her apron. "So he be in no danger, no matter where he be run off to."

When Isabell Fothergill saw the innocent nature of the problem, she but shrugged a shoulder and gave Anny a knowing grin. Then she returned to her baking.

The house was comfortable. Entirely of stone, as were all northern houses, Tarn House had been one of the district's earliest, in the family more generations than any could yet count. "A long time!" was the popular expression. Nor could their neighbours count. Education animal style, a 'let them learn by watching' attitude, was almost universal in the district—learning letters and numbers much rarer. Two other Fothergill families were near neighbours, one in Lockholme, the other in Brownber—both brothers of Rainold. Tarn House was two-storied with rooms enough for comfortable living when the several months of snow were even too thick for going to church on Sundays. There were also, of course, the usual 'work' buildings.

The cookhouse and fuel-store had a raised slate pathway with 'ambulatory' type shelter to the right of the house, while the sizeable byre had the same to the left. The byre, nicknamed 'Cow-House' by Rainold, housed not only all the cattle in winter and hogs and chickens for the table but stable and farm workshop. Fieldmice in the byre, however, outnumbered all other inhabitants to remain a nuisance that decried answer. Beyond the byre were billets for resident workers, although most farm staff were people of the village who came in daily.

Also in the byre was the water well and pump, alongside which was the trapdoor to the 'safety-cellar,' covered by a carpet and carefully placed furniture. The 'safety-cellar' hid children, women and older sons when the Scots invaded. Mostly they continued down the valley into Yorkshire, yet they occasionally forayed the mile to Ravenstonedale seeking food—and, in wartime, to cashier men of fighting age to join their ranks. Refusal meant death, so the opposition army couldn't cashier them.

Only parents remained in sight to meet forces that would ransack the house for whatever could be carried away and ransack the byre for whatever appealed, purloining livestock to take with them for tomorrow's meals. Only if luck and maybe age be with the parents wouldn't there be danger for them, providing they didn't resist. If the young people were found, however, there would be rape as well as murder. Either way, the family would be left the poorer and much distressed.

Right now, however, in the cook-house, Isabell was helping the staff bake bread and cooking up a stew of hog's-head and carrots, sliced green apple and fistfuls of mint and rosemary.

"Smells monstrous attractive, Mother," Rainold told her as she doctored his wound.

"We be yet to add treacle, husband," she informed him. "The aroma when the boilin' is done will then be even more tantalising to 'ee nostrils."

She knew him for a sweet-tooth and catered accordingly.

Few other families comprised the village, so intermarriage into Adamthwait, Fawcett and Busfeld clans over the centuries had abounded, making entire villages blood-related, as were near all nearby towns. Westmorland was simply that sort of district, large in acreage yet sparsely peopled. If a family had too many sons to make a living from the farms, some would move into the towns. Kirkby Stephen, Appleby, Tebay, Orton and Brough were not too far distant.

All considered Kendal, the county capital and largest town, far too far away to be even considered. Few had travelled all those twenty miles. Each local community was its own little hamlet hub with separate small churches making each its own parish. Brough-Under-Stainmore even had its own ruined castle—a feature giving it particular status.

"But being seven or eight miles off makes it hardly local," Rainold would insist.

Churches were community centres. Parishioners flocked to church on Sundays, not only to pray but share news and gossip. Women would gather here while men gathered there. Children would romp and play hide and seek amongst the gravestones. After service, men would assemble by the sundial where those with news from 'outside' could disseminate it. It was the only 'newscast' service the people had, yet few speakers seemed to have more than rumour.

"And how many times has the tale been told before reaching here?" all would wonder.

"Enough to ensure there be little truth left," the more practical would respond.

Yet each rumour seemed basis enough to begin fresh rumours. And even they were pounced upon.

"Sometimes I wish more strangers would visit," Rainold would complain. "That way, Mother, we would have better opportunity of hearing firsthand what new laws the Queen has made."

"Only to leave us again, with the same question, Husband—how much credence can we put on it being the same as that wot left the palace?"

Three

A year later...

A tremble ran down my spine.

Every Sunday morning the family attended service at All Saints. I could never claim it the highlight of my week, but on this occasion Vicar Mabbutt announced from the pulpit that he would not present his prepared sermon.

"I shall instead report from a tract issued from the palace. It is on the recent exploits of Vice-Admiral Sir Francis Drake."

Leyton and I habitually sat together in church, an indulgence depending on good behaviour. On hearing this, we nudged knuckles into each other's thighs, stifling urges to cheer. Vicar Mabbutt's usual drone took on a more exciting air.

"Our intrepid Sir Francis, following the announcement of royal spies that Spain is using Cadiz Harbour to moor, fit out and provision large galleons, embarked on a venture to 'Singe the King of Spain's Beard.'"

Goose-bumps on my arms added to the trembles up and down my spine.

"He sailed with a considerable fleet of small ships, not to engage Spaniards in a naval duel, but to loose fire-ships amongst the vast fleet in Cadiz harbour. He indeed surprised the unsuspecting Spaniards. With the wind behind him, he despatched under full sail scores of small ships loaded with inflammable cargo already aflame. The helpless galleons at anchor, with no sail spread, were all soon entirely ablaze. Sir Francis, with surprisingly little damage to his own ships, returned to England a hero."

The congregation, to a man, rose to its feet, applauding.

"The result of the Sir Francis raid," Vicar Mabbutt then announced, "has rendered King Philip unable to attack England for a considerable time. He must start again."

After service, sons and daughters filed out with their parents so that as a family, we could pay respects to the Vicar. Yet once that duty was performed, all lads gathered to celebrate Drake's daredevil victory.

"What will happen now?"

"Nothing at all. The vicar said Spain must start again."

"We are still at war. Who will make the next move, then?"

"Spain must have a large force, for England is two weeks' sail from Spain."

"Two weeks? Transporting water and food for such an army for so many days?"

"All the armaments and horses his troops will need will mean hundreds of ships."

"Hundreds of big ships."

"As well as supply ships to keep his army fed."

"And horses fed."

"Well, Sir Francis has just burned those plans to cinders."

Among adults over ensuing weeks it also remained the main topic of conversation, mostly across family supper tables, someone during the day having attended the Brixworth square to hear what the cryer had to report. The same was true among household staff in kitchens. And in barber-shops, haberdasheries and ale-houses.

The waiting proved nail-biting. Everyone knew it was coming, and every month's passing meant arrival was drawing closer. England spent the period arming itself and building fortifications along its southern shores and strings of signal fires. Fiery beacons from hilltop to hilltop into the north would summon help.

This was the time when Queen Elizabeth's spies discovered that the Catholic Mary Queen of Scots was, from her prison cell, in secret communication with the Spanish crown. Intercepted letters proved Mary was plotting to have England's preparations sabotaged.

The Queen had Mary tried and beheaded for treason.

"Apart from anything else, Leyton, it is the main Catholic contender for England's crown now out of the way, should Spain win the war."

"Spain win the war?" Leyton cried. He was quickly afoot, snatching the toy pistol he kept tucked in the sash of his tunic. "I challenge you to a duel!"

I too, jumped up. Standing a head taller gave me the advantage. I simply knocked the wooden pistol from his hand.

"You lost, but I can be lenient. I will have my spies teach you how foolish it is to challenge your betters. Apologise, and you can go free."

"All right. But one day I could be bigger than you. I apologise for now."

I wrapped my arm around his shoulder. "For one so young, friend, you have a manly head on your shoulders. You are forgiven."

Yet is this letting him out of it all too easily?

"But remember, even if bigger, I will still be older, therefore wiser. You can never win."

For month after month, the entire country spent its time awaiting the call to rush support south, preparing. To a man, except of course the minority of Catholics who surely prayed for the armada's success, all were sharpening pikes and lances, whittling oaken arrow shafts for iron heads and feathered tails. Men were drilled in hand-to-hand combat. All stood ready to face what they expected to be heavily armoured Spaniards.

England was indeed poorly equipped to combat an invading force with cannon and cavalry, yet patriotism ran high.

Good Queen Bess travelled many miles giving stirring speeches to the faithful, putting the fear of Catholic inquisition into every man.

Spies had done their jobs well, and Sir Francis Drake had his ships, not nearly so numerous as the Spanish but designed for swift tacking and close encounter. Both allowed for more accurate cannonades.

With them, he waited in Plymouth harbour pending the coast-watcher's cry.

~ * ~

With religious differences waning as Elizabeth's rule lengthened, tension throughout the land abated. Faith continued strengthening in favour of Protestantism, and allegiance to Royal Decree continued to satisfy the faithful. On the surface of things, dissidents seemed few.

Little Ravenstonedale, however, had one with a perverse outlook on things. Old Symon Busfeld found fault in every neighbour's opinion on seemingly everything. Argument continued bolstering him into an even greater misfit. Some said he thrived on being simply perverse to whatever seemed acceptable to the majority.

Yet in small villages, such differences went by the board when it came down to realities, so it was a Busfeld daughter that Rainold Fothergill brought in as extra house-help when Isabell was again with child. And this time, poorly with it.

"It is due in the winter, Husband," she warned him. "I worry the snow may keep the midwife from Kirkby Stephen getting to me. My last was difficult because it was twins, and there be no knowing until it happens. With these pains, it could this time be three."

She waited to see if he would comment on her humour, yet he made none.

"We'll be needing a strong woman," she insisted. "If it again be twins and the lifting not done right, results can be damning. Prayer cannot help."

Yet it failed to reach that stage. Late in her confinement, Isabell became violently ill. A physician was brought from Kirkby Stephen yet could do nowt to stop her incessant vomiting but apply poultices and let blood. She became weaker each day and finally succumbed. Her largely pregnant body was interred at St. Oswalds as winter snows were already beginning.

"A man canna rear three bairns so young, Will," Rainold declared at the wake. His friend and neighbour Will Adamthwait was always a tower of strength. "And where do a man find, after this, faith enough to seek God's guidance? He be treatin' me poorly, and I canna imagine the reason."

"Be it that'ee never give 'ee last three the baptism, Rainold? Maybe the Lord be lookin' unkindly on 'ee over that?"

"Ach, man, he dinna seem to mind, when Issaybell and Maythew came, that Steven weren't ever baptised. Did 'ee not now?"

"Aye, ye be right at that. But maybe for one lapse 'ee can make exception, yet three be two too many?"

"Bloody hell, man! Reason I didna baptise them was God takin' Nicolas, who be proper baptised. It were Isabell said Nicolas be likely took because we made him Protestant. Ye know the Fawcett clan be ever waverin' on religion. All over the county, some brothers be takin' their family branches one way while others take th'other."

"But Isabell was ever with 'ee on religion man—Protestant to the core."

Rainold held up a restraining palm. "Aye. Ever she was indeed." He blessed himself yet again. "But maybe her mind retained inherited doubt. Did 'ee know she sometimes had me hear her confession? Sure she deferred to me when we married, went along too, with Nicolas bein' Anglican when Matt Fawcett was Catholic. She had many arguments with her pa over that. She be realisin', I reckon, that once Elizabeth took the throne, there be no goin' backwards. Protestant glue would stick. But maybe some deep-down part of Isabell be still feelin' Papist. So maybe ye be right—maybe the Lord be settin' limits."

"But 'ee need get thee a wife, friend. As 'ee say, bairns need a mother. And 'ee need a woman to gi' thee more sons."

Two months after burying Isabell, Rainold married Dorrytye Chamberlaine of nearby Tebay.

Four

The air throughout England was tainted with rumour.

Rather than honeysuckle, violet, daffodil and roses, it was conflicting facts getting up everyone's noses as well as ears.

"I heard that Spaniards have landed in Cornwall."

"I heard that so many Spaniards have been put ashore in England's south that every town on the English Channel coast has already fallen."

"I heard that Spanish troops are still marching through France, to invade Kent from Calais."

Leyton and I were wishing we were older by five years.

"Oh, to join the Dragoons, Leyton. Just think of the adventure!"

"Not the Dragoons, Richard. The arquebusiers. They fire a lead ball at twenty paces, to pierce even armour. How can the Spanish win a war against the arquebusier?"

"I've heard of them. Highwaymen are rumoured to carry them, but its matchlock can be suspect. That could put you in a sticky situation."

"But we have a cutlass at our belt."

"A cutlass against armour? Sirrah! Give me the Dragoons and a ten-foot lance. A fire-breathing steed under a man's saddle, and the world is his."

"Once a lance has impaled a man, armour or not, what weapon is one left with?"

"The cutlass still. And dagger for when 'tis hand to hand."

"And if your horse goes down behind the Spanish line and you are surrounded?"

"In the same pickle you'd be in with your arquebusier when its matchlock fails."

We fell to the floor, rolling in laughter.

~ * ~

Rainold Fothergill closed the door to his little study. With window shutters closed against winter sleet, it was lit by a lone candle.

Study? Where did I hear that name for a room where a man might sit to consider privy thoughts?

He looked about, not really expecting that this time it might look bigger, yet maybe to give him fresh inspiration for handling worries. The room was but the height of a tall man in both directions, enough for a small desk and a small chair. A wooden shelf hung on the wall over the desk.

Study? And a shelf for what, when a man hath neither letters nor numbers?

So neither paper, ink nor quill were on the desk.

Yet knowing it for the only study in the village gave him a sense of extra height.

Extra to the height Fothergills and Adamthwaits between them seemed to enjoy over most in the village.

It was a satisfaction of sorts in the life of a man who, beyond awareness that two sons lived and his only daughter lived, had nowt else to inspire life since Isabell died.

But not all kinder are yet past the age of five, he mused. *Issaybell and Maythew have yet to see their fourth birthday.*

So he was a man still insecure.

What else be there, in a shire like Westmorland, to make a man feel proud?

The Eden Valley? Surely a land that is God's gift to Englishmen. Yet one the Scots see as God's gift to Englishmen at the expense of

Scots? So a man cannot avoid problems. Why should I surrender me riches to Scots?

His mind pondered deeply on the question that had bugged him all his life.

Yet the bloody Scots, happy too that they've left behind the yolk of Papal problems, insist they want nowt of Anglican religion. Protestant they may be, yet of their own Presbyterian faction. Damn me, but they be insufferable wretches.

He sat and scratched his thinning hair which succeeded in only giving him other worries. He resented every quarter inch of his hair that Dorrytye would so painstakingly trim, keeping only long the little ponytail that added pride.

His hair was russet in colour.

"Descended from the red-squirrels, I be," he would jest to friends.

He even wore to church each Sunday a wig the village wig-maker made from his very own hair. It bothered him nowt that the very people who saw him wearing a wig on Sundays were the same who saw him every other day without it.

When abroad, rather than the wig, he wore the biggest 'cavalier' hat in the village, sitting at a jaunty slant.

Yet he forced his mind back to his study. Simply having one gave him pleasure. It was but a further representation of 'home,' just as was the little brook that flowed through Ravenstonedale. As were his several walled acres—his pastures where his hogs, goats, chicken and cattle grazed. And Tarn House itself. All were his birthright. His forefathers had earned it all for him, so he valued it.

Yet all this be also what attracts the heathen Scot! And why should a man's wife and kinder be as vulnerable an attraction to Scottish loins as be me livestock to their bellies? Just to keep my farm, I must train me boys to first be soldiers. What kind of world be this?

And bloody Symon Busfeld. Who do he think he be? He breeds bountiful daughters yet that be his only claim to worthiness. He be a bloody stitch in every thinking man's side. One can never be sure what mischief his evil mind be plotting. When he gets something evil in his mind he be like a dog with a bloody bone—simply won't let go.

He hounds on about it like it be a fetish. Oh, how I'd like to take that rascal down a peg!

He reached up to the shelf, empty of everything save a bottle of home-stilled whisky and a hand-beaten copper mug. He poured a drachm and sat over it for several minutes, simply breathing in the odour before taking a sip, his mind still on why he was singled out to live so confused a life when he would be content if only it offered small pleasures.

And the useless Dorrytye! A man marries again to sire more sons, yet she dies in childbirth! And takes the unborn tot with her! And with Maythew but still only four! With my luck, it be likely a son Dorrytye took to her grave. So where do a man look now for wife? One young and strong enough to rear boys virile enough to live past five?

Sons were the mainstay of a man's life in a world with few achievable goals.

It was a time when not only was childbirth a horrendously dangerous ordeal for a woman, but when history had conditioned people to expect most children to die early. It was the way of things, one without answer. Also pertinent was also the fact that sons were essential, once grown, to expend physical labour to help feed the family.

And, of course, to see the family name continue.

Maythew should be the one to get a different start in life from mine. He should earn some letters. Surely education gi'es a man opportunities closed to me. If brother Henry in Lockholme can send sons to school in Kendal, so can I. And if he can live a few years with the pain of not having his son under his elbow, so then, can I.

Rainold made a pledge that on Sunday he would take brother Henry aside and talk on it.

He flexed his fingers, using them then to repair the ponytail his scratching fingers had dishevelled.

What happened to that ribbon I tied it with this morning?

Oh, the trials a man must survive to carry him through life!

And Symon Busfeld? What evil might that troublemaker be cooking up for me right now?

Five

When the Spanish Armada's one hundred and thirty galleons sailed into the English Channel, beacon fires were lit. Word was spread not only along the entire channel coast but north, that men and weapons could be rushed south.

"Will you have to go, Henry?"

His Joanne was frantic. She'd never believed the armada would actually arrive. She had thought the Queen would have successfully negotiated peace with Spain. The thought of being left with three fatherless children had her devastatingly frightened.

"No," replied thirty-eight-year-old Henry Bray. "Middle-aged men are no good in hand-to-hand fighting. And when a man hast no letters, he can be no clerk. I know nowt but farming. I be needed here to provide food for the army. James Burgess and I both sworn to lodge root vegetables in a food-bank set up in the market."

At All Saints come Sunday, Vicar Mabbutt had the latest tract. The Spanish had not landed any troops. English ships waiting in both The Solent and Plymouth harbour, once the enemy had passed, sped up behind them, harrying, striking quick blows of cannon-fire. The tactic worked. The nimbler, smaller ships outnumbered the galleons, contrary to earlier reports, darting in and out of their formations with cannon blazing at the waterline.

"A score of galleons were sunk, and the rest of the armada made east toward Dover."

~ * ~

I pledged to my parents that Leyton and I would act responsibly if allowed to visit the market square each day to hear the cryer's news. We promised to quickly return home once he'd left for Market Harborough, the next town north.

We were given the nod and raced to the village square each day before noon.

But the news was most concerning. The Spaniards had made no attempt to land troops. On reaching the Flemish coast, Commander Drake having retired to reprovision his ships, the Spanish fleet had anchored.

"Why, oh why?" Leyton pleaded.

No friend could answer.

"Why would they come all this way and not land their troops?"

It wasn't until the following Sunday that the vicar had the latest report.

The armada had been expecting the Spanish army to meet them on the Flemish beaches but the army had been engaged in sacking Protestant Holland. Once they completed that mission, the Spanish ships would take them aboard and then land them on the beaches of Kent and Essex.

Yet when the armada arrived, no army waited.

"Could they still be in the Lowlands harrying the Dutch?" the vicar read. "Or could they never have got the message from Spain?"

Leyton and I were nudging each other's thighs and butting elbows together.

Only several days later did the cryer bring more news.

Sir Francis Drake again brought fire-ships to attack the anchored armada. With the wind behind him and all the galleons helplessly chained, few could escape the inferno. Those that did, scattered. Many sailed up England's east coast, pursued by Drake. All those left behind were sunk with all hands. The surviving Spaniards had lost their means of communication; all ships were in an 'every man for himself' situation.

Many kept sailing northeast as if making for Denmark, pursued by the English. Others swept to port around the north of Scotland. However, without their army, the opportunity to invade England was lost. They headed home.

Week by week we heard how bad luck dogged the armada remnants down the rugged west coast of Ireland. Strong winds turned to gales, driving the already beleaguered and damaged vessels up on the shore. Those that survived the gales, not having charts of the area, ended up on reefs and shoals to also sink with all hands.

Reports later reached England that only some twenty Spanish ships made it home.

During ensuing weeks, shipwrecked Spaniards who had made it ashore were arrested and beheaded.

"Whose side is God on now?" Anglicans taunted Catholics.

~ * ~

Symon Busfeld would likely be the last person to categorize himself a non-conformist. Yet in that he held no particular affinity for any dogma, that was where others would place him—particularly those professing strong allegiances in a chosen faith, usual in rural areas. Ease in choosing sides when decisions were called for made life easier to cope with. And when all the Fothergill and Adamthwait families in Ravenstonedale, even throughout the rest of Westmorland, were such secure Royalists, it left Symon with few sympathisers.

No adventurer, he had, like his neighbours, rarely risked travelling more than five miles from home—only occasionally suffering the eight miles to Brough-Under-Stainmore, where lived a cousin, the only other Busfeld family in all Westmorland. And because Symon preferred the security of home to adventuring out, intrigue gave his mind something to mull on. So with little happening in Ravenstonedale to excite his mind, it turned to mischief.

Surely a little of it cannot be misplaced?

Whether or no, that was how far he allowed his mind to travel when downcast. He had never got over being left out of local exuberance over the singeing of the King of Spain's Beard. And with news of the armada's defeat not yet penetrated as far north as Westmorland, he still felt dour.

What's it to do with us? If the Spanish invade, why would they travel this far north? Having reached the midlands they will have vanquished any army England can muster—have already won their war. And what if they do return England to Popery? It will prove no problem for Symon Busfeld. They be findin' me but swayin' in the breeze.

He had already settled in his mind what stance he would take in the event of an invasion. Even if Scots from the north again.

I be simply falling in wi' them. I be still hiding my family in my cellar yet will remain astir to greet them with welcome. If I offer to tell where to find other families hidden, the women and serviceable men, they might then just leave my household whole, pilfer only from others. And surely if I point out that others have bigger houses for them to billet in, and larger herds of beef cattle and hogs to plunder, maybe I be keepin' my own outdoors whole?

He stroked his beard, a shiver of excitement rippling through his body.

~ * ~

Lettice, Agnes and I were listening outside our parents' bedroom door.

We knew it for a sin, but they were talking about us.

"Hopefully it will be another boy," my father was saying, "yet I cannot but be amazed. After ten barren years?"

"No more than I, my husband. Yet in my fortieth year, I can still be fertile."

"Should it prove a third daughter, my dear, and your last, we can only then hope that Richard grows to bear many sons, that my line remains secure."

Time was to prove that I had another sister.

They called her Susannah.

Six

By the time the calendar turned over to the 'magical' 1600s, I was feeling more than pleased with myself.

The year would not only bring up my twenty-fifth birthday, the significant quarter-century in a man's life, but we would as well celebrate my father's half-century.

Bray House was the scene of a grand party.

The Burgess neighbours were invited of course, along with other intimate friends, relatives and Vicar Mabbutt and his wife. Lettice and Agnes, now twenty-two and nineteen, had proven close companions during their growing years. Lettice was, by the time of the party, already married and Agnes 'being courted.' Little Susannah, the late and last child then but six, remained the sweetheart of parents and siblings.

"Let alone dreadfully spoiled," all insisted.

When my dutiful toasts to parents were concluded, I proffered one to our Queen.

I stood tall at five feet and ten inches, and my mother always insisted I struck 'a handsome pose' whatever that should signify. I could see it only as a compliment.

"You are broad of shoulder, lad, and you stand with them square. And your back straight."

I wear my fair hair long, for it being curly, wigs are uncomfortable. Agnes keeps it trimmed at shoulder length.

"And your grey eyes match your father's," Mother would insist.

Not only did I note she wore a smile as I stood, but so did Father.

The lad looks almost a gentleman in his Sunday suit, Henry Bray mused. *Lettice had indeed been right convincing him that deep blue velvet with white lace for collar and cuffs would suit him best.*

I felt myself first and foremost a farmer's son and saw myself no more than a farmer for the rest of life, so I was happy enough with my mother and sisters deciding my only 'formal' wear. Formal for me was not jackets with tails but simply a short jacket over a satin waistcoat. White stockings and black leather shoes went with anything. On Sundays I topped it off with a wide-brimmed blue hat. For weddings and formal occasions, Mother insisted on a fluffy white feather pinned to my hat with a broach.

"As an only son you should dress like your father when abroad in the village," she insisted.

I raised my tankard of wine and held it forward.

"Two score and two years our beloved Queen has been on our throne," I declared. "Having led her people through times of great stress as well as great joy, she remains renowned for steering us through the turbulent years of the religious disharmony dogging her term. She seems content for the small minority of Catholics to retain their church and faith and has united our several Protestant faiths in harmony. Through the tenuous years of Spanish threat, she proved her strength as a worthy monarch. May she see us through many more years of harmony and peace."

The toast was carried with gusto. Debate then opened on the Queen.

"For a woman in her three-score and tenth year, she has proved of strong constitution in both health and politics," Father said.

"She had to be strong as well as astute to survive the chicanery of Spanish spies within the palace all those years," Mother added.

"Some even plotting her assassination," said John Knight, Lettice's husband.

"Should we also note how readily, too, she not only had political dissidents beheaded, but any who disagreed with her on anything?" This, from Agnes, brought several sniggers.

"But a spinster queen?" asked Leyton Burgess. "Shall we see our country again tossed to the fiery flames of who will succeed her?"

He turned to my father. "You were still a boy, sir, on her accession. Have you memory of your parents' discussing the mayhem that then ensued? It would be a sad finale to her leadership if such were to recur."

My father set down his goblet. "I remember it well, lad. Catholics were then more numerous and religious argument set many friends apart. Even spouses. Dear God, let us not be cast back into such dilemma. However I am sure that succession will already be arranged."

"It was arranged for Lady Jane Gray!" I interjected.

"She was but a minor, lad," Father replied. "And the dead king had two sisters who, unfortunately for the country, were of opposing faiths. Doors were open to conflict. Surely James of Scotland will succeed the Queen. Not only is he Protestant, but a grandson of King Henry. Elizabeth has striven hard to bring England and Scotland together. Her nephew James is the answer."

"He might be Anglican, yet his wife is Catholic. As is his daughter," opined Lettice.

Many nodded.

"I respect your good judgement, Father," I opted, "yet I will keep fingers crossed. I cannot but see that Catholics are waiting to grasp opportunity of returning us to the Papal breast."

Little did any realise that the spinster Queen was to die in only three more months.

~ * ~

10 July 1603

Maythew Fothergill and John Adamthwait rubbed elbows.

John was standing by him not only in the physical sense but as his groom before St. Oswald's altar. They had been best friends since boyhood, as had their fathers, even both despatched together all the twenty miles to school in Kendal.

They there shared the problems of all young lads denied parental support. The fathers, at the same time, shared the loss of the sons. Absence from family firesides had strengthened the bonds both between the sons and between the fathers.

Now at nineteen, having arrived home equipped with both letters and numbers and a broader view of the outer world, Maythew was taking a bride. Maybell Bland was one of the handful of maidens available in little Ravenstonedale who had ever hoped Maythew might one day note the nuanced and oft-times blatant overtures she'd made since toddling days. He was her knight in shining armour. She'd ever held her scarf ready for him to take on his lance.

From Maythew's viewpoint, she was a worthy lass because not only had she courted him with such flashing eyes, but she was of a family that bore many sons. Also because his father, Rainold, coveted a stud bull owned by her father, who was not prepared to sell.

"When I be a brother by marriage, boy," old Rainold had insisted, "ain't it likely he might think more kindly on't?"

And besides, sixteen-year-old Maybell was as pretty a wench as was Maythew a handsome buck, black headed and already fostering a struggling beard. A further advantage was that Maythew's father owned the wealthiest farm of all about the village, and farmer Bland reckoned that with his Maybell the mother of Fothergill grandchildren, old Rainold would be a softer touch should the stud bull suddenly become available at a higher price.

A further factor was the overall realisation that the two young people were in love—had been all their lives.

Little St. Oswalds was packed. Maybell's sisters stood by her as closely as John by Maythew. And when the vicar asked the important question, each answered "Yes" in turn, illustrating their impatience to become one.

At the Tarn House breakfast, much mead and wine flowed. Speeches were made, and the newlyweds thought anxiously about the lovemaking to come—this time without secrecy!

Every bride and groom and every parent of the day realised how dangerous was bringing a child into the world, danger for both mother and child. It had ever been a momentous event fraught with peril. It remained the time when one child in every three failed to survive its first year—and even then not out of danger. One child in every two died before turning five.

Graveyards had more baby-sized mounds than adult-sized.

For many families, the same given name appeared in church records, three, four and even five times for babies baptised to the same couple. Each indicated that the previous of that name had already become another little graveyard mound.

So over the happiness of marriage, dark clouds of danger always hovered.

Everyone was aware of it because everyone was touched by it.

Old Rainold certainly had been. Having quickly remarried after Maythew's mother died in childbirth, it was more than two frustrating years before Dorrytye conceived. On so many of those near one thousand evenings, he'd gone to bed anxious that the seeds he would give her might be fertilised. And when she finally fell, he prayed a hundred times every day for it to be a son. To then pray that it would survive.

Yet Dorrytye, too, died in childbirth—Dorrytye and child!

He quickly found a third bride, and Margarett promptly delivered him a daughter, leaving the desperate fellow's hopes still unfulfilled. Yet she did, then, give him a son he named William. With hunger now somewhat appeased, Rainold began cosseting the boy from the day he was born, as he had done Maythew.

He was happy, too, to see his Maythew now marrying and hopefully to begin fathering Fothergill grandsons.

Are not grandsons the greatest achievement in life that any man has to hope for?

~ * ~

Faith...

A year later, Maythew stood up for John Adamthwait. Even in matrimony their bond prevailed, and the entire village gathered at St. Oswalds, despite the weather.

It was a bitterly cold February with long-lasting hard frosts and heavy gales. Only the closest of relatives braved the sleet to attend the ceremony.

Sebell Busfeld, daughter of the morose Symon, Ravenstonedale's intractable wheelwright, maker of good solid oak wheels, would likely, maybe, bear sons with good, solid constitutions.

Could it be that the friends were in a race to sire a son of the next generation? Or might it be because Sebell had already delivered three daughters to John before the marriage, and maybe God by way of penalty would deny them a boy child?

In the days of religious turmoil, many ecclesiastical aberrations occurred—some couples married and others didn't, newborns were baptised at birth or not, sometimes the bishop advocated Low or High doctrine gospel. Most differences seemed not that people in the day didn't take religion seriously, but rather that they were deeply loyal to only one of the many factions within the Anglican gambit.

The Fothergill and Adamthwait families of that generation were prime examples of the differences.

Rainold Fothergill, after first son Nicolas died as a tot, had none of his later children baptised. Could it be because he believed God had served him a bad turn in taking Nicolas so young? Or could it have been because St. Oswald's was converting from a Catholic to Protestant regimen? Or vice versa, in that many parishes fluctuated subject to which family in the district exercised most power? Or even that different bishops demanded parishes throughout their see conform to either Low or High doctrines? Some families were fervently Calvinistic in their Anglican faith whilst others not. So could episcopacy be the reason some families declined having children baptised?

Yet during the early 1600s, Will Adamthwait was having every child baptised as soon as born.

And why were Rainold's twins, Issaybell and Maythew, baptised only months before Maythew married? Had there been personal reasons? Or was it that the incumbent bishop had changed, ordering all parishes under his jurisdiction to also change?

Another factor in church records differing as a vicar changed was the spelling of names. It was common in rural villages for the vicar to be the only literate person in his parish. Even at that, his literacy might be wanting in the finesse of spelling. And not only could a new vicar spell the same name differently, but accents made a difference. A vicar could record only what he heard when given the name for the child. It was indeed common that a name recorded at baptism was spelled differently come the child's marriage. And if again the vicar changed, it could be different again when buried.

Certainly the Sebell Busfeld who married John Adamthwait had been spelled Sybell at her baptism. And the first two of Maythew's three daughters during his life were named after the two stepmothers who raised him—the only two mothers he could remember—yet they, all at St. Oswalds, were spelled Dorrytye and Margareth at baptism, whilst Dorryty and Margarett when married. His third daughter was Elizabeth, likely named after the Queen, so the spelling was established. Prior to her taking the throne, the name was most often recorded as either Elsbeth or Elsabeth. And some continued so.

Yet few, in the time, worried over the spelling of names, for few could either write or read. So how religious fervour influenced the baptism of children in the same tiny parish will likely never be known.

~ * ~

In 1603, the Brays of Brixworth was but one English family decrying the death of the beloved Queen.

"Three-score and nine," I sighed.

Age at death was being summed up.

"It is a benevolent incumbency the good Lord gave her," said old James Burgess, "especially one of such religious and political tension."

"Imprisoned just for being Protestant, then once on the throne uncoiling Catholic trappings to convert all but diehard Catholics to her own faith," said my father. "Especially when it brought the country to war. How magnificently she roused the people to ward off the threat of being subdued by Spain."

"And proved her love of her people," I responded, "by abandoning not only her father's practice of burning religious dissidents, despite Catholic Mary when on the throne persisted in it. She realised beheading is more humane and obviously received God's blessing for it. He never did abandon her."

"And she gave her life so wholeheartedly to improving her people's lot. Even denied personal desires to accomplish it."

I raised eyebrows at him. "Did she really, Father? There've been many rumours."

"And every time, boy, denials."

Seven

With the scare of the Spanish invasion past, the period had all the earmarks of a time of peace. Englishmen smiled as Spain continued licking her wounded pride. England ruled the world's waves, and her people felt secure.

The Protestant King James of Scotland indeed succeeded to England's throne. He had been removed from his Catholic mother immediately on birth, to be raised Protestant Anglican. At thirty-seven years of age, having been King of Scotland since boyhood, he ruled over the entire British Isles. He moved to London.

Yet the religion question continued smouldering, even occasionally erupting.

Ireland had been an English possession since the twelfth century, yet it wasn't until Henry VIII declared Catholicism illegal in England that a religious problem arose. Still simmering was the difference between Irish ethnicity and English. Henry had not insisted that the Irish convert to Anglican. Maybe in fear of an uprising when he was committed to wars against France? And the difference between the two countries widened. They differed both ethnically and spiritually. Elizabeth had not interfered with Ireland's Catholicism. But what would be King James' position?

It was a huge question, because whilst he made it clear he was fervently anti-Catholic, he had not only married a practising Catholic but permitted his daughter to be baptised Catholic. Also, as King of Scotland since a babe in arms, he had been agitating to introduce Anglican doctrine in Scotland against the people's preference for Presbyterianism.

So was the combined populace of England, Ireland and Scotland to be thrown again into religious turmoil?

The Gunpowder Plot was developed by extremist English Catholics to assassinate King James, that he could be replaced by his nine-year-old Catholic daughter. Guy Fawkes was not only an educated man but Caretaker of the House of Parliament. He also had military experience with dynamite. It was to be murder by overkill. The House of Lords was due to sit on 5 November 1605 for the opening. Of English Parliament. Fawkes was delegated to secrete in its cellars thirty-six barrels of gunpowder, sufficient to reduce the sitting house and everyone in it to rubble and to plot the explosion.

Government spies uncovered the plot and raided the basement. Many conspirators fled. One was shot dead, and Fawkes and seven others arrested.

Guy Fawkes and his seven compatriots were found guilty of high treason and hanged, drawn and quartered.

~ * ~

My life was soon to change.

Mother died from a lingering illness, and Father declared that having lost two wives, his first having died in childbirth, he had no desire to remarry.

"Which means, boy, that with three sisters, you must remain an only son. Do you remember, as a boy, accompanying me to Scotland?"

There'd always been vague memories of riding on coaches, hitching rides on farmers' carts, strange territories and strange language.

"It was to do with adding sheep to the farm?"

"Indeed, lad. Many elements of commerce have changed in the intervening years, as well as religious factions. With King James now illustrating much of his aunt's skill in developing economic strength, it is time to expand our business."

I wondered what was coming. He had increasingly dropped hints about me remaining a bachelor when he desperately wanted grandsons. I had simply not yet met anyone I could envision as wife. But my mind travelled a wrong tangent. His bent was entirely business.

"We must reduce our dependency on foodstuffs and grow wool in commercial quantities. A thousand other Northants farmers grow grain, potatoes, green vegetables and fruits, yet England must still import wool from Ireland and Spain, both highly questionable suppliers. I suggest we begin converting more fields into pastures and further study the science of fleece."

I was happy at it being business rather than another haranguing about getting married.

"I am not surprised, Father. Observation has indicated of late your increasing indifference to the crop side of the farm. And I take your point. Diversion seems a worthwhile enterprise."

"Having you onside, lad, gives me considerable relief." He sat back. "Pour me a cup of wine, boy? And one for yourself."

I did so, and we talked for hours.

Agnes and 'baby' Susannah were still at home, although at thirteen, Susannah was hardly still a baby. She was approaching marriageable age. The women had, under the direction of a housekeeper, taken over the management of 'meals,' as Father termed the family catering, even to brewing from our own barley a presentable ale. So we two men of the house were able to devote ourselves entirely to not only management of the farm but frequently 'rolling up sleeves' and joining paid workers in the field.

I was also learning about running a successful business.

Having no instruction in letters is of no concern. No contemporaries have the art, even Leyton, yet we all seem to manage our lives by observing those we think worthy. Numbers, however, have proven another foresight of old Henry.

He told me long ago, "Knowing how to make two and two add up to four, boy, goes a long way in running a business." So he taught me numbers enough to budget a business.

It was agreed I should visit the West Country. In Gloucestershire and Somerset, grazing sheep had already become an industry.

"Go see what they are doing, lad. Find out the full of it. Find your way into graziers' minds. Discover what makes them successful. Befriend some. Learn as much as you can. If it takes a year, it will be worth it. Gauge your time by the knowledge you can return with. Meanwhile I can be turning some of our crop-land into pasture.

We went into detail on the goals, including discovering the hardiest breeds with abundant fleece, purchasing a few rams and a score of ewes and having them herded to Brixworth.

"During your absence, lad, I shall scale down our plantations and have several of the stone walls torn down, creating larger fields, especially in the Naseby property. Write me every week. Find yourself a scribe and keep me in touch with your progress."

~ * ~

A King James goal was the strengthening of English–Scottish ties.

Wales had become an integral part of England during Henry's reign, so the entire British island comprised but two states. And with the King being James I of England as well as James VI of Scotland, union was inevitable. It was 1606 when James was declared King of Great Britain and a new flag was unfurled. The Flag of Britain was the red cross of England on a white background and the white diagonal cross of Scotland on a blue background.

Henry, when King, in order to reduce the power of the Parliamentary House of Lords, for it had a casting vote, had denied membership to abbots and priors. This severely limited Upper House numbers. The only clergy left in it were the archbishops of Canterbury and York, the bishops of London, Durham and Winchester and a handful of appointed diocesan bishops.

The Parliament had, over the centuries, developed from a mere panel of advisors to the monarchy to a governing body in its own right. Henry VIII had, during his long reign, granted it use of St. Stephens, the chapel of Westminster's White Hall Palace as a venue for meetings. Henry Tudor, however, proved the last monarch to use White Hall as a residence, yet Parliament continued using its chapel.

Over time, White Hall Palace, so named after the distinctive marble in its construction, was simplified to Whitehall, and after Henry's death, remained the home of Parliament.

King James proved a dedicated supporter of the arts and made a personal friend of William Shakespeare. In fact Whitehall became the stage for the opening performance of *The Tempest*.

Certainly a tentative peace reigned in an England where the majority lived by subsistence farming, a livelihood with little opportunity to expand standards of living. Such remained beyond reach because tenant serfdom, by its very nature, ensured lowly men remained lowly. Tudor monarchs had fervently believed in the Divine Right of Kings, and the relationship of palace and parliament remained on edge. King James, however, a Stuart, was making gradual changes, despite the lords of the land continued protecting their own investments by maintaining the feudal system.

Here and there, a few fortunate families could acquire a small farm on village outskirts. For the nimble-fingered, trade work rather than farming was also emerging as an industry. These were so few in numbers that it could not yet be recognised as change. The Brays became part of it.

Large landowners held considerable advantage. They gave serfs housing and the right to retain as much produce as tenant land produced in return for labour on 'manor lands.' Seldom did the serf community see coin in the palm. They lived on the barter of produce for finger-craft. And the crown continued to levy village taxes, so because few commoners had coin, the poor must pay their tax in produce or livestock.

Yet it was also a time when gentlemen with money could double investment overnight. Colonies around the known world were providing not only tobacco but tea, coffee, sugar and spices that were adding great taste sensations to bland English fare. England was the greatest seafaring nation, and trade was decidedly profitable for investing—again, a benefit solely for those with coin in hand.

Despite continuing arguments on religion, a confidence in the future was unfolding.

For the first time, small landholders could find opportunity to at least dabble in investment. What the people had no way of realising was that here was emerging in history a middle class. One instance was the crack appearing in opportunities for children of literate families. The gentle class, being called on to expend extra time managing investments, created opportunity for those with numbers and letters to act as clerks. So new skills were being acquired.

Yet there are ever downsides to surface advantages, and a significant one in that instance was the need for cheap labour on production sites. To provide England its colonial products, armies of cheap labour were required in agricultural colonies.

The easiest source of cheap labour was slavery.

So as agriculture developed in British colonies, so did slavery.

Scores of thousands of slaves in the time were being transported in British ships. It became an industry of its own, yet because of it, offshore colonies, especially in the Americas, flourished. The day arrived when England suddenly awoke to the realisation that, whilst it had been engrossed in chasing profits from these very colonies, the two million English settlers and traders there ensconced, and the property holdings that contributed the profits, were at risk. British America was surrounded by French America from Louisiana in the south to Hudson Bay in the north—a realisation brought frighteningly home when Catholic France again began sabre-rattling against Protestant England.

The government warned that war was again likely. Strengthening settlements in far-off lands and along England's southern shoreline became priorities. Across England, young men rallied to join the nation's defence.

"Oh, what happened to Elizabeth's years of peace?" bewailed parents of sons and sons' wives.

~ * ~

"Maybe it be God's response to'ee eventually marrying Sebell," declared old William Adamthwait to young John. "Thy bastard children all were daughters, lad. It be only straight after marriage that she give'ee a son. But ye didna have him baptised. I told'ee ye run a risk. Consider thyself lucky the boy still lives."

John wasn't as church-minded as his father. He hadn't had the boy baptised because he couldn't afford the fee. He was the elder of his father's two sons, and the family lived comfortably, yet old William didn't believe in paying his sons for labour.

"I pay them what come from outside when ye and Edmond hain't the foresight to plan work so all can be done between'ee. Ye get free keep and free raiments. And I be keepin'ee wives and bairns. What more can'ee expect? The farm be yourn one day, boy, then'ee can decide where to spend its pennies. Until then, boy, ye work for'ee keep."

"Well, at least give me the fee to have Edward baptised. Sebell is in child again, and as a family, maybe we should not be risking God's displeasure further," he pleaded.

The old man nodded. He'd overlooked that detail.

Old William paid Ravenstonedale's vicar to baptise the boy while its big-bellied mother stood by. St. Oswalds was well attended by friends and neighbours, for church functions were most of the social season's events.

So when the next child, a daughter, was born, and it coming up Christmas so the tot faced five or six months of snow and sleet to live through, he paid again for it to be quickly baptised. Old William didn't want the village casting slurs that his penny-pinching cost the lives of his boy's children.

And exactly a year after Issaybell was born to face the next winter onslaught, Sebell at last gave John another son. He was quickly baptised Thomas.

Eight

Oh what a smug feeling.
Or is that being too simplistic? Surely I must also consider a little unease.

On the road far from home, I was conscious of dangers as well as adventurous delights. When travelling to Scotland as a child, I hadn't the challenge of everything being strange—I had the security of gripping tightly to Father's hand. Now, the farther I went, the more I become a stranger. No matter how many faces I looked into, I recognised no-one. Even all the countryside was unfamiliar. For the first time in my life, I was severed from everything familiar. I had lost all sense of belonging. I was not only very much alone but had only my own judgement to depend on. No father, no Leyton.

I was fortunate when setting out, chancing on a farmer hauling produce to Northampton. He gave me a lift and we chatted. But the feeling of helplessness as soon as he dropped me off was indeed frightening. In that huge square, I was both physically and mentally lost.

How am I to find my way out of the bustle surrounding me? Find the city square?

Father had given me directions from the city square to Broad Lane Inn, but I could not ask directions until at least on a street. Only there could fingers be pointed.

My first decision had to be freeing myself from the milling throng—the mayhem of gaggling geese, honking hogs and stampeding strangers.

My only baggage was a light leather valise on a strap over a shoulder. I needed travel lightly enough to ride astride for much of my journey, so I was not hampered by too much to carry.

Northampton's marketplace was indeed huge as well as busy.

Why is it city people all seem in such a hurry? Can there be some calamity befalls them if they go about their business in a leisurely manner?

And Father's warning on highwaymen?

"Both in crowds and lonely places, boy, they are present. Take care that you venture abroad only where other people are about, yet not so many that you can be attacked and robbed and the villain able to hide himself amongst them."

I can smile, however, at that moment of panic before galvanising myself to gain a street. Or at least laneway.

It was no Brixworth High Street that I discovered, rather a muddy lane rutted with the tracks of heavily laden drays and curb-kennels where all sorts of litter flowed. And oh, that biggest dray I have ever seen, drawn by four great bullocks, its solid oaken wheels, all seemingly overladen with great sacks of grain. Everywhere were husky brutes of considerable muscle in leather aprons toting every conceivable thing in barrows.

At least I can visualise what happens to the corn, fruit and produce we sell to itinerant merchants.

I looked about. Having gained the lane, I could stop a passerby to ask directions.

"Stare strangers in the eye, son," Father had cautioned. "Ye can tell a lying man or a confidence man, for he is the one who will cast eyes away when answering. Only ever take the advice of a man who holds your gaze, boy."

The fellow approaching seemed considerably more couth than the labourers about, picking his way through the mire to avoid getting his shoes mud-laden.

And he has no large holes in his stockings, as had all the others.

"Excuse me, sir. Can ye direct me to the town square? Or even to Broad Lane?"

"Indeed I can, sir." He pointed where he had come from. "Back that way, turn left on the corner where stands a brightly painted barber's pole. Then ask directions to the church of St. Sepulchre. It is but a half mile and comfortable walking all the way."

He then grimaced, using his cane to wipe more mud from his shoes.

"Certainly more comfortable walking than here," he lamented. "Broad Lane is within the vicinity of that unique church. Anyone thereabouts will direct you. Is it the Broad Lane Inn you seek?"

"Indeed so. I have travelled from Brixworth and have been recommended to it."

"A modest inn, sir. Yet admirably comfortable, I believe."

He kept his eyes right into mine as he answered.

I found his directions easy to follow and on arriving at the church discovered the reason for his word 'unique.'

St. Sepulchre was a large stone church, all quite circular. I then remembered as a child learning that St. Sepulchre was the ancient church, quite circular, built by the Crusaders on Jerusalem's Calvary Hill, the very hill where Jesus was crucified.

This must be a replica.

And as promised, Broad Lane was easy to find.

I took a small room in the inn, paying sixpence in advance for dinner, bed and breakfast.

"When travelling, son," Father had advised, "always pay in advance. It is safer to risk being taken down by your host or salesman and losing that minor value than have the misfortune of being robbed in the interim, losing all."

I had several golden guineas sewn by sister Susannah into the linings of breeches, doublet and even of my valise.

"If attacked by highwaymen, boy, you will, that way, lose less," old Henry had summed up.

And oh, how frequently I already have had to indulge in risk, in order to safeguard my family's money. Even to that fellow directing me to the church. I can now see what Father meant when advising that I always stare strangers in the eye to assess honesty. Oh, how thankful I feel for the advice given me by Mother and Father over the years. And old Grandpa Willie Bray when he lived.

And getting to Cheltenham? Asking the advice of my landlord? He certainly didn't approve of Father's suggestion that via Banbury be best.

"The only road to Banbury is rutted and is lonely country all the way," he told me. "A lone traveller is but taking risks using such a road. It is one on which Gypsies camp, so is fraught with chance."

It just shows I should depend on local advice as I move.

Father considered it some three score miles to Cheltenham and said I shouldn't expect to ride more than a score in a day, even in good weather. Yet, I had no real measure. I knew only that it took some two hours driving from home to Northampton, subject to the state of the road. And that was seven miles. But ride I should, for waiting on chances to share could treble the time of the journey. Then there would be extra costs for inns. And should I strike wet weather, I could not shelter. So I should ride.

At least I knew to travel via Stratford. A tad longer than via Banbury but by only a mile or two. And once in an inn for my first night at Cheltenham, I could enquire about hiring a bed with a family as permanent accommodation.

And Father's advice on spending my sovereigns?

"Don't be in a rush to spend them to save toting them, boy. The sooner you run out of money, the sooner you must be home, having learned less. And you shall need coin in your pocket to transact purchase of stock when leaving. Set your cap, once arrived, at hiring out your labour to a grazier. That will help our cause greatly."

At least the advantage of being able to figure numbers will aid me. Oh, how I sometimes wish I had as much skill with letters. But then think on the many hours in every day I would need spend closeted in study with literate monks. It would be a severe cost burden on the family.

Being an only son, my every waking hour needed be spent in the fields rather than with monks. Maybe in later years, if grazing sheep made us rich, we could afford such luxury. And it must certainly be a goal to sire enough sons that I could afford at least the younger to spend their days in study instead of labour.

Now, however, I can but hope my present challenge will help make all such possible.

Nine

    Riding on to Stratford-on-Avon gave me considerable hours to not only think on other aspects I must lend my mind to, but even to a few conclusions. This satisfied me greatly, for each added to confidence. It took two entire days to cover the distance so far. I had ridden slowly, much taken with the new surroundings. I stopped on hilltops, taking in the view. I could then, while watching, fumble about my saddlebag for the hard-boiled eggs sister Agnes had packed for me.
    "For when you feel like snacking, brother," she said, tossing in as well a tasty roasted shin of mutton. Our introduction of 'fleece on foot' at the farm, albeit small, had indeed added much to the Bray family diet.
    "Take the road through Weedon Bec," the ostler at the livery had told me. "Time yourself to make Daventry by midday, sir."
    I chose a gentle mare, for I had no ambition to test either horse or myself in a time trial. I was content to take advice from those who knew the best route to Cheltenham, and how it should be taken.
    "Those in livery stables get daily reports on each road leading from it," Father had advised. "Riders arriving know its condition. Livery people will know the distance to your next port. Always take their advice, lad."

"From Daventry, young sir, take the Southam Road, timing yourself to lodge there. There is a small inn by the Southam livery. My colleague, Timothy Twotrees at the livery, will direct you on come morning. Change your horse at your discretion, sir."

And come evening I enjoyed an ale with the verbose Timothy Twotrees, who, it seemed, after handing over livery responsibilities to his 'night-watch,' made a habit of visiting the inn before hieing home to wife and family.

"Many a travelling gentleman I've enjoyed an ale with here in the evenings, Guv," he told me in a dialect half Cockney and half Midlands. "Helps a man learn wot goes on in the world beyond his ken. Keeps a man's mind alert to things wot help him cope with troubles, Guv. Ye hail from where, Guv?"

"Brixworth is my home, Master Timothy. I travel to Cheltenham."

"Well, that be an adventurous journey, Guv, it really be. They tell me the deeper Cotswold is beautiful country, the home of many gentlemen and many a sheep man. I've not travelled so far. Farthest I've been in that direction is the very heart of sheep country, Chipping Campden, the wool centre of all Gloucestershire. A jewel of a town in my opinion, Guv, that it be."

"Well, that is interesting, Timothy. The sheep industry is the very purpose of my visit to that part of England. I was of the impression that Cheltenham is heart of the grazing industry."

Timothy Twotrees was unruffled at hearing a different opinion.

"Well, so it may seem to some, Guv. As I say, I've not ventured so far as Cheltenham. Chipping Campden is the place glued in my memory as a very summit in the world of sheep. Even built themselves a trading house, they 'ave, where they 'ave sheep auctions and all manner of money exchange to do with fleece. That's what I've seen, guv. Are you into sheep grazing yourself then, sir, in Brixworth, might I ask?"

"In a small way, Timothy. The purpose of my visit is to learn more about sheep husbandry and wool trading."

Timothy plonked his empty tankard down on the table with a loud bang.

"Well, maybe I can be of some assistance to'ee, sir. I might be an 'orse man, yet I know summit of sheep. If my throat weren't so dry, guv, maybe I…"

"Can I buy you an ale, then, Timothy? Please share one with me?"

"Well, that's right gentlemanly of'ee, sir. I would feel most honoured to accept so fine an offer."

Mine host behind the bar already had his eyes on me.

Do I sense he might just have been waiting to hear Timothy plonk his tankard down?

"Two more, please, innkeeper," I responded with a smile.

His eyebrows rose almost to the ceiling before proceeding to oblige.

Actually there proved little more that Timothy Twotrees could add to prove of interest.

In fact I thought it likely the exuberant Timothy had a little something by way of helpful hints on every industry a travelling gentleman could be involved in.

Very convenient of him to have his livery stable next door to an inn.

I took no umbrage. He was indeed a fellow of good cheer. And a few minutes of companionship was indeed the right sort of ending to a lonely day.

And who knows, I might yet find there is some meat in the information he has given me.

So I was not surprised when, having emptied his second tankard, Timothy got to his feet and expressed his apology that it was time he hied home to wife and children.

"Will you want a change of hack come mornin', Guv? I can offer somethin' more lively, if you've such desire?"

Yes, and no doubt at threepence more than my gentle mare costs.

"Thank you, Timothy, but the mare suits me admirably. We have established an understanding on pace and temperament. Thank you also for your company. Ye shall have her fed and saddled by eight, come morning?"

"Yea indeed, Guv. Have a pleasant evening, Guv."

~ * ~

Come morning, having broken fast with porridge and ale and armed with the inn-keeper's suggestion of what should be a fair price to pay Timothy for lodging the hack, I proffered it.

Timothy Twotrees gave a wry smile that told me nowt. However, he thanked me when pocketing the coins, which itself gave the answer.

I looped my valise over the saddle-horn and mounted.

"This road takes you into Leamington Spa, Guv. I recommend you not tarry there. It is an expensive town. Ask for the road to Warwick and take your refreshments there."

"And from Warwick?"

"There are many roads, so be careful to take the one for Stratford. Once there, Guv, do not cross the river. To do so you must take the punt. But there are inns for your lodgement on this side. Tell them at the inn that you go south to learn about sheep husbandry. Ask them the best destination, and I think they will recommend Chipping Campden before Cheltenham. It is a safe road, but keep wary, Guv, just in case."

I proffered a salute to the fellow and rode out, thankful for such honest men in the world of business. When I passed a bakery, the odour of fresh-baked bread had me falter. I reined in and purchased buns and some cheese to serve as dinner in the saddle.

I looked forward to seeing Stratford-on-Avon. One of the best-known names in all England during the last decade had become William Shakespeare. Stratford was his home.

"The man writes poetry and plays to be acted on stage and has earned notoriety for both. And the bard is but ten years older than me," I told the mare.

I had begun talking to her because not only did it help bypass the loneliness of travel, but she never contradicted, simply plodded or cantered on without the slightest show of pique. On occasions she would whinny as if in reply.

A tribute to my patience with her?

I'd been told when hiring her that her name was Gypsy, yet I thought of her as Whirlwind. It somehow appealed to my sense of fantasy.

Whirlwind whickered gently, patiently, as if reading my thoughts.

She brought me safely to William Shakespeare's picturesque town, and I paused on arrival, hauling up a bucket from the town well to splash water across my tired face.

I shall pay for a basin of warm water and soap at my inn once lodged. A thorough bath will do my body the world of good.

Ten

I had always known the title *Chipping* attached to villages and towns was the Saxon word for bartering. A business exchange. And at Chipping Campden I learned that *Campden* is the derivation of a Saxon word designating 'A Field in a Valley.'

Which was extremely apt in this case, and the fact it was but half the distance to Cheltenham was indeed appealing. After two full days of riding, the thought of a third consecutive day was quite undesirable. A three-hour journey, in lieu, held considerable appeal.

So here I was, my first duty to find bed and breakfast overnight and then, come morning, find a scribe to write Father. Then I should seek an economical boarding house. How long I would stay depended entirely on the prospects for achieving the goal of my enterprise. My first few days of enquiry were most important.

I set about achieving at least the short-term programme. It began by looking into the mirror on my room's washstand. The stubble of a beard four days old stared back at me. I had become lazy about this at home, what with spending every hour in the fields for days at a time.

And it's not as if I grow darkened feathers that are easy to spot, even on tanned skin.

Being so fair in complexion, I'd ever had the problem of having to avoid sunburn. I turned my face about, trying to establish how untidy it looked from different angles. I had to face the fact that I was not at home working alongside familiar hands and family. I was here to make an impression, gain confidences. Far be it that I should impress as slovenly.

I had packed my razor, it being neither bulky nor weighty, and some lather. I called to the kitchen to ask for a bowl of hot water and partly shaved. I bared the cheeks with clear-cut lines, leaving the line of a budding moustache and beard. As it grew, it would be easier to keep trimmed, or have trimmed, into a goatee. Surely preferable to seeking hot water for shaving every day.

So having completed ablutions and breakfasted on the same as yesterday, I enquired on where I might find a scribe to take a letter to Father. Having dusted my tricorn, doublet, breeches, stockings and shoes of the dust of the last three days, I strode off just several yards to the village High Street to begin my quest of a new career. The name 'Grazier' certainly had a welcoming ring to it.

What considerably enhanced my chances of finding Chipping Campden a firm contender for my seat of study became evident within minutes of leaving the inn.

The entire High Street was blocked by a flock of what seemed a thousand bleating sheep. Two shepherds were having great difficulty driving them forward where the street narrowed to wade a ford. The only alternative was but a narrow wooden bridge for pedestrians.

Also obvious was that the local populace was not turning a hair. It seemed an occasion of considerable familiarity.

I had come up behind it. Had I been ahead, I would need to dart into the nearest open door, to then quickly close it behind me. Shopkeepers just ahead of the flock were hastily closing doors against the bleating ovine intruders.

And as was village wont, it seemed, I was quickly in conversation with others whose progress had been halted.

"This happens often?"

"Oh, indeed. You are newly arrived, then?"

I tossed off a knuckle-touch to my tricorn. "Aye, ma'am. Only yesterday at dusk. Yet early enough to have seen, along the road, flocks of sheep wherever one's eyes fell."

"This is a sheep town, sir. Has been for centuries. You are passing through?" This from the husband of the woman who had answered first, seeming quite the gentleman.

"I am yet unsure, sir. I come to the Cotswolds for the purpose of learning sheep husbandry and the marketing of fleece. My family has an experimental flock in Northamptonshire."

"You have indeed arrived in the right place," the husband replied. "My name is Calfe, a name almost symbolic of the place. Been here for centuries, we have."

I again touched a knuckle to my tricorn. "Richard Bray of Brixworth, sir."

"And you arrived only yesterday?"

"Yes. My inn recommended a scribe up the High Street. I need to send a letter off to my father on whose behalf I make this study, to let him know of my safe arrival."

"Gad, man. Save your coppers. Our housekeeper can do that for you. And maybe I can point some fingers for you—people to talk to and that sort of thing. I am secretary of the Chipping Campden Graziers Society. I know where to point. I would be happy to be of service."

I was flummoxed.

How lucky I am, falling into such an opportunity in my first several minutes? Secretary of the local graziers? So he's no Timothy Twotrees. This fellow is genuine. And not seeking favours. And he holds my eye while in conversation. What have I to lose by accepting his offer? And maybe he's just the man who can recommend a lodging house?

I couldn't believe my luck. I should further test it and then, if it seemed advisable, use him.

As the flock moved on, we three began following. Calfe introduced his wife; then we together strolled on slowly.

He'd be about Father's age, middle-fifties to sixty.

It was Mrs. Calfe who next spoke. "Brixworth, Mr. Bray? Isn't that the home of All Saints Saxon church?"

"It is indeed, ma'am. My family has generations of baptisms and marriages there."

"You were married there, Mr. Bray?"

"I was baptised there, ma'am. I am yet a bachelor."

"My reason for asking is that my husband and I are patrons of the Gloucestershire Saxon Preservation Guild—both avidly interested in Saxon buildings. Your church is a gem among gems, of course. We have never visited, yet I have read much of both its history and architecture."

This woman has won my heart.

"You have won my heart, ma'am. If you both can find your way to Brixworth once I have returned, I would be happy to escort you through All Saints. My father is its Sexton."

She wrapped her gloved hands over her cheeks. "Oh, that would be such an adventure as well as honour."

I realised I had it made, here. I had always imagined that venturing out on a long-term project meant weeks and months of frustration and disappointment. Yet it seemed opportunity was knocking loudly on my door.

"Please let me buy you a cup of wine or mead, Mr. Bray," said Calfe. "You've captured my wife's immediate attention, and I'm sure she shall want to entrap you. There is a mead-house across the street. Have you time to repair there?"

"Time? I am on a project for which all I am sure of is the objective. I am a stranger in this world of mutton culture, if I can coin such a phrase?"

"A jolly good one at that, sir. Can you join us?"

"I would be honoured."

"Mornin', Squire." The mead-shop lady tripped a little curtsy as he pushed open the door.

"And mornin', ma'am," she added as Mrs. Calfe followed.

"And mornin' to ye, sir," she added to me, tripping another little curtsy.

Eleven

With Richard Bray abroad, Brixworth was managing to survive. Leyton Burgess, however, felt the loss, even after only three days.

How is he surviving his adventure? He could be bludgeoned by a highwayman in some strange town or some brigand on the road by now. How are we to know if he's been purloined to join some ship's crew, or is a body in a bog? How are we ever to know?

The times and illiteracy were such that people could disappear and families could only wonder why they hadn't heard. Small compensation for those wondering where a loved one, or even friend, had got to. Or if they might ever return. A situation to prove time a dreadful enemy.

And Leyton loved his friend like a brother.

What would Richard do now if in my shoes instead of his own? Would he panic? Or simply put it aside, hoping he might hear something in the not too distant future? Could that be all he thinks of me?

Leyton gave himself a mock smack over the jowls.

Bloody stupid thinking. I have more respect for my friend than that.

He really began wondering the practicalities of himself taking off for Gloucestershire's Cheltenham, asking along the way if any stranger had been found dead in recent days.

Or should I just give it a few days to see if a letter arrives? Or ask if his father has received one? After all, Richard is on a project of responsibility, one he's already committed to taking seriously. He will surely be on guard against highwaymen.

Yet, then, how can any man take precaution against a pistol ball discharged into his back? Or a musket ball fired from hiding as he rests his horse? And highwaymen will know the best places, like atop a rise when a horse needs to simply stroll until getting its breath back. And Richard has such respect for horses. All that makes him vulnerable.

"Do you need me any more tonight, Father? I thought I might ride over to see Emma. Play some piquet.

"Piquet indeed. I was young once too, boy. I used to lie to my father just like that. If you are going to see Emma, it is more likely because your cock is throbbing. I know how it is. I lived through premarital pressures too, you must realise."

"I'm worried for Richard, and I need diversion. I do really intend to play piquet to get my mind off it."

Leyton Burgess and Richard Bray had once amused themselves by sharing memories of who in their district had simply 'gone missing.' There had been several. Having questioned friends and neighbours, most being devoutly religious, they had come to the agreement that it seemed just too coincidental that all had been advocates of dogma even higher than the High Anglican Church, the Puritanical body that considered modern distractions heretical.

"How can such entertainments as music and dancing be heretical?" they asked of each other.

The problem was that whilst All Saints services were considered 'High' Church, the parish comprised many with a more liberal attitude to life than did extreme Puritans. Extreme Puritans were in fact the minority.

"To proclaim that pursuits other than only those mentioned in the Bible are heretical, deserving castigation to the extent of execution, is ludicrous," the friends insisted.

"Every missing Brixworth person has been of the Puritan guild, Richard," he could recall saying.

"Do you think, then, Leyton," Richard had replied, "that maybe all have been murdered by the more sane of the community?"

"Highly likely, is my opinion."

And now that another had gone missing, Leyton missed Richard all the more.

And a councillor at that, he mused.

The news had Brixworth in great turmoil. Alderman William Smithers had not arrived home in the nearby village of Naseby after a council meeting.

"Could he have been waylaid by a highwayman?" some asked.

"Ye mean kidnapped?" from another.

"No missing man's family has received a ransom demand," reasoned yet another.

So again, it was a matter of waiting to see if the fellow would turn up, or simply become another mystery—one but three miles distant.

~ * ~

Ravenstonedale was enjoying the promise of a glorious summer. Red squirrels munched happily under leafy canopies, young sons baited fox-traps, older sons stripped to the waist to attack their work while maidens minced through the marketplace in search of being noticed.

Spring was in the air.

Rainold Fothergill, William Adamthwait and Symon Busfeld had just come from sipping mead in the dappled shade of budding trees on the town square, each celebrating the recent baptisms of first grandsons.

Maythew Fothergill and his Maybell had their first child, a son they named William, just as the snow had begun to melt. Old Rainold had rushed to have the tot baptised.

John Adamthwait and his Sebell Busfeld baptised their first son Edward as green shoots of grass had begun struggling up through the saturated earth. Old William Adamthwait had made sure his son had the small change needed to have the tot baptised.

All grandfathers' chests were puffed out in pride.

They lent hands to the several chores needed for glorying in the village sweat-house. On the square, right alongside the town stocks, the sweat-house had been a favourite haunt for village men since Viking days. Built of local slate, it was igloo-shaped. Whoever wanted to use it simply brought fuel, closed themselves inside and set the fire. It had an iron grill over the fire on which river-stones were laid. Once heated, bellows were supplied for keeping the fire livened. Merely sprinkling water often enough was all it then needed to soon have hot steam so thick that no man could see beyond his elbow. It was a highly popular aid against the pains of rheumatism, gout and any other worth complaining of. Especially in winter when the outdoors were freezing.

And even if not in pain, it was a fine venue for swapping tales such as the merits of having new grandsons.

All basked in the joy of spring these years, for Good King James, himself the Scot, ensured no border-raids. Not only parents and grandparents but children from toddling tots to pimple-faced teenagers could live carefree lives for a change. All could look confidently forward to a summer of peace while hoping for good crops and fattened ovine, bovine and swine.

Old Rainold, that evening, feeling so relaxed after his lazy day, put his arm about his Margarett's shoulder.

"With summer upon us, Mother, how be'ee wanting a water pump in'ee cookhouse? George Fawcett reckons'ee can run a pipe from the barn well in exchange for a bull calf. He be having no male calf this year and we be gettin' three, one can be spared. Exchanging a bull calf that we can do without makes a pump a bargain."

Twelve

Whilst England's Northerners had always been influenced by the politics of Scotland, the Jacobean era began a surge of Scottish influences throughout England. When Jamestown was established in the Americas, not only did more Scots than Englanders migrate to establish agricultural industry there, but it meant laws that had previously differed in the home countries began falling into a more common format. So the influence touched everyone.
Me in particular!
I gave my temple a thump with the heel of my hand.
What was it put all that into my head?
It made me feel that my temporary change of habit and habitat were of small consequence. Certainly I felt divorced from all familiar, yet at least the people here spoke my language, albeit with an accent. And lived the same sort of lifestyle.
Oh, how much more those settlers in Jamestown must miss all the familiars in their lives? I find it difficult to imagine. They certainly have my sympathy. The realisation puts my falling in with the Calfe family in a more practical light than one of fortune and fancy. I see it not as luck on which I can chance building; it is rather opportunity to take advantage of.

It was in that sense that I began formulating plans.

I didn't need to depend only on what Squire Calfe might, by chance, tell me and show me. I could surely craft what I sought to know, prepare questions that influenced what he told me and what he showed me. It was what made his enterprise a success that I needed to hear and see in practice. I had no desire to spend the entire year Father hinted at for the project.

I don't see why I shouldn't be able to glean everything I want that Chipping Campden can contribute, then hie to Cheltenham or anywhere else that is recommended for good reason, all within that time. What is to be influenced by season will not differ from one area in this home of the wool industry from another. So I don't have to spend a season here and another in any other. Just short visits to other areas will introduce me to the different breeds on offer.

Thirty minutes in the mead-house with the squire and Mrs. Calfe were enough for our conversation to lead to a visit to their home.

Selfish objectives are not only mine. They want to visit Brixworth to see the Saxon gem of All Saints. Each, here, has something to gain from the other.

I was left sitting over a further pot of mead while the Calfes attended the business that had brought them to town, and then the three of us retired to the rear of the High Street. We passed a number of elegantly constructed stone houses to where their four-seater pony trap was parked in a glade, the pony patiently ruminating in its nosebag.

We drove a half mile through fields of grazing sheep as far to horizons as my eyes could see.

"Those sheep are all Cotswold Lions, Mr. Bray. You will note how long-necked they are. It is a breed highly prized throughout Europe for the thickness of the fleece."

I had never seen sheep with such a russet hue to their wool, which certainly looked from the distance a thick fleece for this time of year.

"I shall have you meet my master-shepherd, Mr. Bray. He can fill you in on the detail of their care. Like all sheep, they are prone to maladies, but I guess you already know that. Our Lion, however, is hardy. A winning advantage."

We left the road, entering a broad driveway lined with poplars seemingly centuries old. It soon brought us to a mansion partly of stone, partly half-timbered. Large bay windows seemed everywhere projecting into manicured lawns and box-hedged gardens.

Certainly bigger than anything in Brixworth. Even Brixworth House!

"We shall introduce you to Beatrix, our housekeeper. You will find her an excellent and accommodating scribe. She is youthful yet efficient. Been with us since little more than a child, who turned into a jewel in respect of learning how to run a house and staff. She can write almost as fast as you can compose your letter in your mind."

And whilst Mr. Calfe went off alone to work on the business that had taken him to the High Street, he left me with Beatrix.

And what a stunner of a young woman!

She was simply dressed yet exuding charm and easy elegance, quite young with delightful dark-brown hair reaching near to her waist. And with a teasingly button nose to set me atremble.

Oh, what happy chance that I shaved this morning. Will she notice how carefully I detailed the line from my facial hair to take in the moustache and beard?

She smiled sweetly while sitting me on a settle in a little anteroom off the kitchen. Then she sat at a desk and readied paper, ink and quill.

She could see I was flustered yet gave no inclination that it either amused or concerted her.

"Please speak slowly, Mr Bray. I shall illustrate when I need you to tarry."

She even speaks like I imagine an angel speaks.

She sat, quill poised.

I could sense my loins tingling. Control was deserting me.

If my loss of composure is obvious, she is certainly not troubled by it. And I'm sure she must have many times, despite being so young—what, ten or more years younger than me—had men coming on to her? Yet she sits ever so politely, simply waiting.

Never had any Brixworth maid caused such trembles to course through my body.

And it is indeed incessant. And the dimples in her cheeks when she broadly smiles give added excitement.

Indeed my loins were more than trembling. I began imagining myself with her in the most intimate of situations, so had to quite battle with my mind to move it on to business.

Might she see my growing erection? Which, dear God, I have no control over!

I snatched my shoulder bag into my lap, opening it, pretending to seek something inside as reason for the manoeuvre.

"I, er, it is a letter to Father."

"Yes," she answered quietly.

Does she know how I feel? Is she just trying to tease me?

"Ah, my reverend father," I began, and watched as she wrote.

Oh why am I in such a dither? Many times I have dictated to female scribes and never felt this nervous.

Yet again her patient smile set me a little more at ease, ease to fall into the rhythm of what I had rehearsed. Her patience was rewarded as I continued...

~ * ~

My reverend father, I had many minor adventures along the road during my three days of travel. I had a quiet hack for the entire journey, which out of devilment I called 'Whirlwind,' not yet to Chelmsford as I shall explain, but to Chipping Campden, where people I met along the way recommended. It was certainly a great distance arriving even here, and I am convinced that the experience advanced my education on life and people considerably. Certainly all the good advice you armed me with stood me in good stead, for I arrived with no loss of chattel or dignity despite temptations to take risks.

I have already discovered great fortune in Chipping Campden in the form of a gentleman of the town by name of Calfe and his lady, who have brought me to their home to study their considerable holding of sheep they call the Cotswold Lion. It certainly seems a hardy creature, as the number of them in the fields I passed arriving here attest. I am to make a study of them.

My objective, once having filled my brain with information on the Lion, is to journey on to Chelmsford as planned and maybe other locations recommended by Squire Calfe, who promises numerous introductions.

The township here indeed illustrates good fortune. I am told it has been a sheep town some three hundred years, and it certainly has made it possible for some grand mansions to be built. The Calfe house is a fine example. It is by the good fellowship he illustrates that this letter is being penned by his own extremely presentable housekeeper, a maiden thoroughly competent with letters and numbers. And who is extremely pretty.

I shall leave off now, you having established that I arrived not only in good order but with worthy people seeming ready to instruct me. I shall write again once having gathered more intelligence.

Meanwhile you have the best wishes your son can proffer, along with the same to his beloved sisters.

Signed as Richard Bray, currently of Chipping Campden in the distinguished County of Gloucestershire, this twenty-third day of March in the year of our Lord, sixteen hundred and eight.

~ * ~

Beatrix dried the ink by gently waving the parchment about and then spread it before me, proffering the quill.

She still carries the twinge of blush she illustrated at my description of her.

I made my mark.

It was simply a pair of vertical strokes some half inch in height and a quarter inch apart.

Thirteen

We chuckled about my comments regarding her, and I could only insist that they were apt. She bade me wait while she folded the parchment and securely waxed it with her master's seal.

"I shall tomorrow deliver it to the livery stable in town where I lodge all the squire's letters. None has ever gone astray. Where is Brixworth, Mr. Bray?"

"Two hours north of Northampton City, Mistress Beatrix. In the Midlands. Some three-score miles from here."

"And the address for your letter?"

Ah! I shuffled in embarrassment.

"Henry Bray, Esquire, Bray House on Brixworth Lake East, Northamptonshire."

And having addressed the letter, she added, "You have travelled a long way, then. I would expect your letter will arrive in less than a week."

"I thank ye, Mistress."

I opened the shoulder satchel, quietly thanking it for its excellent service in my lap. I extracted a small portrait of Brixworth, one with the worthy All Saints towering on its hilltop. I passed it to her.

"This is a landscape of the village. This being my first time abroad from family, I fetched it along to ward off loneliness."

Oh, how I would love to hear her say she wants to visit. Fanciful thinking, of course, yet it surely is nice to dwell on.

My eyes roved her body yet again, forcing me to again lean forward to press my elbows into the shoulder bag.

"It seems right beautiful, sir. You must be very happy there."

"Indeed I am. Are you Chipping Campden born?"

She smiled again. But this time, no dimple. Had I touched a sensitive nerve?

"I don't know where I was born, sir. Both parents died in the great plague of fifteen ninety. My first memories are faces that soon became other faces. My first sense of where turned out to be a convent. I was being mothered by nuns. Then schooled by them."

"Do you know what parish?"

"I never heard its saintly name. I remember it only as 'home.' But then all the priests in the neighbouring seminary got burned after some decree. The convent was closed. Next I remember was being in this house, clothed, fed and given love. It was such a wonderful experience that I stayed, did all work expected of me, heavenly thankful at being with people showering me with attention and kindness."

Ah! What am I to make of all this? To me, home has always been a birthright. To her it seems an indulgence, a gift from heaven. Oh this poor soul! What can I do to show that I care? That I feel for her? Trying to put such into words could well seem patronage, and that I dare not risk.

I so wanted to take her into my arms and cuddle her. Instead, I reached forward a hand and let it rest lightly on her arm. I knew she could see the tears in my eyes.

Yet I don't want her to see it as sympathy.

I put a finger to my lips and then touched it on her forehead. And smiled.

She put her hand on my arm, in turn, and returned the smile. With dimples.

~ * ~

After a dinner of tripe, onions and light ale, my afternoon was spent walking with the squire through barns and shearing sheds and being shown how decisions were made as to which newborn male be castrated at birth 'so it can concentrate solely on growing fleece.'

I was introduced to master-shepherd Christofer, with whom I struck an instant rapport. Christofer seemed naturally attracted to anyone wanting to learn about the Cotswold Lion—a fact not lost on Squire Calfe.

"Why do you want to seek a hostel or some boarding establishment in the area, young Richard?" the squire asked.

"It would prove cheaper than the inn, and I don't want to overextend my father's purse before finding some paying position. I hope to gain employment getting experience on a grazing property."

Mr. Calfe took Christofer's elbow and led him aside, whispering in his ear.

He returned just a minute later.

"Only yesterday, Christofer approached me appealing for another hand. My purpose for being in the High Street today was to have a notice displayed on the town billboard. Would you like that position? Christofer is of a mind like my own, regarding you."

Oh! Another instance of something simply falling into my lap? Another problem so easily despatched? And one offering opportunity of seeing more of Beatrix?

"Oh, Mr. Calfe, sir. I simply don't know what to say."

"Well, say, 'Yes,' man. It will mean you must live in the shepherds' billet, but no worse than if you took such a position with any other grazier. In fact, I like to feel my fellows get a better deal than most. This way you can learn what you need to know, directly from Christofer."

"Well, yes, sir, I would indeed see it a stroke of good fortune. I am a willing worker, sir. I be no stranger to shirt-sleeves and rough doublets in the fields at home, sir."

"Then consider it done. I shall pay you the same I pay my other shepherds. Christofer tells me he will gladly have you aboard. You work things out with him."

"I am gratified, Squire. May I lodge several guineas with you for safekeeping? It is money my father gave me for expenses should I need to supplement my wages, sir."

"Indeed. Whenever you need access to it, ask Beatrix. Christofer will fit you out with working clothes."

And so it was done, everything falling into place simply for the accident of meeting the Calfes on the High Street.

~ * ~

In her room that night, Beatrix struggled with feeling unsettled over the obvious attentions of Mr. Richard Bray. She was no stranger to young men, and a few older who illustrated interest, some subtly, some politely yet forwardly and some even in an outrageously bawdy fashion. And she had her way of treating each. She simply had never felt that she would like the company of any.

Yet Mr. Bray has indeed stirred my senses. Often have I wondered at my ability to shrug off approaches, yet have ever been pleased it is there. I doubt it was a conscious desire to avoid entanglement with a man, for I find it difficult to believe innate desires are born in any person. Surely such only develop through some particular experience. Yet I have had no such lesson. Certainly not consciously. Surely to inure oneself against anything must be a conscious desire?

But Richard Bray certainly appeals more than any other man.

Appeals physically, I mean. I had a great surge of adrenalin as he walked into the house this morning. And he has the most beautiful head of natural hair, blond and, yes, quite beautiful—so bountiful, too, that it is obvious he never wears a wig. My heart fluttered on sighting him. And the flutter persisted as he dictated his letter. And, oh, what a charming letter for any son writing a father. Just its tone illustrated love, respect and an urge to please. All such worthy qualities.

And he is going to work here? He is obviously of comfortable birth, even if not gentle, yet his carriage illustrates gentle pride. And he is handsomely tall. I would have to stand on tip toes should I wish to lay a head on his shoulder, and even then it would be difficult.

And with such clean-cut features for a man approaching middle-age. Also still with such a youthful physique.

And he is a gentleman prepared to work as a herdsman in order to gain knowledge? I wonder if that is a trait of gentlemen beyond my ken? It certainly fits none I have come across. And certainly when alone with me, even when teasing, he illustrates only the traits of a gentleman—so I must believe him such. And that both Master and Madam have warmed to him so naturally speaks well of him also. I have the highest regard for their ability to assess the mien of strangers.

She looked forward to seeing more of Mister Richard Bray.

Fourteen

Maythew Fothergill was suddenly the butt of mischievous rumour.

In small villages in particular, rumours tended to fly more quickly than any peregrine falcon, swift or swallow. And Ravenstonedale was indeed small. In fact, any sort of bad news never broke in Ravenstonedale. It didn't even have to be brought in or even whispered—it drifted in like a ghost story, Everyone sensed it. It was simply on tongues in every household come suppertime.

And this rumour, troubling enough in itself, had Maythew flabbergasted.

Especially so recently after being elected churchwarden of St. Oswalds following the incumbent's death. Everybody in the village knows me as an honourable man, yet now must be reconsidering.

He was both a happily married man and a doting father. His two-year-old Willy was the joy of his life. His Maybell was seen by all as the apple of Maythew's eye and now largely pregnant with what he hoped would be another son while she, naturally enough, hoped for a daughter. She was the first to say that her husband was the last man who could be sexually interested in little girls.

Yet he was the one pointed out on Sunday morning at church—by the child herself.

Maythew had been alone in the church, the small congregation having moved outdoors. He was pulling shutters closed over the stained-glass windows, snuffing candles and generally tidying up when the vicar returned. He was closely followed by a furious young husband and wife with the little five-year-old in hand.

The four walked straight up to Maythew. The vicar stooped down to the little one, putting one hand on her head whilst pointing to Maythew with the other.

"Are you really, really sure that this is the man?"

The child, seeming about ready to cry, what with all this undue attention, looked up at her parents.

"No, child," said the vicar. "It's this man I want you to look at."

He pointed again at the bemused Maythew. "Is it this man who played with your botty?"

Maythew's bemusement turned suddenly to shock, which the vicar noted.

Then the child burst into fearful tears as her father, with murderous eyes, reached out both hands and grabbed Maythew by the throat. The two knew each other, had been friends all their lives. Edmund Prince had married a Busfeld daughter, and now they were accusing Maythew of molesting their child.

"Throttle'ee, I will, thou sick monster! Kill ye I must!"

Both Maythew and the vicar grabbed at Edmund's hands, pulling them free with considerable difficulty.

The mother was crying and the child screaming.

"What?" Maythew bellowed. "Where? When? Have you gone crazy, Edmund?"

The congregation surged around the doorway. Indoors, with the candles snuffed and only the few yet unshuttered windows letting in filtered light, and with the nave doorway jammed with people staring, it was quite murky.

Symon Busfeld, to the fore of the melee, pointed accusingly at Maythew, shouting curses.

It was to old Symon that the vicar turned, to try calming him down.

"Please, Symon, desist. Let some order reign in this house of God. And all this noise is distressing the child, when it is her concentration we need. Personally I canst believe this of Maythew, yet we need to come to some understanding."

In tiny villages, the reigning vicar was invariably always uncrowned magistrate as well as jury. He pleaded with the rest of the congregation to go home.

Rainold, however, insisted he should stay in support of Maythew.

"All this can only be this man's evil doing, vicar," Rainold declared, pointing a thumb in old Symon's direction. "He hath the conscience of a devil incarnate."

"Such language inside the church, Rainold. Ye too, man, need curb thy temper. Come in to the vestry. This is my church, and I demand the right to arbitrate."

Rainold and Symon, looking daggers at each other, followed like lambs and were the very two who the vicar directed to arrange benches as he wanted them.

It was not thought bad blood existed between Fothergills and Busfelds, for like the several families in the district, they had, over centuries, frequently intermarried. Yet in this generation it seemed that some friction disturbed the air between Rainold and Symon, just one of those situations without an obvious cause.

Edmund had picked up his screaming daughter and was nursing her, cooing like a dove to settle her terror. His wife wiped away the remnants of tears with the back of her hand.

The vicar directed the Busfeld party to one pew, Maythew and Rainold to the other, the two parties facing, a yard apart. He opened a cupboard on the wall to extract pewter mugs, a bottle of mead and a flask of water. He poured water for the mother, the child and himself, mead for each man.

He asked again of the child if the young Mr. Fothergill were the man who had fondled her botty. Yet he could get no reaction but that she put the knuckle of her pointing finger between her teeth, tucked her bony little elbows into her waist and seemed ready to again burst into tears.

Rainold kept his eyes on Symon, convinced that the sneaky fellow was trying to urge the tot to say, "Yes."

When she didn't respond, old Rainold pointed an accusing finger at Symon. "See, Vicar? Tis this blaggard's scheming mind that be behind all this nonsense. The child hath more honour than he. Here in God's house the child canna commit the felony of lies. So the Lord has spoken."

"She pointed him out when we came into church this morning," said Symon.

Edmund nodded. "Aye, that she did."

"How was it you knew she'd been molested?" asked the vicar.

"The child told us at supper yesterday," said Symon. "To disgust us all that we have such vermin in the village."

"The child does not point him out now," the vicar replied.

"She be petrified of him now," old Symon cried, himself again pointing a threatening finger at Maythew.

The vicar showed him the clear palm of his right hand. His chest heaved a noticeable sigh. "Oh, what a dilemma here! Such an evil charge against a man I have known since his boyhood and have great difficulty thinking he may be guilty of such heinous crime. However, I ask you all to go home. Fortunately, in your separate ways. I wish to talk with God on this, ask his advice."

He had the same two men rearrange the benches, which they did without a word, or scowl, between them.

"And ye, Maythew, please leave alone what you had to finish here. All is well enough that you can depart with your family.

Symon pointed and began to speak...

The Vicar quickly stood. "Enough for now! You will all please leave me to my considerations."

~ * ~

"Ah," exclaimed Maythew as the Fothergills wended their way home, his wife, Maybell, who had waited in the churchyard with the rest of the Fothergill family, clasping his arm tightly "Of course it has to be old Symon Busfeld's granddaughter, doesn't it! Bloody hell! What are we to do with that man?"

Then Maythew walked on quietly, his mind whirring.

Yes, this will all blow over quietly enough, for it is indeed a concocted story.

I be just glad it not be the true dark side of me that Symon's found out about.

Fifteen

Am I entering a period of flourishing friendships that are to influence the rest of my life? It just seems that with the obvious blessing of the Calfes, my relationship with Beatrix is flourishing.

My relationship with Christofer was already one of mutual admiration, and the Calfe family from their early twenties down to Sarah at fourteen were clearly supporting my dedication to a career in sheep-grazing. There seemed neither jealousy nor fear to be considered, unless it be Edgar. Calfe's oldest son clearly had thoughts of a future with Beatrix. He was closer to her age, particularly as time had proven her not ten years younger than me, but fifteen.

Beatrix didn't seem to see that a problem. She'd told me that during her convent years, it was readily recognised how women had more maturity than men the same age and that this had continued to hold a prominence in her mind.

So age may not at all be a pertinent factor in her choice of a partner. She has had opportunity to rate me in that respect and has shown no aversion to spending any minute of her time with me. Is it only wishful thinking that I don't see her paying that same respect to Edgar Calfe? In fact, I've even no reason for feeling any jealousy there. Never have I seen her showing him any affection that could be considered amorous.

So am I worrying unnecessarily on that score?

She also seemed anxious when needing to go into the town in relation to her own work, for instance, to invite me to accompany her. I was thrilled of course. Was it too early to hope she might be concocting reasons to be alone with me?

Yesterday, for instance—taking me into the Woolstaplers Hall on the High Street. It just happened to be Exchange Day. So it became not only the Wool Exchange floor, the 'chipping' hall where wool bills were exchanged and investments traded, but the office of seemingly everything to do with wool marketing.

"The building itself is a gem of architecture like your village church," she assured me. "Although not so antique, of course. The Woolstaplers Hall was built nearly three hundred years ago, so it proves to you how long this has been a wool town."

I came away convinced she had contrived the visit. It thrilled me, of course. I had to desperately try separating her involvement in my mission from what was her normal business programme for Squire Calfe. Yes, he had told me that Chipping Campden had grazed sheep since the fourteenth century, even boasted that abbeys and monasteries even then grazed Cotswold Lions.

On another occasion, she pointed out Grevel House, home of the town's richest grazier.

"Claimed to be the first house built in the town," she said, "and it is still home to the Grevel family. Look, Richard, see even the stone gargoyles gracing the walls? Just as the Romans built?"

Of course I would rather have Beatrix as my guide, but then I'd need to be trying to steal time from being with Christofer.

It is all so bloody confusing—especially when I don't know how I should go about asking what she thinks of me.

I regularly attended St. Catherine's Church with them on Sundays, and she would even use these visits as opportunity for taking my arm.

"Built during the fourteen hundreds," she told me about the church. "And there are many ale houses. And did Mrs. Calfe warn you of the water?"

"No," I could only reply, "she has made no comment about water."

"Even the town pump where the brook still fords the road, delivers contaminated water, Richard. The brook meanders through all the hollows in the valley, fed by seepage from grazing land. So the water it delivers has a high content of sheep droppings. Drink only the water in the big jardinière in the cookhouse when at home—it has been boiled ready for drinking and cooking. The natural water will serve you ill."

Christofer, on the other hand, talked as deeply with me on animal husbandry.

"We can make more opportunity to talk," he explained after only the first week together, "if we share digs. There is a spare cot in my room above the toolshed if you care to move in there."

I was delighted. All too often, as I grew, I had wished for a brother. My three sisters shared a room across the hall, and I often heard giggling, even raucous laughter, every time envying their sharing confidences. Friendship with Leyton Burgess had ever been my only compensation, but nor did I have him here with me.

I grasped the opportunity, knowing also that this meant I could have more time for walks out with Beatrix.

"And I can respond, Christofer, by unfolding, for you, some of arithmetic's tangles."

~ * ~

Beatrix, meanwhile, was having her own thoughts.

Is it jealousy I feel at the time and attention Richard gives Christofer?

I have to be careful, however, assessing, because after all, the elder of the two is the student and the younger the master. Richard is here to learn. I read his goal clearly enough, for in his letters to his father he hides nowt from me relative to the importance he places on his time here.

She knew she, too, was on a mission. And didn't all missions comprise elements of doubt and subterfuge?

~ * ~

"God spoke to me last night, Rainold."

"So you've come to confirm what I already know, Vicar? That my boy is guiltless?"

"God does not sit in judgement, my son. That is St. Peter's role, and he does not talk with mere clerics. If I were archbishop, maybe he might speak to me directly. But God did send a messenger in the form of a woman who talked with me. I now want to tell thy son that in the eyes of the church he is innocent. Yes, something you and I have known all along. I now know where the lie began and intend taking it up. Yet I want thy resolve, if ye really be the man ye claim in thy prayers, that ye will take the Christian approach. Ye will seek no recompense against he you think is the real culprit here."

"What? Let the slippery eel swim off to whatever heavenly pond he seeks as if free of the mischief he hath made? Made in God's church? Demeaned my son before all the county? You want him walking away smiling?"

"This is the Christian way, Rainold. It is the way it must be done. I am he who talked with the messenger. Only I know what should be said to the culprit to help him see the folly of his ways."

"What, this woman? An angel?"

"I think so."

Only the vicar knew it was Edmund's wife who came pounding on his door, pleading he would tell no-one she was betraying her own father.

"This angel treads the path God made for us, Rainold. She exonerated your son. She wants to set him free of this disgrace, this burden, for she knows he is innocent. She has promised she is ready to tread the Christian path of taking no umbrage out on the guilty. That is how you too must accept it, my son."

He blessed the air that hung between their foreheads, that Rainold might more clearly see how things must be.

"So be it, Vicar. Ye hath ma promise."

And the vicar talked with Maythew. "God sends me with the news of your respite in this terrible matter, my son. I have your father's vow he will take no umbrage on he who manufactured the lie. I will not be so kind, however, for I am the Lord's messenger and will speak my mind to the misguided fellow. But ye owe God a favour now, Maythew. Ye take care to raise thy offspring in the way of the Lord. See they hold the faith. Bless ye and bless thy good wife. God will bless ye with three daughters, Maythew, and then another fine and healthy son. I feel it."

Maythew felt trembles, almost of fear, surge through him.

Does the vicar even suspect my antipathy to his Puritanical cant? That I have vowed to seek the names of all in the parish who are of his detestable sect? That this is my reason for becoming churchwarden?

Yet he was left with his doubts.

The vicar concluded the interview and then called on Symon Busfeld.

"God sent me a messenger, Symon, telling me of thy guilt. And I tell ye now, the Fothergills will only inwardly snigger every time they see ye. Never will ye hear a sharp word. Ye will then each time know how they simply smile inside, knowing you know they know. This be your penance."

Sixteen

A year later...

"An excellent friend heads the consortium owning the Bibury Woollen Mill, biggest in the land, Richard. Would you like to visit? Learn firsthand how buyers of fleece prefer it treated? Even down to how they prefer it baled?"

"Oh, indeed, Squire. But where is Bibury, that I can get there?"

"Still Gloucestershire, lad, some ten miles south on the Cirencester Road. From Stow-on-the-Wold it is an old Roman road, so you may want to fossick for relics, eh? Many are there to be found."

"I would dearly like to visit the mill, sir."

"So you shall. And so shall Edgar. And so shall Christofer. The three of you are worthy of that touch of education. And you students will have a passenger to escort. My friend's daughter has pleaded that her close friend Beatrix might accompany you for a short stay with her. I shall loan you all my coach and coachman for a few days."

So considerable rejoicing was evident at Calfe Manor. Here was opportunity for the menfolk to add to their learning curves and opportunity for Beatrix and her friend Elsabeth to share time together.

And it is so timely for me!

I'd been scratching my head over the problem that I should be returning home. I had fulfilled the purpose of my visit yet not found the courage for proposing to Beatrix—how to persuade her to leave the security of this household to become my wife?

So could an absence from it afford a better atmosphere to convince her of my love?

I could see two advantages in this travel opportunity. One to learn about fleecing, the other to be with Beatrix away from the Calfe home.

After vespers that evening, all four of us joined the family at supper. Many questions on the visit to Bibury were yet unvoiced, and this was the time to discuss them.

Many details were established. All four would be given a half day prior to departure to shop for clothes in the town. We would stay at the FossBridge Inn, where the Stow Road crossed the Foss River, the waters of which drove Bibury Mill. Beatrix and her friend would share one room at the inn, the three men another.

Next morning I grasped Beatrix by the hand.

"Can you please allow time before we go shopping for me to write to Father? We can post it whilst in the town. He will be excited that I am visiting such a mill."

So early on the shopping day, I repaired to Beatrix's little office.

Dear Father and sisters,

Squire Calfe has arranged for his oldest son, two of his staff, and me to travel south to Bibury, Gloucestershire's biggest woollen mill. We leave in a few days.

I feel greatly honoured. Such an experience will add considerably to all I have gleaned. How I am to remember it all is threatening to become a conundrum. Maybe the pretty scribe Beatrix, to whom I become increasingly enamoured, may make some notes for me to that end. Such would ease my burden considerably.

Apart from looking forward to learning what I can at the mill, it will also be a further travel experience. We are told that the Stow Road continues on to Cirencester, the town of Corinium built by the Romans. That in itself will be adventure.

Must away now for shopping. I am sorely in need of clothes for visiting.

The way things have gone with my studies, I feel it purposeless pursuing the same experiences in other towns. Whatever further is to be gleaned may well not warrant the extra expense of time. I am recommending that I return to Brixworth within the next month. If in a year's time we consider it an advantage, I can take a further excursion.

My love to you all. I earnestly hope all are well. My particular regards to my dear sister Agnes on her marriage. I eagerly look forward to seeing her and her John together in their new life.

I keep well; it must be all the lamb and mutton I am fed here. I have discovered how this succulent meat gains added pleasure when laced with mint trappings.

Signed as Richard Bray, currently of Chipping Campden in the distinguished County of Gloucestershire, this 14th day of August in the year of our Lord, sixteen hundred and nine.

Beatrix's first comment was in respect of my "...to whom I become increasingly enamoured."

"Should I be pursing my lips and indicating embarrassment at such a statement?" she asked with a teasing smile.

"It was no statement," I answered with exaggerated pomp. "It was a declaration."

I took her hand and sat on the arm of her chair. "I have little doubt that you know how I feel. You have simply become extremely dear to me."

I held my breath, conscious that her own feelings were much in tune, yet also conscious of other influences in her life threatening to cloud it.

Apart from the considerable age difference, there are the other admirers. She obviously has plenty, here at home as well as in the town. Whenever abroad together, any number of beaux tip hats to her. Even the odd gentleman kisses her hand. And there is her attachment to the family here. It has taken her in, made her part of it. Could she leave all this affection simply to come away with me? And who knows if the Calfes already see her as wife to Edgar?

She sidled sideways in her chair to give me a more comfortable perch. She rinsed the wet ink from her quill before it could dry and then gave me one of her hands.

Neither of us could see the other's eyes unless she awkwardly turned her face upwards, which was too much of a strain, yet each realised that sitting so close I could smell her lavender cologne and she my shaving scent. Neither wanted to be the first to move apart.

We sat quietly for what seemed an age, yet would have been but a minute. We sat so close, then, for several minutes, chatting and letting fingers illustrate that neither wanted to move.

Inside, we both were trembling, and we both could sense it.

Nor did either want the senses to finish.

She leaned back at arm's length, her eyes taking in my entire face...

She despatched her voice to a joking old style...

"Sit thee achair, there, Master Richard. I shall make thy beautiful hair most handsome."

She moved to the desk and picked up a brush and scissors.

I 'snuggled' into the chair, abandoning myself to whatever she had in mind.

~ * ~

Maythew Fothergill and John Adamthwait continued pacing each other's lives.

Maythew's Maybell gave him first a daughter, then a son. John's Sebell had given him three daughters before marriage, then a son and then another of each. Both couples had been fortunate in births coming easily and safely for the mothers. All the children continued healthy. Yet only John and Sebell's first, of all the eight between them, had reached the nail-biting fifth birthday.

In the main, however, smiles were on every face.

Yet Maythew worried that his and John's friendship was feeling strained.

John seemed to be changing.

Is it over Symon Busfeld's prank? It was when Edmund came to me after that affair, with his apologies, that John took an attitude alien to his personality. It was a wretched trick for old Symon to play on his daughter and son-in-law, just to make trouble for me, but is it this that has John off-side?

"The old bugger not only put the child up to it," Edmund had told Rainold and Maythew, "but told me my child had confided in him the tale of being abused. Naturally, Maythew, I was incensed. I wanted you burned at the stake."

Maythew, conscious of his promise to the vicar, took no side.

"It is over, Edmund. I have been found not guilty and rightfully so. Let us leave it be."

Yet Edmund didn't want to leave it be. "The old bugger is giggling in his gut. He be seeing it a joke on all Fothergills. He be even lying to his own daughter. My wife was just as much the dupe as me," he pleaded.

Maythew invited Edmund into his father's house, and they shared wine.

Peace had been made between Fothergills and Edmund. The vicar had done his job well.

Yet John Adamthwait could not see it that way. Despite not having been involved, he wasn't prepared to accept the incident over.

"From where I sit, Maythew, Symon is getting out of this too easily. He should be in the stocks with the entire village reviling him. God knows that this late in winter there is a surfeit of rotten fruit and excrement both waiting to be buried. He deserves it. Does it not gall you to see him go free?"

Maythew must conceal his promise to the vicar.

"And surely the vicar should not have taken it on himself to play God. It demeans the very function of the clergy. He is as guilty as Symon."

Maythew put his head in his hands. *If I tell him the truth to clear the vicar, who is indeed the hero in this, despite I, too, object to him believing he can play God, I break my promise. If I do not, my best friend sees me a coward, or quitter, for walking away from such a damning insult.*

Oh, how evil secrets can lead to undermining good intent in life!

Seventeen

"It should be needless to say, gentlemen," Squire Calfe spelled out slowly as the family assembled on the front steps, "that all recognise the responsibility entrusted to you, that the two young ladies you will escort over the next several days are given due deference?"

We awaited the carriage from the stables.

He smiled, knowing his warning would indeed be carefully tucked away in every mind and that strong cocks would also have to be as carefully tucked away.

Beatrix was under our care to FossBridge Inn, after which it would be her and Elsabeth.

I at least felt all agog. I had high hopes of ensnaring the seat beside Beatrix.

I will jostle to ensure I am head of the queue. It will be easiest if I am in conversation with her when the coach stops.

As it turned into view, I had inveigled my way to the front, where Beatrix willingly let me take her hand. But Mrs. Calfe quashed my clever plan.

She excused herself, taking Beatrix's hand from mine into hers. When the coach stopped, the footman urged his way to the door to open it.

Mrs. Calfe ushered Beatrix inside. "Sit facing the front, dear. You see the view that way."

She then turned to the men. "Edgar, sit by Beatrix. You know the road. You can point out features to her."

Bloody hell, thought I. *Could Edgar have asked his mother to do this?*

I couldn't see Beatrix's face to see what she might think. I had to satisfy my mind that at least the second prize wasn't bad.

I will have her to look at all the way. And maybe we can play an eye-contact game?

We changed smiles and the odd wink, although Edgar demanded much of her attention.

The blighter points out odd cows grazing and ravens jostling for carcasses or such.

The eight miles to Stow-on-the-Wold were comfortably covered by midday. Beatrix, as secretary for Mr. Calfe in respect of expenses, informed that all would there partake of a light luncheon.

"We can then treat suppertime at FossBridge Inn as today's dinner," she advised.

All were ready for refreshment. Every minute farther from work at the Calfe property had made it seem like a holiday. I resolved to create time together with Beatrix.

Edgar was indeed out to make the very best of his opportunities.

I must break that plan.

Stowe-on-the-Wold was a pretty town. Typical of Cotswold, buildings mostly of stone yet retaining much of the popular half-timbered structures of buildings north—all emblematic of what people were beginning to call Tudor Style. It had a homely ring to all save me. I was used to buildings using more timber than stone.

It was a busy town and, like Chipping Campden, a wool town. Its market square was immense, the town pump and stocks side-by-side on a little central platform like an island. Around the square were ample eateries.

"Your choice, Beatrix," I proffered. "You will know the squire's mind."

Her smile was despatched when Edgar loudly proclaimed, "I'm sure my father would recommend the cheapest restaurant. I cannot imagine he expects this venture to appear magnanimous."

I saw Beatrix's eyes roll across the heavens. It did my heart good.

"I have already been instructed, Edgar," she replied, "to seek a happy medium on all expenses. This venue before us seems invitingly adequate. Will you join the rest of us here?"

Oh, you quick-witted little darling, I shouted to my alter-ego.

Christofer, too, had a quiet smile on his face.

"Well, if you insist, Madame Secretary," Edgar exclaimed, seemingly suddenly conscious of his ill-chosen outburst. "Yes, it looks and smells admirably adequate."

And it proved so. *Oh, how tidily would this young woman fit in with my family! She so frequently makes me feel how much my type of woman she is. In every way, she is my type of woman—years older than her age, yet young enough to be totally desirable.*

My mind was more than ever confirmed in wanting her for wife.

Oh, how proud I would be to have her so.

~ * ~

The journey down Stow Road was more comfortable than expected. The Calfe coachman chose to follow in the ruts of a side road rather than proceed along the Roman cobbles. He had mentioned as we boarded after lunch that cobblestones laid more than a thousand years ago today presented a not too comfortable surface.

"Greatest advantage those roads are today," he insisted, "is but fodder to tourist hunger. They've moved or sunk here and there so much that they prove highly unsuitable for the modern coach and four."

Nor for ploughmen's wagons, thought I, the only farmer present.

And so it proved. All such vehicles were, that day, choosing the rutted side road.

Eighteen

Leyton Burgess was still wishing Richard home.

Alderman William Smithers, he who had gone missing near a year ago, had been found terribly dead—'terribly' in that what was found was a corpse so mutilated it was already part skeleton. A stiletto was found buried between the shoulder blades.

And Richard isn't here to talk it through with. And with Pater and Mater both interred, I have only sisters who seem unprepared to discussing what makes people tick, rob and murder. Only marriage is ever on women's minds.

Leyton had kept in regular communication with old Henry Bray on Richard's letters, Henry relaying whatever he could remember of what the scribe translated.

And old Henry's mind is beginning to waver on memory, as had Pater's. Oh how I do wish Richard were home.

Leyton had married his Emma to make love as frequently as they played piquet. Often. Yet neither made up for the loss of Richard's company. He had, by now, quite overcome his fears of Richard succumbing to the traumas that leaving home must introduce in a life.

He will by now have overcome most obstacles in every essence. His letters quite illustrate a command over how he finds life in

Gloucestershire. And this Beatrix? He seems quite in love, yet is it responded to? I just wish he were home. With her or without her.

Leyton had, during Richard's absence, become a Brixworth councillor. It had indeed given him a further interest, one in which he wished Richard shared. Even to put his name forward for the next election?

It would give us so much to debate opinions on, so much more to cement our brotherhood. We could help each other, results contributing to Brixworth's advantage.

I do hope he will soon return.

~ * ~

The road to FossBridge Inn passed through delightful rolling hillsides. I considered it the most beautiful countryside ever witnessed. All was a verdant green carpet patterned with sheep. Pastures had small copses of trees here and there, although indeed sparse, as if the grazier were deliberately denying his flocks the benefit of shade.

They clearly seek it, for wherever it exists they cram tightly under every inch. Yet it certainly gives the pastures an essence of space. And Gloucestershire indeed illustrates space.

FossBridge Inn lay just across the little river. The coachman had opened the hatch beside his seat on the box to report it in sight—a delightfully rural little inn, also structured of both old stone and half-timber, even to its tiled roof of black slate.

Floors throughout the downstairs were stone, and the staircase awkwardly uneven. "Two hundred years old," the mine host told us as he cautioned about the uneven risers.

I, nevertheless, stumbled twice. Then even the floor of our room had a distinctive slope. Edgar made sure the cork in his bottle of Scottish whisky was secure before laying it on its side at the 'top' and letting it roll. It quickly passed under my bed, alighting against a leg of Christofer's. The scotch was re-opened and a drachm poured for each.

The garden setting was a delight. Spacious gardens and lawns had a family of parading geese holding court. Age-old willows dipped branch tips into a pond fed by the Foss River, a fast-flowing stream teeming with trout. A waterwheel directed fresh water to the inn.

Not only were Mr. Elwood and daughter Elsabeth waiting, but a maid from the Elwood household, who would share the ladies' room.

"Gwyneth will show the ladies around the district while you men are engaged in business," explained Mr. Elwood. All 'men' realised that Gwyneth's first obligation was, surely, chaperoning the ladies.

The inn's taproom that evening was jolly. Visitors nearly outnumbered locals, and the presence of two gentle ladies had the district rustics on best behaviour.

"I am sure the language on other evenings is considerably more boisterous," opined Beatrix. Mr. Elwood agreed.

"Indeed, my dear. I have been here on occasions when, with only as many locals as are here on this occasion, one can hardly hear himself think. Most is in good humour, for it is the only social life they get. They quieten down when the inn has guests. Especially with gentlewomen present."

Yet the occasion was for him to outline the programme he had for us students.

"Tomorrow you visit Elwood Mill. I shall walk you through the processes of cleaning fleece, carding it and spinning. Great strides are being made throughout Europe in cleaning wool, and we have lately introduced a mechanical wheel for spinning. About half our production is now spun this way, and I am wanting to purchase a second machine. Yet every day, it almost seems, are rumours of yet further advanced technology. It does indeed seem that machines are going to replace many hands in every type of mill."

I found it extremely exciting to hear that machines could do some things more efficiently than even the deftest hands.

"I will be apprenticing my younger sons to carpentry," Elwood added. "Inventive carpentry, that is—designing how finely crafted cogs and wheels can undertake an operation ten times as quickly as can a pair of hands. Damn me, if one day soon, factories will begin operating more machines than they employ people."

~ * ~

Supper had proved a delight. Broiled pigeon was on the menu, enough prepared that all could indulge in the delightfully gamy taste.

Faith and Frenzy

Dessert was a new menu sensation—a French concoction called *choux* pastry, fashioned into balls stuffed with cream whipped to stiffness.

"A memorable experience," mine host promised. And it indeed was.

"Become quite the order-of-the-day up in London," he declared.

After supper the three ladies adjourned to their room, and for the next hour Mr. Elwood questioned us on new technologies in sheep husbandry.

The Chipping Campden lads had much to help him there.

"I've none to offer," I answered. "This is why I am here. Sheep grazing at home is yet a sideline to farming. Most operations are trial and error. There is no science to it, I'm afraid. All that seems here in Gloucestershire."

"It extends farther, Richard," he continued. "In Somerset, Devon and Wiltshire, grazing is becoming popular. There are vast areas of Europe where sheep farming is growing, particularly in Spain and the German states. I hear, also, that in South America the Peruvian and Chilean Indians cultivate the fleece of the llama and alpaca, a softer wool than ours."

Mr. Elwood then also retired. He was staying overnight.

"No one rides alone at night," he explained. "Highwaymen are then more active. Few residents will venture their coaches out after dark. It is becoming common for hosts to provide overnight accommodation. Bloody bothersome it certainly is. I advise against you fellows walking abroad at night. An early night at home is a worthwhile habit."

So we three men were left alone. We talked for seeming hours.

"I doubt this science," Christofer proffered. "Mr. Elwood calls it progress, but I doubt traditional methods can change as quickly as he predicts. Man will think as he does things. Machines cannot. If woollen yarn becomes tangled in spinning, machines cannot run backwards to untangle the tangle. No more than can the waterwheel driving the mill suddenly wind backwards. A machine can only be making the tangle worse. Do'ee not feel?"

"We should wait to see this spinning wheel, Christofer," said Edgar. "Neither can I imagine it working in the first place. Yes, your comment on it not having a brain is apt. The entire concept of 'machinery' leaves me quite in awe."

I had little to impart. "Millers can grind corn and flour from the waterwheel. I have seen such operations. A machine turning a wheel, with meshing cogs to other wheels, is indeed clever. But a wheel spinning fine wool from a fleece? Neither can I imagine it. I look forward to what Elwood Mill has to offer."

~ * ~

About St. Oswalds was invariably a scatter of horses: those of the verger chatting with the women polishing altar brass-work, of men toting slate shingles to hoist up the steeple where a storm dislodged some, of grave-diggers ankle-deep in water.

And if it weren't horses it was simply barrows, somebody wanting clay from the grave-diggers' pile to make sludge to patch stone walls where randy bulls broke them down trying to service reluctant cows.

Today, however, it was only Edmund Prince's horse. He was at the altar, praying.

Edmund had not only become a nuisance at the Fothergill door, repeating time after time his apologies for being party to Symon's impious deed against Maythew, he was as frequently begging forgiveness at the altar.

"He tells me," said Maythew appealingly to John Adamthwait, "that he desperately wants to become Churchwarden in my stead. Or turn to lay preaching. He seeks not only God's blessing but help in atoning for his dreadful sin. His wife, being Maybell's sister, tells her all. And 'all' includes self-flagellation. In what he considers the privacy of his bedroom, having bolted his door, although she can distinctly hear everything, he takes the bullock-whip to himself, lashing his back until bloody. And seems unconscious of the fact that she sees the results of it, not only when he bathes but the blood spattered about the room that she must have her maids clean."

"Ah! Could the woman be turning as demented as her man? That all sounds too crazy for a sound man like Edmund."

"Might the Gypsies have breached his reason? Cast a spell on his common sense?"

"The vicar attests to his demented state. Edmund plagues him, admitting his sin over and over, pleading for any sort of work he can do in the church, offering free service for menial tasks, threatening to crawl on his belly to Pennine Point and the Cross of St. Mark. The man is indeed demented."

"It is clear Symon is trying to avoid thee, Maythew. But why do ye not approach him on it? Insist he owes it to Edmund to help him through the dilemma."

"Symon is too selfish. Edmund inviting so much attention to himself eases the rancour still directed in Symon's own direction by the entire neighbourhood. Anyway, Edmund wouldn't listen. I know how it is with him. He comes to our door often enough. He is wrapping himself in deity shrouds. He has let religion take hold of his entire life—almost in a Puritanical sense.

"He seems to have insulated himself from normal life. He has withdrawn into a cocoon."

Nineteen

Bibury was but two miles off.

The ladies stayed at FossBridge Inn to enjoy its gardens.

"I am sure we shall find feeding bread to the geese and drinking in the scent of daffodils and rhododendrons more amenable than watching women pluck brambles from greasy fleece," Elsabeth insisted over breakfast.

"And not seeing each other in so long, we girls have much to discuss," added Beatrix.

"I thought you would have accomplished all that overnight," I tossed at them.

"Overnight we were too busy discussing you men and your foibles," teased Beatrix with a wicked purse of lips. "Besides, after an entire day travelling, sleep was inviting."

"What foibles?" asked Edgar, seemingly unaware the comment had been a joke.

"Ones of which each is obviously unaware," teased Elsabeth in turn.

And that was all that was to be told of it.

Oh, how devious women can be!

Aboard the coach, we sheep men had that to mull over while traversing the seemingly endless pastures of Cotswold Lions. I was waiting for either Edgar or Christofer to make remark on the attention Beatrix and I paid each other, yet neither did.

Maybe the presence of Mr. Elwood diverts their attentions? Surely Beatrix's comment was introduction to such.

I happily let it ride.

~ * ~

Bibury was a delightful village; a long row of stone cottages lined a road by the river, the Elwood Mill just beyond. Its big waterwheel squeaked and groaned, scooping up water in great leather buckets to pour it into the mill's very bowels.

"Washing the fleece is a major part of the process," Mr. Elwood informed us, the first instruction in a day of wonders.

Christofer and Edgar had seen small mills close to home, but this was a large mill.

"Likely the largest and most modern in England," declared its owner with more than a hint of pride. "It has been in my family some hundred years, growing not only larger in each but adding more modern skills with each generation."

We were to see four distinct operations. Fleece off the sheep was 'greasy wool' containing natural oils from its body that must be washed out. Also considerable dirt from soil, brambles and vegetable matter from shrubbery. These contaminates were washed out in repeated soakings of soaps and chemicals.

"Each chemical claimed better than any other," explained Mr. Elwood with an exasperating sigh. "Each must be tested."

Then came 'scouring.' Left in the now non-greasy wool were thorns, twigs, petals, tiny stones trapped in wool tangles and snippets of loose bark from trees the sheep rubbed against either accidentally or deliberately to ease an itch.

"You may have noticed the pastures are sparse of trees. This is deliberate. Fleeces are naturally cleaner. A grazier can demand a better price from me in such an instance. I pay it willingly, for it reduces the amount of labour I must pay for scouring."

He had some thirty ladies and children simply combing the fleece with fine wooden combs, then picking out stubborn items with hooks made from fish-bones. Older operators inspected results on large tables before committing each fleece to soaking in hot water overnight. It was then pressed dry in clamps before being delivered to the 'carding' room.

With but two of the four operations concluded, I was thumping my temple trying to settle each detail into respective brain cavities. Then it was time for dinner.

Ah. Do I ever need some respite in trying to confine everything so far seen to memory. I have never felt so harried. I want all the detail to tell Father, particularly ensuring cleanest possible fleece. No wonder we are paid so poorly by our local mill. The pastures Father is nurturing right now we will have to not only thin of shrubs and trees but start again by sifting the soil and replanting grass.

Then a relieving smile brightened my face.

I shall, as soon as back at the inn, commission Beatrix to seek a quiet room where I can dictate all I have learned. That will relieve my mind. It also gives me reason she should journey to Brixworth to help explain everything to Father. Ah. Yes!

Up until now, I had thought only of reasons with loopholes. Now I could offer her a paid assignment.

Her presence will be worth the expense.

At dinner I was to find how such industry influenced traditional routines.

"This mill employs near every man, woman and child living hereabouts," Squire Elwood explained. "So dinnertime here is held at the end of each day rather than midday. Employees bring light food with them, similar to many farming communities."

I described the traditional 'ploughman's lunch' of bread, cheese, pickled onions and ale. "A typical lunch on the Bray farm and orchards."

Then it was back to more discoveries and more to remember.

"A common phrase is 'on tenterhooks,'" Elwood explained. "This is a 'tenter.'"

He held up a wooden frame with metal hooks attached every half-inch.

We students were shown women stretching each still damp, clean fleece, fixing it to every hook until the entire frame was filled with wool as tightly stretched, in all directions, to almost breaking point. It was then dried in the sun if sun were present, or indoors by open shutters where breezes helped.

"Carding is the first process of converting wool to a continuous fibre."

'Cards' were pairs of wooden paddles, their surfaces etched in furrows and ridges. Handfuls of clean wool, dried and stretched, were torn into small pieces and spread across a card. Its partner card was then placed atop and, by careful manipulation, rubbing the cards together, the wool tangle inside became a series of long shards in the trenches.

We spent considerable time watching carding. It was a highly skilled operation by men, women and children. The all but final part of carding was to lay the edge of a hand at one side of the bottom card, to slowly, at just the perfect pressure, roll it forward, compacting the straight fibres into a bundle.

Indeed a handicraft learned over much practise, I tried adding to memory.

Bundles were then grouped to form a cylinder some eight or nine inches long and three or four in diameter. Already it was beginning to look like the wool my sisters used to knit the very scarf I wore.

These were 'rolags.' And rolags were sent to the spinners.

"Spinners don't work here," we were told. "Spinners work at home, and each seems to have his or her own way of drawing the wool from the rolag, turning it into a skein or ball of wool every man's wife, mother or sister uses. We shall see this operation tomorrow."

During the drive home, he explained that countless ways of spinning had been derived. He reminded us of last night's dinner subject of mechanical spinning wheels being trialled in Europe—our amazement at machines replacing the skill of the fingers witnessed in the Carding Room.

"Spinning is the same principle for making rope. Ships' tars join ropes by intertwining thread ends and rubbing them between their palms or on their thighs until so tangled in the same direction that they cannot be pulled apart. Stretching them only tightens the bond."

"But by machine?"

Doubts abounded.

~ * ~

Vicar Elwin Mabbutt usually asked a donation for reading mail to the illiterate yet not from the parish's senior verger. Henry Bray was considered an indispensable part of All Saints. He could see how excited his friend was at the news from Chipping Campden.

"And this young lady he has writing his letters, Henry, has delightful penmanship. The even consistency of her writing is unique. All her characters are remarkably distinct. I wonder where she learned her craft?"

"Probably locally. Gloucestershire would have many monasteries, Elwin."

The vicar was as much family friend as village vicar. He had been in the role more years than Henry cared to count. They had quite grown up together. The rapport established over years had them as close as family.

"I certainly consider young Richard, too, a close son of the church, Henry. I have hopes of the lad soon assuming a verger role. He is certainly here often enough helping you. And it is clear he is using us in courting this scribe, to cover what he is likely too embarrassed to infer directly."

"Lad, Elwin? The fellow is thirty-four—high time he was married. Especially when an only son. I sincerely hope he is courting her. I am as anxious for a grandson as I am for his return. I'm inclined to think he is playing delaying tactics, just to prolong his time with her."

"If he delays his return for that reason, Henry, he can but believe that an acceptance remains a possibility."

Once home, Henry recounted the news to Susannah. The two presently comprised the entire Bray family still in residence.

"Your brother continues finding the right people to help his survey. This last letter says he is leaving to inspect a large woollen mill. He is likely there even now."

"What does this one tell us of his Beatrix? Still hints of romance?"

"Yes, Susannah, dear. This time he is calling her 'the pretty scribe to whom I am becoming increasingly enamoured.'"

"Oh, Papa, he sounds quite in love. That he dictates such thoughts to her proves it."

"She must surely return his advances, or he wouldn't keep making them."

"Does he say when he will return?"

"No, my dear. But earlier letters illustrate it may be soon."

Twenty

On hearing the carriage arrive, Beatrix and Elsabeth came to the door.

I was first to alight and felt all a-tingle at the broad smile on her face.

And Edgar and Christofer have yet to appear!

She approached, wearing her dimpled smile and holding out her left hand.

I took it with my right, and she immediately swivelled to be beside me. We walked together, to the door, hands still clasped.

Elsabeth was watching us, eyes raised as if in bemusement.

I wonder, then, if they have been discussing me?

I felt a slight tightening of her grasp.

Elsabeth moved aside so we could enter together. She then went to the carriage to welcome Edgar and Christofer. Mr. Elwood would ride to his home astride, and return for dinner.

"I have missed you," Beatrix whispered. "This is the first time in more than a week that I have not seen you several times in the course of each day."

"You have been counting?"

"Almost. Did you find the mill interesting?"

"Oh, indeed. I learned much. Did you feed bread to the geese?"

"Yes. They kept following us so closely that we had to come indoors to find relief from their gaggling."

I laughed. "Can you spend some time with me before supper? There are two reasons why I would like a half hour of your time."

Now her eyebrows were raised as had been Elsabeth's. "What two reasons?"

"One, that I'd like you to take dictation. I have so much crammed in my mind that I want its headlines recorded."

"Well, we can even get some detail down too. And the second?"

"So I can have you to myself for a time, keeping those other two wolves from your door. They make me so jealous."

She chuckled.

"On the first, yes. I will be as much help to you as I can in noting your memories. And on the second, at least one of the wolves will, I am sure, be otherwise distracted. Elsabeth is wolf-hunting Edgar. She is quite smitten by him."

"So you girls have been discussing us? Did you tell Elsabeth I have been dropping hints to you in my correspondence?"

She chuckled again. "Hints? I told her how shamelessly obtrusive you have been."

"And where did that lead?"

"She told me Edgar Calfe is her type of man and has pestered me all day with questions on him."

"No. I mean where did that leave you and me?"

"I told her I like you."

"You *like* me. Not that I'm your type of man?"

"I told her you seem my type of man."

"Seem?"

"That you are very much my type of man." She squeezed my hand hard.

"And you, dear Beatrix, are without doubt, my type of woman. I have pledged myself to marry you."

"Ah!" She stopped, not letting go of my hand yet turning to face me. "Please say that again?"

"I said I want us to be husband and wife. I am convinced of it. Would you marry me? Please, oh, please say yes. I can go down on my knees right now? Or publicly in the parlour? Tonight during supper? All three? Just nod, and I shall do so. You have only to give me leave."

Only then did she let go my hand, to wrap arms about me.

"Yes. Oh, yes, dear Richard." She squeezed me tightly. And I, her.

"I am much older than you."

"Yes. Isn't that wonderful? I am so lucky."

"But your years with Edgar? Both he and Christofer want you, you know?"

"They are my brothers. That is how I feel about them. All the Calfes are family. I do not have for them the affectionate love I want to give a husband. To you." She squeezed me again.

"I shall take you away from your home. To Brixworth. I am an only son so will inherit. I can offer you only a farm in a delightful little town."

"A farm and sheep run. That will make it seem like home."

"We are not nearly so wealthy as the Calfes."

"But you will be. I will help build your sheep pastures. And I know..."

"*Our* sheep pastures. They will be yours and mine. And you know what?"

"I know the business side of a grazing property. Once back in Chipping Campden, I will take you to the Woolstaplers Hall. There is an auction come Friday. We can inspect the quality of fleeces on offer, and I can grade them, suggesting what I believe they will bring. You might find me a reasonably good sort of judge."

I stalled for a moment. "If you do well at that, maybe I shall marry you. Does that sound all right with you?"

She grasped me even more tightly. "Yes, Mr. Commerce, I'll take that as a promise."

We slipped quietly into the hotel's linen room to kiss long and deeply, sensing the thrills passing through each of our bodies.

Then she again took my hand. "Come. Let's attend to your dictation before you forget everything that happened to you today—except, of course, for the last several minutes."

~ * ~

The next hour was a blur.

Having dictated everything I could remember about my day at Bibury Mill, we agreed that whenever further thoughts came to mind, I need only mention them and she would hold them in memory until noting them.

"I shall keep a list open for further items, my dearest."

"Then I shall endeavour to keep racking my brain so it will happen often, if you promise to each time call me 'dearest.'"

"I promise."

"One thing worries me." I grabbed both her hands, straightening my arms so she leaned far back while I stared into her eyes.

She could clearly see the frown in my forehead.

"What worries you?"

"What if the Calfes want you wife to Edgar? The squire is, in many respects, your father. What if he objects to me as husband for you?"

"It can be an instance when I let my relationship with him be one in which I retain the decision. I am, after all, but a ward by chance. Never was I formally surrendered to him. He doesn't need convincing that I love him like a father, yet there remains the fine line that he is not. I can plead mercy in that you are the only man who can grant me happiness in marriage."

She looks more beautiful as she chooses such words. Surely no man can deny such a plea.

She swished her head sideways, the very movement tossing her hair in a flowing wave, flicking it from draping the left shoulder, to draping the right.

I let go one of her hands so I could run fingers down the deep brown tresses, lifting them to where I could kiss them.

"Even your hair smells divine. Do you nourish it with lavender?"

She squeezed my hand and leaned up again to be kissed.

"May I announce at supper that I have accepted your proposal? That could illustrate where the decision settles?"

"Indeed, my sweet love. Let us be sure we are sitting side by side so all can see us clearly holding hands?"

She nodded. "Let's to your letter."

I needed to dictate a short note to Father and sisters declaring our agreement on marriage. And that I would be home within the next ten days.

...Wedding arrangements are yet to be talked about, Father, including location and timing. Nothing will be decided until both families have had opportunity for consultation...

We took the present opportunity of being secreted in the little study off the kitchen to not only close the door but settle its crossbar into stirrups. There we again kissed deeply. I knew she could feel my hardness, yet it no longer mattered. It made me feel only more proud. She responded by letting me kiss where her bosom disappeared into her gown's cleavage, kiss, smell and tongue-taste. Such that we both were tingling all over.

Then, hand in hand, we started for the taproom to see who might already be waiting for supper.

"Oh," she exclaimed, suddenly stopping. "I told Elsabeth I would come to our room when finished your dictation. She is waiting there for me."

She leaned close to whisper, "She is wearing one of my gowns because it has a lower bodice-line than her father allows. She wants me to maybe pin some tucks or something. She is eager to impress Edgar."

I grinned. My hour and world were already made.

"Then you must go. However, in the taproom, why don't I make a point of insisting I want Edgar and Christofer on one side of the table while I face them. I will ensure it is Edgar who has the spare chair alongside him. Before you girls arrive, word up Elsabeth to make for the spare chair by Edgar before those fellows decide to move. And you immediately come to the chair beside me. That way, my dearest, to make our announcement, we are facing all three. Now how is that for an Eros inspiration?"

"Oh, what a cunning knave you are. I see I need be careful. There seems a cunning rascal side to you."

"Indeed so. It's both my Northampton upbringing and my added years of experience that make me so. Now upstairs. Off you go. I'm on my way to organise seating arrangements."

In the taproom, Edgar and Christofer were perched on stools at the bar.

Mmm. How to break this up? They might even insist we leave moving to the table until the girls arrive. And who knows how long it might take before Elsabeth has enough breast showing?

"Ah, blow the bugle," Christofer joked as they espied me. "The hounds are now a'ready!"

I laughed. "Aye, but are the mounts yet assembled?"

"Which are you looking to ride, Richard?" asked Edgar.

"I shall need to look them over first, Edgar. Have you a choice?"

"I've a pouch of sugar in both hands, Richard. I'll see which nuzzles me first."

"And Christofer?"

"I am used to taking what is left. Maybe it must be this buxom one behind the bar."

"Well, she's making enough eyes at you. Methinks you would have no hurdle to clear."

I ordered a pint of light ale, then saw two more rustics arrive to join a half-dozen at the far end of the bar.

"Let's take ourselves to a table, lads," I said. "We noticed last time that if we take that by the window, the local lads will give us clear berth. And they could get rowdy."

"Good thinking," exclaimed Edgar.

We moved off to the table with, already, three chairs either side.

I claimed a centre chair. Please, both of you sit opposite. I have a list of questions about today for you sheep men. I want to be able to read your eyes."

They politely moved to the far side of the table, Edgar taking the middle chair.

We were straight into sheep-talk and had covered but a few questions when Mr. Elwood arrived.

I rose. "Come sit by me, Mr. Elwood. We are talking fleece, and you can give me support."

With both Edgar and me in middle chairs, it made no difference on which side of me he sat.

Snug. All set for the girls to choose their respective places!

Sheep-talk continued until the ladies arrived, both looking stunning.

Elsabeth's dainty breasts literally bulged over the lip of her gown's tight bodice.

The men rose. I put out a hand towards Beatrix. "Come sit by me, Beatrix, should I have more notes for you."

Elsabeth eagerly pushed Beatrix towards me. "I shall sit by Edgar. All right with you, Edgar?"

She gave him no opportunity, hurrying for the sole remaining chair.

She stood waiting for him to pull it out for her.

I turned to Mr. Elwood to note his staring eyes fixed on his daughter's bosom.

To quickly break the moment, I called the buxom wench at the bar, asking her to bring paper, ink and quill for Beatrix's notes.

"But surely we are not going to talk business over dinner," Edgar asked, tearing his eyes, for the moment, from the same sight that mesmerised her father. "Surely our work stint is over for the day?"

"Indeed," added Elsabeth, no doubt anxious to keep conversation flowing before her father had a chance to speak.

She called to the girl behind the bar, "Forget the writing material, Lily. What do you have for us to eat?"

Lily quickly came to the table. "Mutton-kidney stew, Miss Elsabeth, with potatoes, onions and carrots. Cook has fresh spinach to boil up if someone wants it."

Beatrix leaned around me to hail Mr. Elwood. "How does that sound to you, Mr. E? Like a veritable feast? Do you like spinach?"

I had to swallow hard.

And she called me a cunning knave? *I shall surely have to have my wits about me for the rest of my life. And she expounds her questions so invitingly!*

Her smile at Mr. Elwood was the full-on one, the smile with dimples.

I was already holding her hand under the table, so squeezed it hard.

Her expression didn't falter.

Not only cunning, but brave.

I then felt a responding squeeze from her hand.

"Yes, that sounds inviting. Same for everyone?"

There would be no choice. In an inn so remote, supper comprised whatever was available. And often its cooking began hours before suppertime anyway.

Whatever problem had been in danger of erupting seemed suddenly repealed.

"Just to talk sheep for another moment," Mr. Elwood parried, "we will tomorrow see various methods of spinning the wool from rolags. It should take us through the entire morning, and then you young people can spend your afternoon relaxing. The following morning, those for Chipping Campden leave for home. Elsabeth and I also return home. I sincerely hope you are finding your time worth the effort of having travelled so far?"

He was heartily assured such by all.

Hmmm, thought I. *He's obviously changed his mind about not staying tomorrow night. Could Elsabeth's cleavage have influenced that?*

Then, with most all but finished our entrée, and the rustics already departing, Beatrix again grasped hold of my hand under the table.

"I have an announcement," she declared.

All looked up in surprise and expectation.

Beatrix paused while the buxom Lily served wine.

"It is news I am exceedingly proud to share with my brothers and dear friend Elsabeth." She paused teasingly, long enough to attract meaningful stares from all eyes.

I noted her particular use of the term 'brothers' in the instance.

"I have, earlier this evening, accepted Richard's proposal of marriage."

Gasps emanated from Edgar, Christofer and Mr. Elwood.

Elsabeth's hands flew to her cheeks.

A long silence seemed to follow, although it was but several seconds. I realised it was up to me to break it. I raised Beatrix's and my clasped hands to rest them on the table, still joined.

"Beatrix has made me the proudest man in the world." I said it so quietly that it demanded attention.

"We realise what a shock this might be to you all, as it will no doubt be to the rest of the family at Calfe Manor. However, we share hope that all the combined family can meet as often as possible in Brixworth. Bray House is a delightful little manor by as delightful a lake on the village outskirts. We shall indeed be increasing its accommodation, to make visits possible."

I let it rest at that, awaiting response.

Beatrix quickly added, "We shall need added accommodation anyway. For I'm sure Richard will agree that we intend having many children."

This brought surprised faces, led by Elsabeth, who of course was not surprised, and then laughter. Everyone suddenly seemed eager to be first with congratulations. Mr. Elwood stood, proposing a toast, to have all quickly on their feet, goblets to hand.

With both Edgar and Christofer's responses appearing positive, the topic dominated conversation for quite a time.

Certainly Elsabeth took advantage of the situation by clasping Edgar's hand as tightly as Beatrix held mine.

Twenty-one

"Oh, how life is becoming a trial, John."

"What, Maythew? Edmund's fantasies? You do seem morose of late. So unlike you. Have you other burdens, then?"

Maythew Fothergill and John Adamthwait were on haunches, swinging hammers, breaking rocks for repairs to a wall of a Tarn House paddock. Each was used to hands-on outdoor work and helped each other when it provided opportunity for sharing problems.

Maythew looked about before answering, despite aware that the only others present were young sons, both apples of each father's eyes.

"Indeed I have a heavy weight pressing on my mind, John, apart from Edmund's persistent badgering."

Edmund Prince had given Maythew no respite from apologies for "grievous sins" against his brother-in-law, now a year since. He had become almost a persistent joke in the village over his self-imposed penance. Even then, he was building a huge wooden cross in the village square, magnificently carved, woodcarving his chosen career. It stood several feet above his own height, in solid oak. Every hour of the day, and even of many evenings, he was carving, carving, carving.

"It is to be my funeral pyre," he kept explaining, yet none believed he was yet deranged enough to set himself ablaze.

"What heavy weight is that, my friend?"

Maythew said nowt for as long as a minute, then sighed deeply.

"I am afeared for our church, John. William Parsons has been a beloved vicar all the years he has been with us, as all can attest. Yet a year ago, I began realising that he was delicately testing where my faith stood. He was propositioning me to adopt several Puritanical practices. When he urged me to nominate for churchwarden last year, I accepted, mainly so he would have the more faith in me to openly declare his ambition of St. Oswalds becoming Puritan. Do you understand what I am saying?"

"Well indeed, Maythew. I've always seen ye a dedicated Christian, also pleased that Vicar William kept adopting more High Gospel policies."

"You noticed?"

"Aye, friend. Indeed I did."

"You never mentioned it."

"Because my family, except for old grandfather William, is not church-minded. Ye know it nary bothers me much, one way or another."

"Aye, I know that. And knowing it is why I am now to declare my fears to you. Most about here hold strong feelings even between Low Church and High Church, knowing it be an Episcopal leaning of whoever be bishop. It of course also influences whoever be vicar. Yet Vicar William is now seeking my co-operation to influence the entire parish in adopting the full Puritan dogma, a vast step beyond even High Church ideals. It is an immense worry. It would drive wedges into every family in Ravenstonedale."

"Why so?"

"We will lose the good fellowship that exists. We are a small, tight community and lifestyle between High Church and Purity calls for vast change. We may play no games of chance, no piquet, no chess or draughts..."

"No trump and ruff?"

"None. We may not dance, play music, read or write poetry. We may dress only in black and white livery. There can be no more breeches and stockings and certainly no embellishment to clothing like feathers in our hats. Puritans declare all such Popish trappings. Our lives must be one of only Purist thought. We must never have sex with our wives for enjoyment, only as a means of procreating children. We…"

"Hold, hold, hold, dear friend. What is this? The church interfering in my bedroom practices? My Sebell and me enjoy romps of pleasure. Damn me if we don't! I want none of Puritanism if this is what Vicar Parsons is angling towards. I recognise your fears, friend. It will be the death of life for many men and many wenches in our community."

Maythew clasped his arm around his friend's shoulder. "It gladdens my heart to hear you say this, John. People come into our lives for many reasons, reasons that keep us together, reasons for letting friendships lapse. Yet always reasons for something. Our friendship remains strong because we think alike in so many ways."

"What do we do about the vicar?"

"Knowing you stand on my ground, I put this to you—my contribution to saving this parish from being led into it by our bishop and vicar, is to find a voice in Parliament. Vicar William hints that is where Puritans are gathering strength, that Parliament will pass laws imposing these restrictions on all. King James is sickly, and he is all that is holding out against the Purists. My thinking is that as many of us more sane people could have a say in Parliament is the only way to stop this terrible trend."

"Ye speak of the House of Commons, of course. Yet must not all its decisions be approved by the House of Lords?"

"Aye, dear friend. Yet not all members of the Upper House are Lords. Many of the bishop class have automatic appointment, and many bishops find fault with the Royalist bloc. The Royalist bloc is the greatest strength in the House of Lords, yet its power is dwindling. More and more bishops are becoming disenamoured of the King's power over the Church. I have a dreadful fear that all is counting down to a crunch of voting numbers. Puritans seem to be gaining. It is in the House of Commons that warnings must be raised."

"Are those outspoken against the Puritanical trend, then, laying themselves open to assassination?"

"Indeed. And it may be happening. How do we, up here, really know what is happening in the south? This is why I should seek the chance of gaining a seat—help re-establish the Royalist bloc in the Lower House."

John Adamthwait was silent as he took back a stone to chip at a pimple preventing a neat fit.

"I am but one who will do all I can to help you get elected, Maythew. We both have broad families in the district, many entitled to vote—all who would want to save England from Puritanism. What is involved in gaining a seat?"

"I know not. I will soon travel to Kendal to make enquiries, and I would like you with me."

"I will come with you if you need support. It will be good after all these years since school together there."

"We need do it quickly, John. I am not sure when the next election is due. Nor even how many seats are available in Westmorland. Vicar William claims Puritan candidates are already being sought under cover. A new Parliament, it seems, can sit only under Royal decree."

They spent several quiet moments watching young Thomas and George play.

"It's these children I have in mind, John, in wanting to help keep the Puritans out. How sad a life it will be for our sons and daughters if they cannot enjoy music and dancing."

Neither was to know that that very evening, Edmund Prince was to make this day his last.

~ * ~

Less than a mile away, at his father's farm, Edmund stuffed dried hay into a sack.

It took two trips to tote sacks of hay, bracken and thin logs to the village square.

He sat for his last supper with wife and children, giving them confidence to believe that maybe he was casting off the evil spirits that had stolen the love and attention he had always given them—that had turned him into almost a madman. Over supper he had somehow illustrated a happiness again, at least enough to raise hope in their hearts that their husband and father of old could be returning.

If he had any positive thoughts in mind, none could deter him from his intent. They were that his wife's very father, old Symon Busfeld, who had caused all his dilemma, was not poor. He had a sizeable enough herd of beef and dairy cattle, and his expertise as a wheelwright, to take his little family in, give them a proper life.

After supper he declared he was going to climb the scarp behind the village, to pray in the silence of the upland, and that he would be late home.

"I shall take the pony and trap, for I shall want fuel for a fire to keep me warm in the upland chill," he told them.

He had decided that a pony and trap would save him yet a third difficult trip carrying fuel to the square. Especially as he had since decided on chains to bind his ankles should he have a final urge to spare himself.

Hmf. I want to be well dead before the logs catch—logs to ensure there is nowt but bones left for the family to fetch to the churchyard.

He felt entirely serene as he let the pony walk all the way. He needed to be sure the square would be free of people before burning himself on his cross—the magnificent carving that had earned so many compliments and congratulations.

At eleven o'clock, when darkness hid all, for the sky was, as often, covered in thick cloud, he wrapped the chains about his ankles, twisting ends for securing with staples. He was thankful for his supple physique, supple enough that he could properly stack the base of the fire about him. The fuel needed deft stacking, that even if his knees were twisting and turning in his agony, they could not dislodge anything enough to slow the fire's intensity. He wanted to be taken to heaven before the pain of life on earth surrendered.

His flints and flint box were in the fob of his doublet, along with the pinch of salt he invariably kept in pockets to ward off evil spirits. On the solid cross-bar, at reach-height of his oaken cross, he'd carved handles in which he could take a solid grasp.

And pledged myself that despite the severest of pains, I shall never let go that grasp.

As he finished adjusting the bracken and logs, his ankles and calves secured by chains and all from sight by the fuel, he felt closer to God, his family and the Maythew he had so wronged, than ever before. He struck a flint, and the spark quickly caught.

He quickly struck another on his other side and let it as deftly fall.

He sniffed in the aroma of the burning larch-wood, relishing it, fully realising it would be for the last time.

BOOK TWO:

Twenty-five years later

Twenty-two

King James was dead. Charles I sat on the throne of England, Scotland and Ireland.

England and Scotland were at peace except for bickering between Anglican and Presbyterian dogma, yet Ireland remained rebellious. The two previous monarchs had been prepared to allow it its Catholic religion until the urge for independence exploded into rebellion. It was put down with brute force, and in reprisal England despatched recalcitrant Irish landowners from properties throughout Ulster, offering titles cheaply to English and Scottish settlers. Thousands took up the offer. The entire northeastern corner of Ireland became a Protestant settlement. The rest of Ireland had, ever since, seethed.

The new King Charles, a twenty-five-year-old playboy, on the one hand immediately married by proxy his Catholic French Princess and on the other declared himself violently anti-Catholic. He began tossing inflammable fuel on the already simmering fires of Presbyterianism in Scotland and Catholicism in Ireland.

Charles had already disenchanted royalist followers in England by dismissing Parliament.

All at Bray House were feeling quite betrayed by our new sovereign.

"The man has cast our political structure back a hundred years," I declared at our dinner table. "Progresses made in relationships with Parliament by Henry, Elizabeth and James have been all for nought. Charles even claims Divine Right supersedes the constitution."

Even twenty-one-year-old son Soloman was incensed. "I thoroughly support Parliament's attitude to persistent demands for funds to satisfy his exorbitant lifestyle. They should have begun refusing years ago. I agree with you too, Father, on his fervid adherence to the Divine Right of Kings. His father and Elizabeth before him were never as irreparably averse to Parliamentary prerogatives."

"There is also his approach to the European wars," said Dickie. "How can he refute claims by our allies on the continent that our army is unreliable? How many battles have we lost?"

"Every one we fought in, boy," I told my eldest. "He sends his Personal Guard and Royal Cavalry in answer to requests by fellow monarchs, yet instead of chasing fleeing opponents, lets them race to freedom and to fight another day. He remains on the battlefield to loot the pockets of fallen enemy and raid cellars of nearby homes. Quite irresponsible conduct in wartime."

At the far end of the table, I could see Beatrix smiling, her eyes on me.

We had ever encouraged the children to be outspoken on matters common to all. Our dinner table was our debating stage. My Bea had elected to educate all as soon as old enough to sit still and not disturb lessons. I was indeed proud of her successes. Successes wanted for strength in some quarters, of course, yet all now responded to thinking on matters before proffering opinions. We talked freely as all families should. We held that siblings not only learned better by partaking in reasoned argument but bonded more strongly.

I was surprised at Dickie jumping in like that. Despite being oldest of the eight, he usually sat back to judge the flow before casting his fly.

That's why I so readily chose to support him, afore all the others.

"Dismissing Parliament for refusing his demands is certainly an insolent response," opined Frances, putting down her fork so she could wave a finger. "Does he really believe he can waive a century of tradition just by waggling a finger like this? Such arrogance! I am shamed by it."

Beatrix mused.

I can read my eight children near as clearly as I read my own mind.

Haven't I taught each and every? Drawn from them their reasoning on statements? Encouraged debate in each so all can consider the effect of their own words on others?

She looked around the table.

My dearest Richard at the head, of course, first son twenty-five-year-old Dickie on his right and twenty-one-year-old Soloman on his left. Next to Dickie is elder daughter Frances and by her, her husband Ted Gunnell, then young Henry at fifteen. Opposite and next to Solomon is younger daughter Jane at fifteen, John at nineteen and little William six, but who takes quite an interest in all our topics.

Across her mind flashed baby Beatrix they had buried when a tot in arms and Cecille, who had succumbed to influenza when three.

We are just so lucky that all others are vibrantly healthy.

I put up a finger, calling for the floor. "I recall the King sacking Parliament for the third time in as many years. 'I shall rule alone,' he declared, and did for eleven years. Every time he had recalled it was to appeal for money for his wars, his parties and his amours. He is sadly losing popularity. It is not as if Parliament could trust him to use funds for the purpose granted, for he has proved flippant in the past. I feel very sad at having to question my royal instincts."

I glanced at Bea, and already her eyes were circling the table to see who would jump in.

"He further confounds supporters, Father, by his attitude on Presbyterianism. Not only does he swamp Scottish churches with copies of his father's *English Prayerbook* but decrees Presbyterian liturgy illegal. He spends Parliament's grants on alienating allies."

John is the studious one in our family. He is a ready helper at All Saints and seems happy to spend personal time with the vicar, so maybe his future is in the church? Soloman was like that, yet of late he has switched interest towards politics.

"Not only *Prayerbooks*, John. Also English Bibles," Soloman responded.

"Where did you hear that?"

"From Mary Allen. She said her father was told it at the Freemasons Lodge."

William giggled.

"What makes you giggle, William?" Beatrix asked.

He sang to the tune of a lullaby, "Mary is Soloman's girlfriend."

Soloman threw his serviette at his 'baby' brother.

"I saw them holding hands when walking home from church last Sunday," William added.

"I get girlfriends, young man, because I don't have as many freckles as you. I guess that's why you only get boyfriends to walk home with."

William was about to reply when I noticed Bea's arm move—an under-the-table nudge at William's knee, a "that's enough" nudge.

~ * ~

Old Rainold Fothergill and his Maythew had, after twenty-five years, somewhat recovered from the heartbreaking experience of burying their son and brother Steven—especially in such a tragic circumstance. They had considered Edmund Prince burning himself to death should have been enough to cope with. Yet to be burdened by Steven, arriving on the scene after spending the early evening making love to his paramour, dying in the very same fire, proved a hurt to forever plague them.

"The brave fellow had desperately tried to release Edmund from his chains," onlookers told them.

Rainold was, by now, showing both his age and hurt. He had never been sure of his age, numbers ever having proved a conundrum. His hair had always had a tinge of russet. "Because maybe you were really sired by a red squirrel," his mother had always joked to him. Or so he claimed. Yet it had considerably thinned. He invariably bundled it tightly behind his head, hanging in a pony tail.

"Wigs are a bother," he would insist.

"The village wig-woman gets my shorn tresses," he would explain. "She uses them to make wigs for Fothergill brothers. She claims that nobody else in the district wants russet hair, in fear of being taken for a Fothergill."

He always enjoyed telling that joke, especially when in his cups, which, of late, was often.

Yet he rued Maythew's interest in Puritanism.

The lad claims it a ruse—that he involves himself only to discover who, in the district, harbours the deceit. "Father, please desist!" he admonishes when I question him on it. "I strive towards its downfall," he claims. "It will be the death of our very religion if it prevails. It has become my pledge in life to contribute to its downfall."

Maythew had endeavoured on three occasions to gain a seat in Parliament yet suffered the disadvantage of being too little known in such a large electorate.

"I weary of life, boy," Rainold would tell him. "When I am gone, you will be master of Tarn House. Your boys will carry the Fothergill name down the centuries, so your aspirations are more important now than ever. It is you who must prepare your sons to take hold of the reins that steer our future."

Maythew had aspired to his fiftieth year, and his Maybell had only last year died in childbirth. He had no desire to remarry, because he had too much concern for the future.

"The world is going mad," he insisted "People today play with religion like a bouncing ball."

By spending the rest of his life a widower, he realised that his William at twenty-nine and George at nineteen would remain his only two sons.

If a man were to have more now, the boy could quickly find himself fatherless afore even finding faith and common sense. He would be left vulnerable and be influenced by fools. Better I take Father's advice and spend time ensuring William and George follow rightful paths.

The daughters Maybell had given him all survived.

An unusual circumstance, but one to please me no end.

Margareth and Dorrytye were married and raising broods in neighbouring towns. Third daughter Elizabeth, twin to George, was yet unmarried.

She be a lass comely enough to make an easy match. I'd like to see it an Adamthwait, yet John's young Thomas be already betrothed. Also I must be sure William be ready to take up Tarn House when my time comes.

Maythew also had the responsibility of seeing old Rainold off properly.

His body tires, despite both his mind and temper remain fertile enough to drive our household to frustration.

"He will surely take that temper of his to his grave," he told John Adamthwait.

John's Sebell had also given her husband twins, a boy and girl, and then young Thomas.

Thomas looked forward to his imminent marriage to Ann—another Busfeld maid.

My George is to stand by Thomas at the service, same as I stood by his father.

George Fothergill and Thomas Adamthwait had grown up together playing opponents at war. A further favourite pastime was shaking ground peppercorns over cakes cooling on kitchen sills, ready to take to the village fair. They had hearty laughs when all who partook burst into fits of sneezing.

They then attended school together as had their fathers.

Yet sharing adventures were nowhere near finished.

They would have many more adventures very soon—when the country would erupt in Civil War.

Twenty-three

"A letter from home, dearest."

Home had had various meanings for my Beatrix. Yet every one a joy—the convent, Calfe Manor and Bray House.

I was grateful that her Calfe family had been ecstatic at her becoming Mrs. Richard Bray. "We can see how deliriously happy you are at the prospect," they'd told her.

The entire family had travelled from Chipping Campden and lodged at Pitsford Inn, Brixworth's finest, Beatrix's beloved filly Sweetness trotting behind.

"She will leave a dreadfully broad cleft in our home," bewailed Squire and Mrs. Calfe to Old Henry, "yet there is no-one we could be happier seeing her take as life's partner as your Richard, sir. He is indeed a son to make you proud."

Sisters Lettice and Agnes arrived with husbands and bairns, squeezing into Bray House.

"We shall be having so many children," Beatrix assured her family, "that Richard has already declared he is to build a further wing to the house."

All could see how delighted she was at her prospects.

She had excitedly agreed to All Saints for our wedding.

"With its long history in your family, dear Richard, it would be sad not to also see you married at its altar. And I will be proud to see my name appended there, especially in that the names of all our children will feature there."

The Calfes, of course, as patrons of the Gloucestershire Saxon Preservation Guild, were not only agog to see All Saints but to witness their Beatrix married in it. Over the next several days, Vicar Mabbutt, Father and I gave them considerable time inspecting every detail from its cellar to spire. Squire Calfe had us seek out Northampton City's most renowned artist to paint a large canvas of it as a wedding present. It remained a feature of the gracious new stairway built when adding the south wing.

My Bea, as I had recently dubbed her, fulfilled every dream of our life together. She proved a skilled housekeeper and a doting and capable mother as well an exciting and loving wife. Sadness crossed our path on occasions, yet we could begrudge none—no-one could expect life to be perfect, and we had times to enjoy in abundance. Baby Bea died of 'cot sickness' at three months and was laid tearfully to rest after simply failing to wake up one morning. Cecille was ever sickly and died at three. We took almost personally, too, the sadness of London's renowned Globe Theatre burning down and but three years later, the bard himself passing on.

"An ever such sad loss," Bea bewailed. She had become an avid Shakespeare fan. Our library shelves held all his plays, and she had read every one to me.

At her insistence, every Bray son was encouraged to perform with the Brixworth Morris dancers. Her Chipping Campden had been famous for its Morris dancing, and she convinced me how grand an experience it would be for them to play such a part in Brixworth's heritage. John and William were both still part of it.

Bea now admits to being a matronly 'forty-something.' She persists in wearing her tresses long rather than as most mothers in their middle-age, piling it atop their heads to cover it with a bonnet.

"It may be beginning to show streaks of silver," she admitted, "yet I consider it a salutation to my age."

She steadfastly insists on me retaining my hair at shoulder length rather than wear a wig.

"Your fair hair remains delightfully handsome on you," she always insisted. "It complements the grey in its midst."

She has ever continued dressing it and now insists on being barber to my goatee beard.

"She immediately became a familiar in Brixworth society," I today tell visitors. "From the start, unlike most new brides, she chose to be seen abroad, except at church, riding side-saddle on her golden-hued Sweetness. Since the mare's demise and when the weather is toward, you will find her afoot with a large creel on her arm. It seems as much a part of her attire as her bonnet and loose tresses. Sometimes it holds flowers for decorating the house or All-Saints, sometimes fish and eels from our lake for the poorer villagers, sometimes cheese, bread and pickles for men in the field. Also sometimes empty as if carried out of habit."

I too accomplished much in the interim. I became a council alderman, rose to chief verger at All Saints and saw 'baby' sister Susannah marry. Just five years ago, we had the misfortune of burying our beloved Old Henry. Bea felt the loss as much as me. He had always illustrated as much love for her as had I. It was a tragic time. Dear old Vicar Elwin Mabbutt contracted a wasting sickness and died. He had taken a caring interest in me all my life—baptising me, appointing me verger and marrying me to my Bea. And he had been such a great friend to father. We buried him with considerable pomp. The bishop appointed another High Church rector, Anthony Torrens.

With my inheritance money, I purchased the property of Vallentine Judkin, just three miles of Bray House. I established it solely as a grazing property for Cotswold Lion stock. My dear wife, of course, persistently tried teaching me to read and write, yet I as persistently declined.

"I have the most intelligent, capable and literate woman any man could want as wife," I kept reminding her. "I am a busy father, grazier, farmer and businessman with two properties to manage, leaving me little time to dwell on the luxuries of learning to write. And with all my children so well tutored? Surely my brain has enough to endure."

She at last found it sound argument

"So long as, then, dearest love," she would croon, "you still spare time for loving your wife and mother of your children."

What more compensation could a man ever ask?

~ * ~

My personal feelings on the King's failings had been confirmed when he chose Bishop Laud above more learned and deserving men, as Archbishop of Canterbury. It was only too convenient that Laud championed the Divine Right ethic.

It is but further evidence that the country is dividing. Factions in royal favouritism returning as strongly as in the great Queen's time? When King James was so successful in creating it but an unhappy memory?

That night Bea and I sat in our private sitting room, created during the Bray House extensions as our very hideaway, talking on it. My confidence in this King's abilities was growing ever weaker. At our dinner table debates, I was finding it difficult to take an unbiased view of him.

"The last thing we had in mind when developing these debates," I told the children at breakfast, "was that they might divide our family. It concerns us that some may choose to follow me simply out of family loyalty. We would prefer it being a conviction in your own minds."

"We can support each other here, dearest," Bea had told me. "I have been in the fortunate situation, during their schooling years, of drawing out their real convictions on any matter as a classroom exercise. Yet now that applies only to young William. Yet all those hours have taught me how each mind works. It is likely, given the situation you raised tonight, that I can help. I can either support you or raise a question requiring further debate. One calling for reconsideration?"

We agreed such a course was not deceitful; rather a positive approach to our children avoiding a wrong decision for the wrong reason.

~ * ~

On the Faith front, as head of the English Church, Charles continued accusing the Calvinistic Puritans of returning to many old Catholic doctrines. He began making things so uncomfortable for them that many Puritans emigrated to New England in the Americas.

Charles and Archbishop Laud were both pleased to see the back of them.

Yet tension between Parliament and the Crown continued simmering.

"Oh, what a flamboyant poppycock the man is, Leyton. And politically blind. Can he not see the dangers of using force of arms against a Scotland rejecting Anglican rather than Presbyterian prayer books? Surely he should be wooing them to the goal."

I was lounging in Burgess Manor's library, Leyton having just poured brandies.

"Next, Richard," he responded, "we shall hear that infuriated Scots have renewed invasions in our north, begun a Viking plague all over again."

"Charles is so besotted in his faith that he blindly builds hurdles in his own path. His obsession with being God's champion on earth riles both Scots and Parliament. In council meetings, am I alone in noticing how several traditionally Royal supporters are beginning to take Parliament's views on things?"

"Which in particular?"

I smiled inside at the snide influence.

"That if he were to win this fight against Presbyterians, he would then start on Ireland's Catholicism."

Leyton moved to let down the heavy bar sealing the library door against even staff.

"Are you so seriously finding your Royal instincts wavering?"

He was now drawing windows closed. "Instincts don't easily change, Richard. I too admit the King's behaviour shifts from surprise to concern. For the first time, I too harbour doubt on our monarch's wisdom. It seems to be approaching blind insanity."

"I am sure this conversation is being held behind many sealed doors, dear friend. Even amongst the King's noblemen. And Royal Guards. Many must be looking more kindly on Parliamentary views."

At dinner the very next evening, it was again Soloman who made the opening gambit.

"Father, I cannot help but wonder what will become of the archbishop's propensity for High Church dogma. Will it not only further widen the gaps in Anglican lore? Further separate its elements? What is Vicar Torrens' attitude?"

As senior verger at All Saints, I took time to answer. I dunked my napkin in my fingerbowl and wiped spilled juice from my velvet breeches.

Is Soloman pressing to see where I stand in the matter, rather than just the vicar?

"We agree that Laud is simply obeying a direction from the King. For an archbishop to deliberately make such a ruling in dogma without formal consultation with bishops, is not only unusual but, in the present atmosphere, inflammatory. As you suggest, boy, it widens the gap not only between High Church bishops and Low, but the growing Puritan element. Particularly as the latter becomes an increasing strength in the Upper House. Fervently anti-royal at that. It but exacerbates the rift between the Crown and Parliament."

Frances raised a finger.

"All Saints continuing with High Church lore puts us outside the national argument. Yet I agree. Religion seems no longer binding people together—it is rather driving faith asunder."

She let her eyes rove all around the table, inviting comment.

Bea answered. "Certainly, we are all involved, child. Our sovereign no longer maintains harmony in his nation's faiths. The harmony was once split by only the Protestant-Catholic row, yet it now splits Protestant harmony. For more than a century, Protestantism has been mainly Royalist, as has been the gentry. Aristocracy dominates the House of Lords, so Parliament is also dividing more widely—House of Lords for King and House of Commons against him."

"And it is the House of Commons that makes the laws," Dickie added.

I raised a finger. "Even so, son, it is the Lords who must ratify them. Anything controversial to the King is readily defeated."

"Well, why is the King worried? If laws cannot be passed against him, he remains secure," asked young Henry.

"Because, lad, the King's expenses must be approved by the Commons. The country's constitution clearly gives it the right to approve all monetary grants to a sovereign. Charles has expensive tastes. He demands three times the monies sought by past sovereigns.

"Let me inform you, children all," I added quietly, having gnawed off a further succulent knob from my mutton-leg, "of a recent development...

"A lawyer and renowned polemicist, William Prynne, a Puritan Presbyterian, along with two supporters, were just a few years ago convicted of seditious libel. Prynne had previously had his ears 'cropped' as penalty for Seditious Libel against High Church dignitaries, and on this occasion, all three had their ears lopped entirely. Both Prynne's cheeks were as well branded 'SL'—for Seditious Libeller. All three were returned to the Tower, where they had been writing their pamphlets of protest, this time without paper or ink. They are now allowed but one book, the English Book of Common Prayer, which, of course, they refute. Let me also add that all three are adamantly British to the core, their greatest crime writing pamphlets condemning what Puritans see as anti-Christian—the upholding of feasting as a Christian practice, even Christmas, and claiming that theatre treats life only as imaginative playwrights might conceive it, rather than acknowledged biblical facts.

"So many people feel treated too harshly—that this King's attitude goes beyond what is considered reasonable. Even justice. Especially those of us who believe feasting a fair enough pastime and who are adamant supporters of playwrights like William Shakespeare. Your mother and I believe these are not crimes demanding loss of freedom and physical torture.

"Now, note that the House of Commons has ruled that the three were 'Illegally treated.' They have been released from the Tower and are free to write their Puritanical theses. So keep these examples in mind when comparing life under Charles or life under Puritanism."

Soloman again raised a finger. "At least the Puritan Parliament, Father, offered them the right of speaking freely, when the King kept them confined and under torture."

Bea and I smiled.

Twenty-four

George Fothergill was in the doldrums.

Trying to soothe the burdens on my best friend's shoulders keeps me sombre. And my father's advice is added complication.

Maythew had been pleased at George coming to him for advice, yet the lad's reaction proved disappointing.

"I've never seen Thomas such, Father," George had appealed. "He tells me he can no longer face the world. You know how much he loved his Ann. Her death has sent him near berserk. His spirit has been kept alive only in the boy she bore him, and now it too has died. Thomas will not eat. He drowns himself in ale and wine."

"Death of a loved one, dear boy, is the hardest thing in life to bear. I feel it now too. Your grandfather's life is quickly fading. He no more complains of gout, rheumatism and arthritis because he has given up on life. He gives all the signs of wanting release. Seeing him so distresses me deeply."

Old Rainold had had enough, and his son was devastated.

"This Puritan wretch of a vicar," Maythew continued, trying to illustrate to George that others had problems too, "gives him no respect, let alone help. He tells him to pray to God that the King may yet see his proper responsibility is to Parliament. He is under instruction from his bishop to write sermons vilifying what he calls 'the evils we persist in.' He insists it is God's wrath that has befallen not only your friend Thomas for his Royalist tendency, but every soul in our village but those who have committed their lives to Purity. He will be the death, George, of our very church!"

Feeling utter defeat, Maythew raised his palms to hold his sagging head.

George had never seen his strong father so forlorn. He let a long minute pass.

Grandfather's ageing is a burden for us all, yet age cannot be denied. We all must face it. If Grandfather's time is come, none can do aught but accept it

George wasn't seeing his father's distress as a weakness.

I shall surely feel the same about him when at that stage of life.

Yet he avoids my question. It is his help I need, not another lecture on our Puritan vicar.

Father has ever declared me the family realist, rejecting notions of fairies and elves, of the gremlins Grandfather blames for all the unexplainables in life. Even God. I sometimes wonder if Father frets over the possibility. And should he ever realise that I too, doubt God, it would shatter him. I simply cannot see that if God is so good, how can so many evil things befall so many good people—Uncle Steven, Thomas' Ann, Grandfather's incessant pains.

"...we are cursed, today, with such a romantic fool of a King."

George was amazed, as his mind popped back to his father's surprising declaration. "Sorry, Father. My mind was adrift."

Maythew shook his head, not annoyed that George had lost concentration, but as if his subject were some sort of bad dream. "I bemoan the facts today invading every man's soul. A good King or Queen, as Elizabeth proved and James proved, had their people at heart—saw it a duty to build a strong nation, strong people, enhance our lives. All our family, George, your grandfather especially, has ever been a devout Royal. And me. Proud of it, we ever were. But this King lives in a dream-world, thinks only of personal pleasures and power.

He uses religion not as a guide to man's morality, but a tool to be carved into any shape he desires."

George was shattered at his father's frankness, even in his own home.

"Father, for the sake of us all, shield that fear from others. There are spies everywhere. They will have your head on a pike for people to gawk at and for us to weep over."

Maythew rose and put an arm about his son. "Never fear, boy. I realise the dangers. I shall continue careful, for I want no shame on my family, nor give you the pain of seeing my head on a pike. Nor do I want to give this bad King the pleasure of killing me over his poor judgements."

George clasped his father to his breast and hugged him.

Maythew's sadness suffered more when, despite it being expected, old Rainold conceded life.

He had pulled his sole remaining son's head to his dying lips to whisper regrets at Maythew continuing churchwarden to a Puritan vicar.

It was a bitter blow.

Had I not remained churchwarden, the vicar would have recruited more converts. I at least saved many neighbours from turning affections towards Parliament and Purity.

He was not to realise that it was happening all over the nation.

~ * ~

Only a week later, the people of Edinburgh rioted.

King Charles was Scottish born, and his turncoat attitude against his own father's doctrine inflamed all Scots. Not only Presbyterians in Scotland, where it was the dominant religion, but also its adherents in England revolted. They found he had been raising money from wealthy adherents to take an army to Scotland to suppress the Presbyterian religion by force. Also to then remain in Scotland to ensure subservience was observed.

A growing intolerance saw Parliament continuing to refuse a grant of cash to spend on what Charles saw his God-given right. He took a desperate measure.

I shall have them cut their own throats.

He wanted a war that would forever quit the country of both Parliament and Puritanism.

Every King in Europe will send armies to aid my royal cause!

Yet Parliament was even more clever. It agreed to advance him his claimed money if he agreed to several principles. He must refrain from imposing taxes without Parliament's consent. He must convene Parliament to sit at least once every three years. He must refrain from arbitrary imprisonment of dissidents. He must refrain from quartering troops in people's homes, from imposing martial law in times of peace, abolish his newly created special courts. Final demand was that the Earl of Strafford, the King's sheriff of all Ireland and most outspoken minister against Parliament, be executed.

The list indeed cut deeply into the King's gut as well as his enormous pride.

Yet he was desperate. He signed the execution order of the friend who had ever given only devoted service, and he conceded to all demands. Parliament paid when Strafford died.

~ * ~

"Is it any wonder," Beatrix asked over dinner on the day we received that news, "that people are turning against the King? In the market square today, Cook and I couldn't believe our ears."

She told us Cook had also informed her, on their ride home, that every member of the staff was already agreed that the King had lost their support. "He ain't worth a quarter of his father's royal station, ma'am," she had insisted.

"Well, I agree with her. Executing such a loyal supporter to get his money is the last straw for me, too."

Soloman was the first to give me a little clap of hands. "Surely, Father, you would find yourself in the Tower if publicly airing such thoughts."

A quiet fell over the entire table, every eye on me.

"Not at all, lad. Firstly, a Bray dinner table is not public. I should be the first to expect loyalty from my family when each of our very futures is at stake. My strongest duty is to lead you to prosperous and satisfying lives. Such ideal the King has lost sight of. Parliament seems to be increasingly supporting free speech—the William Prynne episode taught us that."

All but little William were smiling. It seemed he found the ant climbing up and over his stockinged knee of more interest.

The family was smaller now, Frances and husband having moved on to their own farm.

Dickie spoke first. "Father, only a month ago I would have thought such a blasphemy against your Royal principles. You've been illustrating, of late, a marked change in your philosophy, and all, dear Father, are in agreement. We have been discussing it."

The candles flickered as butler Robson, at that moment, came through the door carrying a tray of apple pie servings. He hesitated. I noticed it and beckoned him to proceed.

"There can be no one-side or the-other-side in today's problems, Dickie. These are enticing loyalties either way. Yet I agree that divisions are dividing the people."

Robson set his tray down on the sideboard and retired.

All realised he was likely listening at the other side of the door.

"Some, like you, Soloman, apparently reached your decision some time back. I commended you at the time. It is unfortunate that all Englanders are being forced to face the fact that both religion and politics seem spiralling into a vortex."

I waved my hand around the table.

"Your mother and I have always been Royal supporters—luckily lived under sovereigns with their subjects at heart. Sure we suffered minor disappointments in some decrees, yet in the main, we believed ourselves lucky being English. But we too have been questioning King Charles' morals. He is too self-centred. His policy forces only personal views on us, views not necessarily best for any of the three countries in our nation."

It seemed an age before Dickie again spoke. "Thank you, Father. You have ever taught us to think for ourselves, question values before doing as told. As eldest, I feel it my duty to recommend to all siblings that we follow Soloman's example. I am with Soloman."

John stood. "Me too."

Jane stood. "Me too."

Henry stood. "Me too."

Seven-year-old William, already crossing to the sideboard for his slice of pie, called, "Me too."

~ * ~

The Tarn House sitting room was converted for a wake.

Curtains were drawn, tapestries were gone, portraits removed, window shutters closed. All was in darkness twenty-four hours a day save the lone candle atop the bier.

Only other furniture was a dozen pews borrowed from St. Oswalds. Many villagers declined entering a church adopting more Puritan rules. With the bier closed, a Royal Crest carved into the oaken lid, all sat in the flickering candlelight, murmuring quiet farewells. Margaret and Maybell served tasty treats in the dining hall, where ale flowed freely.

Maythew mounted the wake at home so friends could see his father off with dignity. He was afeared that if the eulogy were entrusted to the vicar, little justice would be shown.

When the time for burial came, despite the chill, the many dissenters remained outdoors until the service concluded. They wanted to see Rainold Fothergill laid to rest, yet declined the Puritan service. Dissenters were now so common around the country that in many parishes, provision was made for them to avoid sermons. Puritan vicars used sermons to laud Puritan standards and to revile non-believers and dissenters. Come sermon time, dissenters could move outdoors until a bell was rung, signalling the end of the sermon.

Yet a funeral service offered no such facility.

"But ye may attend the burial," Maythew told them.

"The bishop hath agreed that as churchwarden, and the deceased being my own father, I may conduct the interment ceremony."

So his service to a Puritan vicar, whilst reviled by old Rainold, made it possible for his dissident friends to see the old fellow on his way.

~ * ~

With his plans to take troops to Scotland with the granted money nipped in the bud by Parliament's conditions, Charles turned again to the nobility.

Many Lords responded to the threat of losing Royal support by offering, rather than money, their private armies. All knew that losing Royal support could mean their house and land would be confiscated, leaving them poor. Charles even pandered to the Irish Catholics. He promised them that from then on, should they support him in a war, they may practise their Catholic religion. None of these agreements broke his pledge to Parliament.

He totted up his advantages…

My English Lords are taking their armies to put down the Edinburgh revolt.

I am now able to withdraw my loyal Royal army from Ireland.

My spies insist that the Scots, whilst avidly siding with Parliament, will wait behind their borders to see if Parliament can hold its own against me before joining any action.

And my pockets now bulge with money.

The frenzy seemed, now, highly probable.

Twenty-five

When Dickie decided to marry his Mary, it was unanimously agreed they should make Bray House their home.

They moved into the suite built for Bea and me in the south-wing addition. It had its own little sitting room. We had moved into Old Henry's suite when he followed Mother to their grave at All Saints. Our previous suite had, in the interim, been a guest suite.

"It served us so well, dearest, after dinner of an evening," Bea reminded me. The 'dearest' expression had, over the years, become part of an intimate game.

"The King may well set bad examples for the younger generation by keeping an entire troupe of mistresses," she had insisted. "We should give our own young the same opportunity for establishing a binding love."

"Indubitably, my dear. I am highly conscious, after our score and more years wedded, that some wives still offer husbands satisfaction in their *boudoirs*. Especially when lacking the King's ability to afford such royal luxuries."

She stared down her nose because I sat while she stood behind with hands on my shoulders. She decided to ignore the risky jibe.

"Have you talked with Dickie about restoring the old Naseby house? You said when buying the property that you would. I think you even said, 'When Dickie has proved himself a capable manager.' Has that time not arrived? I could use its space as a studio for Jane and me with our painting, modelling and weaving."

I rolled my eyes across the ceiling. "You continue to intrigue me in asking two things in the same sentence, my dearest. Is it because it has so often proved successful?"

"Of course, dearest. Why should I change?"

I pulled her into my lap. "If I weren't wearing these thigh-high boots, my dear, I would make eager love to you."

"If I weren't wearing a twenty-hook corset, dearest, I would comply."

We settled for several giggles and some kisses, conscious of how neither had tired of physical love, even after nine children.

"I shall talk with Dickie on it. It would mean more staff. Can you do with fewer here?"

She kept pushing on my shoulders, for I was actually rising as if to begin shedding boots. "What if the children should see us?"

"It would further cement their belief in our happiness. Can you afford fewer servants?"

"We have but two in the kitchen and two cleaning, apart from Robson, who you insist is essential if you want to continue hands-on work in the field. I cannot afford to release staff just because Dickie moves out. But if they were living on Naseby money, we would save on feeding them. And do we want crying new babies here?"

"Save enough to cover the costs of hiring a cook and a housemaid for Mary and increasing Dickie's salary?"

"Should we see it as the cost of helping our children find their way? It would be good for Dickie if Naseby were established as a separate business. Surely agriculture has scratched grazing's back long enough? Surely grazing pays its own way?"

"You are indeed an absolute although delightful scoundrel the way you twist things. Why relate the need for Bray House servants to separating our business into two companies?"

"Both are pertinent family matters, dearest. We have many children whose futures need considering. And all must relate to our income affording it."

"We cannot split our farm five ways between five sons, dearest. It is a shameless wile to treat me this way."

"Of course it is, dearest."

I let a moment pass while gathering thoughts.

"You are right, of course. We should split it in two. Soloman obviously has no wish to farm or graze. At twenty-five, his head is into books on law. Politics is a likelihood for him, despite being a brewing storm these days. Nor is John for farming. You tell me he has taken to figures well, and when I consult with him on farm-work, his approach seems only on how we should be handling this or that to make the operation more profitable. He is for something academic rather than farming."

She too let a long moment pass.

"He grasps a business concept more than Dickie or Soloman. Maybe his future is accounting?"

"That still leaves me boss of the farm, at least until Henry and William begin illustrating aptitudes."

"Maybe when splitting the operations, dearest, we include John sharing the grazing business with Dickie, while managing the accounting of both? That would free you of considerable work too."

"An excellent suggestion in the longer term. But I will certainly look now at dissecting the two farms."

"Maybe you might find the agricultural side of the farm on its own unprofitable? We could then either consider here raising alpaca, or mohair, or digging for Roman coins?"

I recognised this as her way of asking 'Any other business'?

And she has never been wrong. She sees things more clearly than I who remains too close to my father's ways. Maybe we should consider mechanical spinning-wheels for Naseby?

Just the memory of Bibury and our betrothal brought another happy smile to my mind.

~ * ~

The year 1641 brought trembles of war jitters to every breast.

"It's that Englishmen are training to reach for the throats of brother Englishmen," I expounded over dinner—our farewell dinner to Dickie and the pregnant Mary.

Dickie was confirmed manager of Bray Grazing Company.

I had spent much time with both Dickie and John on the various arts of running a business, handling staff, monies and risks encountered in my self-taught past. Beatrix had arranged with Edgar Calfe for Dickie to spend a month in Chipping Campden at old Christofer's knee. The old Judkin land had a cottage on it that we extended to a comfortable home for a moderate-sized family. It was but three miles of Bray House, in fact closer to the village of Naseby than Brixworth. Dickie and Mary wished to retain the old name of Naseby Cottage.

"You will like it," Naseby neighbours told them. "It is the sort of place where nothing happens."

So it would suit them well. Happily, too, the area still fell within the Parish of Brixworth, and All Saints would remain the entire family's place of worship—an important factor in days when different parishes were adopting different dogmas.

"And," pointed out Beatrix, "it means our family will be separated in the future no longer than six days."

It didn't apply to me. I would be riding to Naseby every other day.

Yet war jitters remained a dampening influence on all.

The family still at home seemed small—Soloman coming up twenty-six, John twenty-three, Jane nineteen, Henry sixteen and William ten.

Jane was being courted by her William Penn. Young William, we felt, was the only son likely safe from having to take up arms in the event of war. The thought of any son having to march into battles of hand-to-hand combat, however, was a shivering fear in each of us. Battles were so much a one-on-one fight to the death.

A desperately fearful thing to face.

At least my sixty-five years would keep me safe.

"Only consolation on that point," I proclaimed before Sunday dinner ended, "is that I am relieved of finding abhorrent the taking up arms against my country's King. I remain shattered, however, that I am left with supporting a Parliament that could force Puritanism on us. That possibility keeps roiling in my gut. We could lose so many freedoms. Even suffer greater spiritual hardship."

On Sundays, Dickie and Mary dined with us.

I walked to the other end of the table and raised my Beatrix to stand by me.

"Your mother and I would like to hear all your comments."

Bea sat, and I returned to my studded saddle-back carver, raised my tankard of wine and took a long draft.

We sat expressionless, most eyes on Dickie. Yet it was Soloman who raised a finger. Dickie gave him the nod.

Beatrix seems pleased at Soloman having first voice. She has tutored all, knows their separate natures, their different approaches to emotional problems. Soloman is most like me, can see both sides of an argument, always considers possibilities outside the box.

"My strong feeling, Father, is that Parliament remains the lesser of the two evils. I too feel guilty standing against the King, yet he behaves abominably, has proven shamefully untrustworthy. Parliament too, has faults, in particular the one you mentioned, the embargo on religious freedom. A military victory for Puritans could begin a war amongst parishioners, wars of emotional stress. Yet whilst being the first to assist Parliament win victory, I shall be the first, once that task is achieved, to seek a seat in the House of Commons. It is the one legal area where one can speak against compulsory Puritanism. If the King should be granted undisputed rights by victory, there will be no opportunity for free speech at all."

I quietly clapped my hands.

"Dickie? You with now a wife to protect and a baby on the way?"

"I favour Parliament. Should the King win a war, I would be happier with his brand of Anglicanism, yet by insisting on it, we should again be quickly at war against Scotland. And have the Irish again rising. There could be no peace."

John interrupted. "Surely in a war, Irish and Scots will support Parliament? The Irish will realise that with Charles ruling supreme, there will never be a Parliament again, that the King's next target, once Presbyterianism is abolished, will be the Catholic faith. A King with absolute power is dangerous. Especially this king. Look back on King Henry. He forced all English to convert. Charles would do the same to both Scotland and Ireland. I cannot see the King winning a war against such odds."

"He can call on Royal armies from European monarchies," interposed Bea. "He has sent English armies to help in the wars there."

"To be beaten every time," John added, caustically.

My Bea gave a wan smile. "You have studied modern history well, boy. However, monarchies help each other. I think that with the exception of only Spain, all Europe will come to King Charles' aid."

The discussion went on into the night. Even Henry and young William included.

Jane pleaded out. "I have every intention of having my Liam's proposal before you shortly Papa," she declared confidently. "And should I happily marry him, I must side with his wishes. I would rather, for now, remain neutral. But whatever you decide, I will not let it divide me from my family."

Beatrix and I smiled wanly.

"With your mother's powers of persuasion, my daughter," I said, "you could well influence him."

All brothers giggled.

I was highly pleased at the boys' votes being unanimous.

I was anxious to talk with Leyton Burgess. We had liaised that each family would, on this very night, affirm its preference.

We both knew war could not be avoided. And we were both for Parliament.

~ * ~

When Parliament ruled that William Prynne's sentence was without British law and released him from imprisonment, restoring him to the magisterial bench, King Charles raged. Tensions between The Crown and Parliament reached boiling point.

The King led his Royal Guard into the very House of Commons to arrest his several worst enemies. Yet typical of 'royal secrets,' the intended victims had been forewarned and fled. Charles was further vilified by Parliament for having 'invaded under arms' the sanctity of that establishment.

Charles, however, furious that his quarry had escaped, and supported by the fact that Divine Right had God on his side, made the momentous decision to raise the biggest army he could scrounge. He directed every county lieutenant to raise forces to march under the King's flag. He despatched requests to European monarchs to send armies to England—both foot-soldiers and cavalry.

Parliament followed suit, hustling around the country for volunteers. Its forces would be dubbed Roundheads because of the pudding-basin haircuts all were given so metal helmets could be worn.

The King's major assembly point was Leicester in the Midlands.

Accordingly, the enemy Parliament made its assembly point only a day's ride south: Pitsford Water, a large lake on Brixworth's southern outskirts.

However, the first skirmish came from minor forces of both sides en-route from the west country to the Midlands.

At Worcester, the Royal Cavalry, swash-bucklingly clad in uniforms of velvet, lace and dashing plumed hats, were all well-trained and seasoned swordsmen, All were accomplished horsemen, their mounts trained for battle.

Parliamentary cavalrymen were raw—quickly put to flight.

However, rather than chasing and reducing their numbers, Cavaliers tarried to loot and plunder not only the fallen Roundheads of their pocket contents, helmets and sabres but the local farmers' poultry and piglets.

Meanwhile, the Royalist infantry, vastly outnumbered by Roundheads and with no expected cavalry protection, was decimated to a man. The King abandoned his holding of Worcester, and such was the opening gambit of England's great Civil War.

Parliament had taken its first city.

Twenty-six

If one wanted to divide the map of England in a straight line that had on its left side those who were content to live in a 'follow the leader' world, and on the right those with grudges enough that a stand was worth taking against Divine Right, loss of religious freedom and taxation without representation, then one could be drawn.

A line strung from Torquay to Hull could well be 'a rule of thumb' separation.

The eastern half had most population, most of the nobility, most of the educated, most of the trade centres. It was indeed most of men with the ability to measure political values. It supported Parliament and provided the vast majority of its Roundhead army. In general, only the moneyed nobility within the eastern zone were for the King.

West of the line had the sparser population, least of the nobility and most of the illiterates, especially in the north. It supported the King and provided the vast majority of his army of Cavaliers.

However, the Royalist Cavaliers had two further advantages, ironically mostly drawn from east of the imaginary line. One was the majority of generals with experienced troops proud of their royal uniforms; the other was their ready stash of armaments.

The Scots, incensed at the King's badgering over what they considered their political rights and at his 'illegal' taxes imposed on their pockets and produce, were for Parliament. It had promised them that, in the event of war, should Scotland support Parliament and it was victorious, Scotland could retain its Presbyterian religion without interference.

So the Scots retired behind the border until the trend of war became evident. If the Royalists seemed to be winning, Scotland would invade. If Parliament had the upper hand, Scotland would still invade even if just to clearly illustrate support, that they could earn religious independence. Scotland had nothing to lose.

This meant that Englishmen of the northern counties, fervently Royal, were trapped.

~ * ~

In Ireland, the people had only two enemies. The Puritans supporting Parliament were vehemently opposed to anything Catholic and had even declared that, given the power, Catholicism in Britain would be abandoned. The King had equally declared on accession to the throne that he was also vehemently opposed to anything Catholic.

However, the King had, in his desperation, promised the Irish that if he were to win the war, he would permit the Catholic religion in Ireland. The Irish signed the agreement, and Charles withdrew all but a handful of his Royalist Army from Ireland, to fight against Parliament.

~ * ~

In Ravenstonedale, the secret Fothergill cellar was stocked with hay for sleeping, barrels of drinking water and as much bread, salted pork, fruit and potatoes as would weather up to a month before needing replacement. Lookouts were posted on the Pennine heights, watching for invaders approaching down the valley. None knew if the Scots would concentrate on marching south to link up with Parliamentary forces, or to first spread out in search of horses to ride, poultry and swine to confiscate, men to cashier into their army and young women to rape, even to take farther south with them.

If no army were present to assist locals, it was futile for any young man to resist. They too must hide or hie south in endeavour to meet up with a Royalist detachment. Any able-bodied man refusing to join the invaders would be struck down on the spot.

It was a bleak, no-win outlook for every family.

"At best," said Maythew with tears in his eyes to anxious sons, "if ye flee ye must keep off the roads. Ye must avoid any gathering of men not bearing the King's colours, even if ye must flee all the way to Leicester."

Messengers had brought news that that was where the King's army was based.

All knew that border skirmishes generally see-sawed through the Eden Valley, subject to numbers of armed men either side. Winners would stake claims on every grain of produce and every head of livestock they could lay hands on, irrespective of whether the incumbent farmer was friend or foe. Each farm could be left devastated, its people hungry.

"This is full-scale war," neighbours agreed. "It be not just Scots raiding, but as well, Royalists and Roundheads looting and burning, stealing our sons for their armies."

Yet the entire north was together in one respect. All were for the King.

"Except our preacher," reminded Maythew.

"And the vicars in other parishes, and the bishop in Kendal," echoed others.

So every northern county was divided on the aspect of religion.

However, some would not race to their cellars to hide. One was the non-conformist, some-time recusant and dissident Symon Busfeld. He was neither for one side nor the other. And his mind had been spinning.

If I offer to tell the Scots where families hide their women and serviceable men on the proviso they leave me and me farm unscathed, it would be to my advantage. I might just sound them out. I've but one daughter married and gone. All the others are here and need protection.

So, yes, he would hide his women and sons in his own cellar, then sit in wait with a primed pistol tucked into his belt. He would leave hands hanging idly so he could quickly grab it in emergencies. He arranged a chair by his front door for the purpose.

Two others of the little village didn't hide. George Fothergill, son of Maythew, and Thomas Adamthwait, son of John. They were already riding for Leicester.

George's motive was sheer patriotism. Thomas still rued the loss of wife and son and sought distraction.

"We should be home again soon," each told his family. "We will return with tales of sweeping victories over the Puritans."

"I envy ye lads," old John had said. "Were I a touch younger, I be ridin' with'ee."

Both had grinned. Old John was past sixty and hobbled with a stick. Gout and rheumatics kept him in pain. But he had been generous. Both fathers had been.

Old John gave Thomas a handful of shillings, and Maythew, never to be outdone by an Adamthwait, gave as much to George. It was sufficient to equip them with uniforms once finding the King's army, even having paid lodgings en-route.

Both fathers choked back sobs in readily conceding that their youngest sons respond to the King's cause. The joint partings were tender. Could this be just that final parting that might be the one too many? The dreadful last?

Such sorts of fear dwelt in every family breast.

Each was given family swords with crested hilts, polished to gleaming perfection by excited sisters who also gave them knitted jerkins, each with teardrops dried into every stitch. And a thousand kisses each.

Twenty-seven

November 1642

"The King holds Market Harborough, but a half day's ride."

The war, having so quickly come so close, had Brixworth in a spin.

"Should we flee, Richard? Will they come here, burn our homes?"

Beatrix and I had never expected the war might endanger the Midlands. Never having experienced fighting up close, we were still trying to grip the fact that Englishmen were fighting Englishmen, their objective to maim and kill.

"And all over politics and religion. Especially over religion," she bewailed.

"Flee where, my dear? We've no idea where they will strike. To go anywhere may simply be jumping from pan to fire. I simply must admit I have no idea what we should do other than stay here. At least we can be thankful our boys are all right. Donating so much wool to the war effort is a Godsend. Dickie's and John's work at Naseby, when most their ages are being cashiered by Roundheads, is considered essential."

I diligently wooed our local civic administrator, Abel Mason. It was imperative I convince him that taking skilled hands away from growing wool meant Parliament's soldiers could freeze. Fortunately, in that respect, temperatures were already plunging, and Roundhead soldiers faced imminent snowfalls. Also that farms growing vegetables and fruits were as desperately important. Experienced farmhands could contribute more to the war effort than taking up arms. I gave him free rein to bring fishermen to our lake shoreline. Even gave him leave to use my boats.

Beatrix and Jane were spending all the time they could knitting Dickie's yarn into scarves, stockings and woollen knickers for Roundhead troops.

Nor did Abel force us to billet soldiers, as was happening to most large houses. Poor Leyton at the manor was swamped with them, and all were proving unappreciative tenants, making free with stables, cookhouse and wine-cellar.

"And for the moment anyway," I was able to tell him, "Abel has given us twenty guards to protect us should Cavaliers attack."

I also persuaded him to send a score of guards to Naseby.

"Oh, how fortunate he is a fellow verger at All Saints, dearest," my darling insisted.

"We are very fortunate. But he could get moved. War is like that."

"I saw you in close conversation by the cookhouse this morning. What was that all about?"

"It had a good side to it as well as bad. The good is that he feels secure about his job because local men are favoured. He knows who are the riff-raff and trouble-makers so can readily assign them to the army. And like our Soloman, direct them to safe yet useful appointments."

"And the bad?"

"To keep up his quota of men directed into service, he must take some good villagers from their families and send them to war. Yet, my dearest, he has a liking for your eel pasties. I suggest you make a point of seeing that he is given some on regular occasions."

The Soloman thing had also been a God-given gift. When interviewed, Abel Mason was so impressed by Soloman's command of literacy and numbers that he assigned him to Parliament's administration office.

"I have been instructed," Abel told me, "to weed out the literate, recommending they apply to the Army Communication Officer at Cambridge."

It was a tremendous relief to us.

"Get from the man, my love, names of his friends he was forced to enlist into the fighting arm of the army. I am helping organise farming wives into ensuring families left fatherless do not go hungry. We can all contribute something to help those left without income. That should lift some guilt off him."

"I knew when I married you that I must keep a watch on your guile. Yet by all means, my dearest, let us feel quite guiltless in using all the cleverness we can. We need to keep on his good side. We still have other sons."

We cuddled closely.

"Anne told me children in the village are raiding at night, stealing not only eggs but hens. She says all children seem to have a way with dogs—instead of guarding, they snuggle up for cuddles."

Anne was Dickie's new wife.

"It was Mary who trained their dogs to bark," I reminded her. "When she died in childbirth, the dogs lost their regimen. When Dickie married again, Anne had no influence over the dogs. They fell lazy and instead of barking at intruders, now, as you say, snuggle up for cuddles. I shall have a word with Dickie on it. John has a better way with dogs. I shall talk with both."

One day, being so short-handed, I was helping my Bea peel potatoes.

"Yesterday," she told me, "I met Emma Richardson on the High Street. She told me her young man is on look-out in the church tower. Seems that overnight he can see the glow of fires not only up Market Harborough way, but south to Pitsford Water. That puts us right in the middle of the two armies, my dearest. Royalists camped a handful of miles north, and Roundheads less than a mile south."

"To see fires so far north, my love, it must be houses burning rather than camp-fires. Some poor souls' homes. I wonder where they shelter now?"

"With relatives, most likely. But it would only be the women. Men will have flown, either to join the Roundheads or escape the Royals. Word is that Cavaliers take no prisoners."

"That puts us all in danger if they come here. Our twenty-strong guard is not going to repel a raiding force."

"With the main Parliamentary army encamped at Pitsford Water, Cavaliers aren't going to walk right into its midst. Surely the King has bigger targets in mind than Brixworth. There is no castle here with caches of wealth to line his coffers. He has Leicester. He will more likely strike north than south."

"He struck and took Market Harborough. And what riches does it have?"

"It is a crossroads and major trading market—an ideal base to support and feed an army. Some of our wool even goes to a mill close by it. It is but six miles of Naseby."

"I cannot help but worry they should come here."

I put an arm about her shoulder. "They wouldn't worry about an old fogy like me. My greatest concern is William. Not sure what be their attitude to eleven-year-olds. They could conscript him as some officer's lackey, or drummer boy."

And we were then interrupted by Soloman's arrival. He had come from Cambridge with messages to the commandant at Pitsford Water.

"That camp is a shambles," he told us. There seems little organization and no leadership. Everyone seems running hither and thither, unsure what to do with all the recruits."

We were thrilled to learn, however, that he was permanently assigned to administrative work in Cambridge.

"Wonderful news, boy. Far better than imagining you toe-to-toe in battle with experienced swordsmen or pike-men."

"I must return on the morrow. Oh, I have seen so many carts on the road, families fleeing from Leicester and Market Harborough, so I should have no trouble hitching a ride. I am to assist with communications between the various branches of Parliamentary forces. But what of you? You seem distressed, Mother. Have you serious problems? And Dickie and Anne?"

We filled him in on our latest situation.

"So many men having been conscripted there is a shortage of labour," Bea explained. "Jane and I are tending horses and swine and milking goats and the cow. Lucy the maid was coaxed to invite her sister to come live in. So, yes, I am tired, yet ever worried should the Royalists attack as they did Market Harborough. You say so many people have had to flee?"

We discussed things in general, explaining that we operated under Parliamentary protection as an 'essential service.'

"Jane's Liam has moved in as farm hand," I told him. "He feigned a bronchial wheeze that would likely save him from conscription either for cavalry or foot-soldier. Abel Mason, who assigned you to Cambridge, is proving helpful. He has assigned a small troop of guards to Dickie. John also falls under his umbrella of shelter, working alongside Dickie. Henry and I are working hands-on in the field, so he too works under the Abel Mason umbrella of safety."

"He seems a handy fellow to keep onside of."

"Luck. I have known him many years. He often helps out at All Saints functions. He is a High Church adherent too, so all that is a fortunate bond."

"We have already invited him and his wife to Jane and Liam's wedding in a few weeks," Beatrix said, looking over her shoulder as if the fellow might be listening. "We will be having as fine a breakfast here as the times permit."

Soloman smiled. "Up to your guiles again, Mother? But no shame on you. I must tell Jane and Liam that I must miss their nuptials. I shall be kept extremely busy in Cambridge."

"Jane is in the cookhouse."

He left to go see her.

"Why don't you go with him, dearest, even start a new batch of eel pasties?"

Twenty-eight

George and Thomas had ridden hard for days.

Ravenstonedale to Leicester was many times farther than either had ventured. It seemed such a long ride. Now, nearing their goal, their hearts throbbed with the excitement of adventure. Yet the question hovering in each mind was no nearer finding an answer than when asking each evening at overnight inns...

"Will the King himself really be there?"

They had expected every innkeeper in England to be as satisfying a source of local knowledge as Ravenstonedale's ever proved. Neither was sure where 'there' might be, for they'd been told at Bradford only that it was rumoured the King's forces were heading to Leicester. Nor were they sure where Leicester might be. They were only following old John Adamthwait's advice to keep on the road for London and make enquiries as they went.

The King was not in Leicester. In fact, as they neared that big town, biggest either had ever seen and that had them eyes agog, they discovered they should be exercising care in proudly informing strangers they were seeking the King's army. It seemed as they moved south that less support was shown for the King and more for Parliament.

"Not as if these people are bloody Scots," George remonstrated. "They're English, like us."

Both found it hardly conceivable that any Englishman could side against the King.

They discovered Cavaliers had won a battle south of Leicester, taken the town of Market Harborough to establish a camp there—good news for the lads in two respects: they knew where to find the Royal Army, and the King was giving the Roundheads a thrashing.

They were increasingly finding the adventure, so heartily embarked on, not at all the easy ride to expected glory. Soldiers in armour meant serious fighting, real personal danger.

George Fothergill and Thomas Adamthwait joked less in ensuing days. New realisations on life were dawning.

~ * ~

I watched Beatrix at her loom.

"I am thankful when weaving blankets, that no pattern requires detailed attention," she had told me.

Many women all over England would be doing likewise.

I wondered if any of the wool my Bea wove could be ours? Dickie knew it for Cotswold Lion, so maybe it was ours.

Twenty-nine

In Oxford, Oliver Cromwell pounded a gloved fist on the table.
"A rabble I tell you! An absolute rabble!"
Arriving unannounced, he demanded audience with Parliament's new Minister for War.
Oliver Cromwell, son of a country squire, schooled in letters and numbers, was a zealous churchman with an unaffected outlook on life. He was both a Puritan averse to all forms of pomp and ceremony, and a man of decisive action. At Cambridge University, he had been tutored in military discipline. He acquitted himself well during the early days of the war, quickly identifying areas needing urgent attention to better Parliament's forces.
"Trial and error will never achieve," he scoffed.
He discovered that men in the field listened to him, were receptive to his ability to recognise the point of contentious matters, dismiss protocol so that sensible argument could be driven home. He could make sensible decisions on the battlefield. They followed where he led, and he led them to minor successes.
Parliamentarians too recognised the common sense he expounded, to listen, cogitate and respond positively. Inefficient generals were

stood down, replaced with men recommended by Cromwell, and better pay was awarded fighting men.

Discipline improved, and Cromwell was given greater command. Improvement was quickly evident. With newly confident men behind him, the tide of war began to change. He took Royal strongholds, blasting apart with cannon castles never built to withstand an assault by anything more powerful than catapults or swordsmen on ladders.

~ * ~

In wartime, risky judgement led to lower morale. In a war tending to be a series of one or two-day battles, winning them was vital in building morale. Most significant towns in seventeenth-century Britain were walled, and sieges were part of weakening the enemy through starvation. Sieges were briefer still when drinking water failed inside the wall. A river or stream flowing through, or seeping under it, could easily be fouled by the attacking army simply tossing slain cattle into it. Typhus and cholera quickly broke down both numbers of fighting men and morale.

So it was usual, as soon as an army gathered outside a town, to begin bombarding the walls. That usually caused the defending army to sortie out, forcing invaders to either fight hand-to-hand or run. Only two classes of combatants were involved in seventeenth century warfare—cavalry and infantry. Terrain played a big part. The army with the greatest number of men afoot needed to attack downhill. Also essential was a high point for commanders to overview the battlefield. Besieged towns with a wall had such an advantage.

Weapons played a significant part. Modern technology like siege towers and mechanical catapults were strong influences. And how strong a cannonade could the attacking army mount? More numerous and of greater calibre than that from within the walls? Or how strong was the cavalry in a town unsuspecting of attack? Or how many of an attacking army might be camped beyond a hillside, unsighted from atop the city-wall so that strengths were under-assessed? All such variables called for considerable spying by both sides. A 'most advantageous' site was available to only one, so guile played a part.

Whoever wasn't ready when enemy bugles sounded 'Charge!' was at a considerable disadvantage—especially in a time when every piece of firing mechanism called for lengthy reloading. When two sides met in the field, firearms were doubtful weapons, subject to numbers. All that could prevent the battle depending on hand-to-hand swordsmanship was one side having available cavalry to join the fray. Attacking foot-soldiers from saddle-height was a distinct advantage.

So was having scores of long-bowman behind the front line raining showers of arrows into opposition ranks. Again, numbers were important.

Risks were great. Most pitched battles had each side with strengths in some elements and weaknesses in other. So good luck or bad luck in terrain and weather were as chancy as timing. A leader with the least number in one element must rely on strengths in another.

Strength of leadership? Experience of troops? Good luck or bad luck?

All played roles.

~ * ~

In early 1643, King Charles enjoyed the tide of war. His forces were experienced fighting units drawn from service in Europe's Thirty Years' War. In the west, he took town after town, even Oxford where Cromwell had harangued his superiors. Charles made it his new seat of government, not only as a snub at Parliament, whose stronghold it had been, but because the city was second to London in facilities offered.

Messengers travelling from town to town tacking news sheets on market-square notice boards had Parliament supporters feeling more dour each day. The early months saw few major battles, merely minor ones against the ill-trained Roundheads. In the northeast, whilst townpeople were mostly loyal to the King, country people favoured Parliament. In Lincolnshire, Charles despatched troops to Gainsborough, and the small Parliamentary force readily surrendered. As did several Staffordshire towns. The first half year proved a period of decisive victories to the King.

Oliver Cromwell was meanwhile establishing his 'Ironsides' directly under his control—special forces named after their armour.

Come July, Cromwell had mixed fortunes at Gainsborough. He established a cannonade on the town walls under the darkness of night, and by good fortune a ball killed the Earl of Kingston. With their leader dead, the defending Royalists immediately surrendered.

Near two weeks later, however, Cromwell received news that more than a thousand Cavaliers were marching north from Leicester and Nottingham. He immediately despatched his Ironsides south.

"We shall meet them in the fields," he declared.

~ * ~

Two pikemen of the Cavalier Infantry in the fields were George Fothergill and Thomas Adamthwait. They had yet to be tested in battle, for on arriving in Leicester and finding the King's army with already several successful battles behind them, they were asked to illustrate their skills with the family cutlasses their sisters had polished for them.

Neither impressed the assessors.

"Ye will not be playing Catch Me If Ye Can, sirrahs," they were told. "War is a killing matter. Ye both would be dead within a minute of closing with real swordsmen. How be ye with the bow? Can ye hit a target the size of a man's heart at thirty paces?"

They failed at that. They were instructed in wielding the pike, the pole-axe and the matchlock musket. They were taught the formation of battles—various exercises involving infantry and cavalry, forming boxes and siege-formations. They were taught how to march without overtaxing their bodies and how to 'read' the bugle signals.

Much of it they found boring and other, fearful.

They quickly began realising glory came at a dreadful risk to a man's very life.

They traded in their beautiful swords to buy leather armour. Leather flaps hanging from shoulders gave the fighting man more ease of movement than metal armour. Pikemen in the main wore metal breast and back plates with thick 'flaps' of leather covering arms above elbows. They were forced to accept that man's forearms and wrists didn't deserve protection.

Training in handling the matchlock muskets had both at sixes and sevens. Loading was intricate, leaving a man exposed up to a minute if something fell or if trembling caused powder to fall to waste rather then down the barrel.

"It's all very well being a musketeer if a man has four or five hands instead of two, what with carrying all the paraphernalia needed to reload," they bewailed. Apart from the musket being heavy, one must tote the plunging rod, the 'rest' or rowlock, the musket balls, powder and powder horn."

"Being a musketeer is not to my liking," George complained. "It all is a tedious to-do."

So they trained as pikemen.

A well-trained army had pikemen shielding the musketeer during reloading, then sometimes even helping him aim by resting the heavy barrel on the pikeman's shoulder when firing.

"All very well if one has ears stuffed with wadding," Thomas insisted.

Musketeers were also trained to use the 'rowlock,' a metal rod, shoulder-height, with a U-shaped 'rollick' for aiming his musket. Yet that was an extra item, cumbersome at that, to carry into battle.

So the two had ended up realising that the pike was the weapon giving most control for men unskilled. "Pikes are the greatest deterrent to advancing cavalry," they were taught.

"Every rider sees his steed a personal friend. All are loathe to charge against a wall of fourteen-foot pikes aimed at their horse's throats."

However, the lads from Ravenstonedale were to find their first battle called for no such cavalry charge. They were stationed in Doncaster and told to march on Gainsborough in Lincolnshire.

"The upstart Colonel Oliver Cromwell, a Puritan if ever there be one," they were told, "has taken the town. We are to wrest it from him."

"Action at last, Thomas? All this training, and we still haven't sighted a Roundhead?"

"Patience, George. We both suffer the pains of realising we can never be heroes. Every muscle in my body aches from having to cross the chasm between the glory we imagined and being ready to fight. Such realism has made my ego hide. Yet as pikemen, we have the best chance of survival. Unblooded we be, yet strong of heart."

George laughed. "At least our dear fathers and sisters are not here to see how we've had to climb down from envisioned heroes. We may yet come close to it, but, as you say, we must first sight the enemy."

Gainsborough changed hands several times. Yet now, Cromwell's spies reported it held by but a paltry Royal force.

Ten miles to its south, the Royal Cavalry saw Cromwell's complement of a hundred horse appear over a crest. Parliament had the advantage of height. It charged, driving the Royals into marshy flatland, where its leader, Cavendish, took a fatal sabre-thrust through his chest. Three hundred Cavalier riders fell to their deaths at the hands of the outnumbered Cromwell, who relished in his first major victory.

Yet it was short-lived.

Next day, word arrived that a force of Royal troops was approaching from the north. Cromwell led off to meet them, driving off two troops of horse, and then, on climbing a hill, quickly called to his equerry.

"Look at that, dear fellow, an absolute sea of them," he declared.

They were indeed facing a sea of some thirty regiments of Foot as well as a great body of horse.

After conferring with God, as before any action, Cromwell made his decision.

"Our troops have little left in them after yesterday's battle. Order withdrawal."

They fought their way back through the remnants of horse they had just slaughtered and fled south to Lincoln, conceding Gainsborough.

Cromwell's first victory over the Royalists was so quickly and easily overturned into a victory for the King's men.

"Do'ee think, George, that we won because they now hast thou and me with them?"

Thirty

The King was in Ireland examining the strength of his military.
Can I pull out more men for fighting in England without leaving Ireland vulnerable to rebellion?
It was a fickle war. It was the day when men made fighting a career—a mercenary killing for whichever side offered the highest salary. Many an English army had many such who couldn't even speak English. Such men would gather wherever two armies assembled, offering themselves like prostitutes in the shadows.
Charles was in the situation that if such clusters of Irish were available, he would hire them. Most were those hired two and three years ago to protect the Scots who settled Ulster. The risk was, of course, that these were they who would be first to cut and run if the going got tough. Also, after the collapse of the Irish rebellion, with the English army controlling Dublin and the Scottish army Belfast, the Irish established its Catholic Confederation, naming Kilkenny its capital. It raised its own army. They also had many friendly nations with armies in Catholic Europe. Charles trod a path strewn with all sorts of difficulties so even encouraged these men.

"All you of the Irish revolutionary movement wanting reprieve are now pardoned if joining my Cavaliers. Choose this or Puritanism," he threatened.

Thousands flocked to him.

Oh, what a fickle war!

Charles, of course, stood alone on an island that itself was in the frenzy of bloody war. Yet the great salesman won agreement from the Catholic Confederation that neither would it rise in rebellion if he withdrew his English troops. It signed its commitment with its Irish seal.

Another major point won! Charles could now withdraw every battle-hardened man who valued his paymaster. He took them all home to England.

~ * ~

The war's turning point arrived with the end of summer.

King Charles' nephew, Prince Rupert of the Ruhr, had brought his army, both infantry and cavalry, in answer to Charles' request. Rupert was a professional soldier with a string of successes in the Thirty Years' War to his credit. His troops were on a high, having immediately on arrival wrested the city of Bristol from Parliament.

Charles' Irish troops arriving from Dublin were also on a high. They had taken Cirencester from Parliament.

Their respective armies met outside Gloucester, home of Richard Bray's Cotswold Lions and one of the few remaining Parliamentarian strongholds left in the west.

Charles and Rupert held a council of war.

"Do we lead our combined armies to take London? Or do we first take Gloucester?"

Rupert was for Gloucester. "It looks easy, Uncle. Let us establish the entire west as safe under our banner, then march on London."

"If you are so sure of Gloucester proving easy, Rupert, you take it whilst I lead my army to London. You can catch up."

"Uncle, dear Majesty, I have a lifetime of successes behind me in making decisions on the strategy of battle. The 'why not' is easily answered. Our decision to attack London was on the basis of having our combined forces. The report of one spy, in my opinion, is not enough to change my mind. If I attack Gloucester and find unexpected delays, you would arrive in London undermanned and vulnerable."

Charles mused.

Don't I have God on my side? He was all the way with me when negotiating with the Catholic Irish. He has been with me all the way in this war so far, so will prove so all the way to London. I have nowt to fear. However, I cannot risk denying Rupert. I will trust God to hold London for me.

"We shall take Gloucester, Rupert."

They drank a toast, and Rupert set about preparing his attack.

On Monday, 10 August, King Charles demanded at Gloucester City's gate, that the defending garrison surrender. It refused, sneaking arsonists outside the city walls to burn every facility that Charles would need in a siege, and then sealed the gates.

Charles first severed water pipes that entered through the wall's foundations and set up bombardments. Rupert set engineers to mining the walls and setting explosives.

Every morning the two expected to see a white flag of surrender unfurled.

They waited morning after morning after morning.

Two weeks later, Rupert informed Charles that his miners were ready to blow the walls.

"Charges are being laid overnight, Uncle."

That very night, the weather broke and the mines flooded.

All the work was undone, leaving them right back where they had started.

~ * ~

"A letter from Soloman, Richard. And a plea."

From the field I had seen the courier arrive in dusty haste so made my way there.

Beatrix, all agog because she had already perused it, read it to me.

My dear parents,

Whilst our Parliamentarians make significant gains in the north, things do not go well in the west. You have likely heard that Bristol has been taken and that the King has returned from Ireland with a large army. We fear for London. Our Earl of Essex is taking his entire London complement west in an attempt to save Gloucester. I have been ordered to Reading in Berkshire to establish communication lines along the Cotswold-London road. I need help, and this is opportunity to gainfully employ a brother. You will have reasons to choose either John or Henry. You will take my meaning, and each has the qualifications I require.

He must meet me with all urgency at the George Hotel, Reading. I am leaving for there now.

May God have you all in his sights.
Your loving son, S.

"The dear boy has our concerns at heart, Richard. Maybe this is indeed God's answer to our worries over Henry?"

"At seventeen, my dearest, he is indeed the most vulnerable. They were saying in the market only yesterday that conscription scouts are active. It may not even, any longer, be in Abel's hands. Henry is indeed the most likely to be despatched to whatever battle they want."

"Should Abel Mason be no longer here, should we consider John?"

"It is already clear Dickie and John are understaffed in the pastures. Taking John away will surely make inroads into supplies of both wool and mutton to the army. I shall not ask the authorities, I shall simply despatch Henry to the safety of Parliament's headquarters and hire more outside help for my fieldwork here."

She smiled the smile of a relieved mother.

"Anne," she called. "Please send your little Richard to call Henry. The matter is urgent."

She turned back to Richard, in her mind the fact that all the troubles of late were ageing him. His blonde hair, now longer and kept in a tight pony-tail, was showing more silver streaks every day.

Yet he continues such a young man for his age. Readily mobile and comfortably active.

~ * ~

With escort provided, Soloman rode hard for Reading. With armies so dispersed, intelligence communications had become a priority. Oliver Cromwell was already making a name for himself in the north, his successes making strong inroads into Royalist holdings in Nottingham and Lincolnshire. Yet the west was proving as successful a battlefield for the King.

Soloman's spies had already alerted Parliament's Earl of Essex, a Puritan general with considerable popularity amongst his forces, of the dangers at Gloucester. Essex responded that he was leaving at the earliest with fifteen thousand men for the relief of Gloucester Town.

Soloman needed to meet up with his army at Reading to establish with its intelligence officer lines of communication. He was to be the liaison link with Cromwell's army moving south to relieve London. He must also organise his spies in respect of the clash at Gloucester.

His need for John or Henry was an extra pair of ears for considering incoming reports.

It must be understood by both to assess the validity of information. Royalist guile meant to throw us on to the wrong track seems to be increasing. I need two impressions coinciding.

At Luton he took a quick supper with ale, and with autumn weather holding fine, and with a change of horses, sped for Reading. He needed to arrive by nightfall.

He did, in a state of near exhaustion, to find Essex's man already installed at The George.

"Captain Neal at your service, sir."

"Soloman Bray, Captain."

They sat over ales, waiting to share a squirrel stew.

Neal was the earl's intelligence officer.

"I have runners galore who will be in contact with you so long as I know where you are," Neal explained. "Whoever arrives with the password 'Albion' will be my courier during this entire exercise. You may give him in return even the most intimate information. How shall he be sure he has the right man in you?"

"I shall respond with the password 'Angel'."

"Can we agree that all other messages where these passwords have not been transmitted be classified 'Unconfirmed Reports'?"

"Indeed, Neal."

"I am new to this, Bray. I am a command man, active in the field. Isn't exchange of intelligence quicker if couriers travelled direct to the recipient? Surely it is wasting time me sending the earl's messages first to you?"

Soloman smiled.

"If you were to send one right now to Colonel Cromwell, where would you send it?"

"Last I heard, he was in Gainsborough, Lincolnshire."

"Well, Neal, I can tell you that he is right now in Peterborough on his way to securing London. With you chaps leaving it unguarded, he is concerned. Not having learned that Gainsborough is already taken, your courier would undoubtedly be travelling via Northampton and Leicester, missing the colonel entirely."

The captain saluted and raised his tankard. "Cheers to you, man. Yes, it adds, now, that the Earl of Essex himself had your name in particular as the contact."

"All commanders in the field are being advised of this procedure. It was proposed by Colonel Cromwell himself. I have been seconded to this sector from Cambridge, solely to speed up communications between him and Essex. You and I will be exchanging couriers frequently—from me to keep you informed and from you to keep Cromwell informed."

"Why didn't Parliament choose London as its wartime capital?"

"As I see it, because London is full of spies—spies for Parliament, spies for Royalists and counter-intelligence spies for both. And after all, as Cambridgeshire is Oliver Cromwell's home, he made that proposal also."

Captain Neal again raised his tankard, and they drank to the man destined to soon become Lord Protector of the British Commonwealth.

Thirty-one

Approaching Gloucester, the Earl of Essex sent scouts ahead to reconnoitre the terrain. They returned to advise a prominent patch of high ground was being guarded by a small Royal contingent. By daybreak, following a scuffle, his army occupied the hill. With the drunken Royal watch uncaring of security, nary a drop of Parliamentary blood was spilled.

When the King's troops discovered the enemy holding it, Charles scurried to Rupert.

"Essex holds the high ground. Where was your watch last night?"

"Trying to quieten your drunken revellers, Uncle Charles."

Subordinates had noticed over the days that the King and his nephew seemed to have slackening respect for each other. They were regularly arguing.

"Well, with London so denuded, Rupert, surely now is the time to make haste there."

"Concede Gloucester?"

"As I insisted two weeks ago, I'd rather have London. You chose Gloucester."

"With Essex here, surely Cromwell in the north has been alerted that London lacks forces. He will, right now, be racing south. We could never make it in time."

"We can if we leave now rather than face Essex. If you don't come with me, God and I shall take London alone."

Rupert sighed. He was beginning to feel annoyed at his uncle's utter faith in the Divine Right of Kings. Rupert was very much the practical soldier. And, being Lutheran, he was at odds with several Anglican principles. However, realising his cavalry would be ineffective against a walled town if the infantry departed, he agreed. So whilst the cavalry stayed to protect the personnel packing up camp, the King began marching all infantry eastward for London.

~ * ~

Soloman Bray set down his quill and rubbed his fingers. They were going stiff partly with fatigue and partly with the cold. The candlelight wavered gently in the September breeze. He had left his window ajar for fresh air, despite dogs barking and horses neighing could prevent him sleeping.

Thoughts galore tumbled around his brain, not the least of which was his wife. When married, they settled in Cambridge because of his work. Mary had quickly become with child, and he was regretting being in Reading rather than with her.

She has some five months before birthing. I feel loath leaving her with winter nigh,, but hopefully I can return before snow begins. Oh, how I wish she could be in Brixworth under Mother's caring warmth.

He wiped a reluctant hand across his brow and snapped his mind back to work. He had spies galore queuing up to report snippets of news, some useless, some dramatic.

He and Henry were billeted with the town baker, who found the queue of fellows waiting to be given their hearing each morning fortunate new business. It was still early when they awoke to break fast with ale, cheese and fresh bread.

And were then soon at work.

"Henry, come sit with me and hear this fellow out."

Soloman pulled a second stool alongside his own. Across his desk sat a man of some thirty years. Apart from a clubbed foot, he seemed in regular health although in the moment gasping for breath. His face and clothes were spattered with mud from hard riding, so he had been quickly rushed to the head of the queue.

He had no password to proffer, yet his news was dramatic.

"I didn't spare me'orse all the way from Newbury, Guv."

"Well, your news, man. Out with it?"

"The King 'imself, Guv. With a huge army. Settin' up camp for the night, Guv."

"They came from where?"

Soloman had, since the departure of Essex and Captain Neal, heard nothing from them.

"From the west, Guv. Swindon or beyond."

They listened for several minutes, yet the fellow had no skill for assessing numbers.

"Many more than live in Newbury, Guv. Maybe twice as many, or more," was the nearest he could figure. "And they're towin' cannon, Guv, a score o' pieces."

Neither Soloman nor Henry had heard of Newbury.

"Where is Newbury, man?"

"Bucks, Guv. Right by the 'Ampshire border. I've rode hard some twenty miles. Some-it of their fellows is talkin' of marchin' all the way to London, Guv."

Soloman eyed his brother. "Do you believe the man, Henry? We get so many false leads."

And even before John could answer, a second fellow obviously in a stressful state was hurried in from the street.

"The Royal Musketeers be marchin' on London," he stammered, slumping on a vacant stool. Henry hurried for water for both men.

"Where've you come from, man."

"Newbury, sir. Biggest army ever I see, sir. The King hisself be leadin' it, sir."

It seems unlikely Royalists would send two false spies with the same tale.

"They both seem genuine to me, Soloman," Henry whispered while the two fellows drank. "Neither one illustrates a mean eye."

Soloman scribbled a note, signed it, peppered it, waved it about, folded it, dribbled wax and stamped the Parliamentary seal into it. He handed it to Henry and whispered in his ear, "Master Cromwell is at Windsor. Leave now and ride hard with this missive. If robbed of it, keep going and give the news by word of mouth. If they ask for my authority, tell them it is from 'Angel.' Time is of the essence, Henry. Ride hard. Apart from his personal army, he knows we also have troops at Winchester. Tell him I am alerting them that they should start for Newbury. "

Whilst Henry was readying himself to depart, Soloman walked along the queue asking for any that had brought him a message with a password.

None responded.

So there is no word from Neal. Yet if Essex were making for Gloucester, and the King was certainly in Gloucester a week ago, surely the two armies would have met? Such large forces cannot move undetected!

He selected three of the 'spies' from different areas of the queue. He brought them inside and then wrote the same note.

The angel is advised that the King is with a large army, camping overnight Wednesday in Newbury, headed for London. Windsor has been advised.

He signed it, sealed it and gave each man a copy.

"Take different roads bypassing Newbury and rush this to the Earl of Essex in Gloucester Town."

He gave each man sixpence.

He returned indoors and gave each of the 'spies' bringing the news sixpence, and sent them home.

More than a week later, he received a message from Neal.

Bray,

We arrived Newbury Saturday 19 September to find Prince Rupert blocking the London Road. On Sunday the King attacked us from what he thought was hiding. Our cavalry had him covered from behind. His entire infantry amazingly ran out of ammunition for his cannon before an hour was up. Every man ran. Only Prince Rupert's cavalry saved them from total massacre.

On Monday we were able to continue towards London. The enemy was entirely in disarray. Prince Rupert made the only attempt to harry us, yet we drove him off.

Hope we meet again,
Neal

Thirty-two

The closing months of 1643 saw several skirmishes in Cheshire and Lancashire resulting in wins for the Royals.

However, once Essex had returned to secure London, Cromwell took his armies north to make considerable gains.

Could the fact of having given every man a Bible to carry into battle along with pistols, muskets, ammunition, pikes and cutlasses, have been an influence?

He carved an enormous wedge from Yorkshire through Lancashire to the Irish Sea. Unlike Royalist forces, he was able to garner discipline into his ranks, particularly evident in the heat of hand-to-hand battle. He proved himself a great organiser and military commander, defeating all before him.

Royal England was now split into the North-East and South-West. The Royalist North was fast shrinking. Charles could see that the future called for a massive change of fortune.

He not only set up Royal Chambers and Office of War in Oxford City, he turned it into a fortress from which he would rule until such time as he could retake London.

The Irish returned to Ireland, the Scots to Scotland, and peace reigned while armies licked their wounds. Commanders, however, never doubted that further warfare must ensue. There had yet been no winner.

~ * ~

The truce lasted several months. By the summer of 1644, however, the strongest Royalist centre in all England, the northern city of York, found itself under severe threat. Parliament's army was camped beyond its northern gate, and a Scottish army swept south through Northumberland and Durham to set up a camp to York City's east.

From the newly won northwest, Roundheads swung east, crossing the Pennines south of a Ravenstonedale now clearing from snow, to threaten York from the west.

To prevent the armies meeting, Cavaliers set themselves up as a barrier south of the city at Selby, only to be captured to a man—an embarrassing and major blow to the King.

"York is the most Royal city outside London," Beatrix exclaimed when the news reached us. "It was the crux of the War of the Roses. That dreadful war's greatest battle was fought at York. It has always stood significantly as a Royalist stronghold."

~ * ~

"Well, the siege still holds, it seems, my dear. If it is such a gem in the Royalist crest, surely any change would be quickly announced."

At All Saints on Sunday, Vicar Torrens based his sermon on the religious effects on the great war. "Let us hope both sides see the importance of avoiding destruction of such a great city."

Yet week after week no further report was issued.

"Maybe it was just a rumour to begin with," Beatrix decided.

Significance waned as silence persisted.

"Is the war really over, then?" I posed when a month had gone by.

"Surely it is not over," she answered. "Nothing has been decided. Hadn't we been told both sides were rebuilding? That one day confrontations would start again?"

A letter from Henry decided the issue.

28 July 1644
My dear parents, sisters and brothers,
I write to say thank you for my birthday wishes and the beautiful waist-coat. It fits me like a glove.

Soloman sends his love and wishes also that he could fit into it. We have been extremely busy, what with battle events in both north and central. Maybe you have not yet heard of the Royal relief of York and Battle of Marston Moor to its south. It was indeed a long siege for the city, Prince Rupert eventually arriving with superior numbers, so it was surrendered fairly quietly. So quietly that he had time to manoeuvre his army into position where our forces were gathered a little to the south on Marston Moor.

The battle was quite horrendous, with many casualties. The feeling here is that it was likely the bloodiest battle of the entire war. Rupert retired defeated. He had saved the city but lost the battle.

And all that coming so promptly after the Earl of Essex had so completely thrashed the King's personal forces at Oxford. Master Cromwell has rubbed salt into the King's wound by declaring Oxford his personal headquarters. The King left behind considerable armaments.

We have no idea where he is now in hiding. It seems he is certainly running out of friends. There is also a rumour circulating that a significant quarter of the Royal Army brass is manoeuvring to have King Charles 'dispatched.' Soloman says you may choose to believe what that word might mean in this instance.

Had you heard that Master Cromwell has been created Lieutenant General?

Must away now, our hope that you all keep well and happy.

We should all be thankful that the war has spared Brixworth and Naseby.

Love and many kisses.
Your sons Solomon and Henry

Thirty-three

"What happened, Thomas? Things were going so well."

"Stop talking, George. Save your breath for running."

They were not far from home.

For week after week, month after month, the relentless Cromwell had driven the remnants of Rupert's army north. Sometimes they would counterattack and regain previously lost ground only to lose it again. On each occasion, farms and Royalist Manors changed hands. Poor and rich alike found their every grain of produce and every head of livestock confiscated to provision either the occupying or fleeing army. In some cases the armies paid with certificates redeemable at county halls, yet it proved a process to seldom work; pledges were not honoured.

Cromwell had found on Yorkshire's Marston Moor that mercenaries Rupert had hired were the first to break. Then the Cavaliers. Greatly outnumbered, they had no option but to flee. For two days George and Thomas hid in the cellar of a burning farmhouse while the Roundheads revelled. Only when a quiet descended dared they emerge, hungry and shivering, to forage for edible scraps.

Since then, they'd been a month running, hiding, running, hiding, up the Swale Valley.

"We cannot be far from home, George. Thirty, forty miles maybe?"

"We must cross Pennines, Tom. Cold it will be, without blankets. Maybe even snow?"

A single road crossed the range, emerging at Brough-under-Stainmore, eight miles of Ravenstonedale.

"Sprinting distance if we had the strength, Thomas."

Thomas didn't answer. He but forced a smile and kept struggling forward.

Travel anywhere in the time was fraught with danger—danger of being caught by the enemy, danger of being killed by highwaymen, even for the rags they were reduced to. Yet across the range was their only way home.

"There be no blankets to find, George. Roundies have scorched all Yorkshire it seems—not a thread of clothing, blankets, food or relic worth even a farthing."

"And every church sacked and burned? Why that?"

"Why indeed! No sign as whether they were High Church or Low Church. Simply all sacked, every idol smashed."

"But why burned to the ground? Why some stonework even tumbled?"

Thomas shrugged his shoulders. "Simply hate, do you reckon?"

Neither had even heard much of the religious war that led to the start of the fighting. They had taken up the call simply because the King called for support.

They again tightened their belts to ease hunger pains and made for the Ure Valley, expecting the weather in the pass might chill them to the very bones.

"Not even a horse in sight for us to nick."

And their uniforms were in shambles.

George cast his mind back to when he had paid a tailor to fit him out. *I cut a dashing figure,* his memory told him—*the feathered plumes, the fine lace at my cuffs, the knee breeches and stockinged calves down to glistening buckles on my shoes.*

He had felt as proud as his image appeared—spent hours strutting along streets simply enjoying being admired by every wench in every town.

Yet now both were sorry sights, bemoaning the fact of returning home not heroes but down-at-heel losers.

They knew not even if their families were left to welcome them. Or the village.

Could St. Oswalds be nowt more than a blackened ruin like every church in this valley? Every sight seen during the last several days illustrates how, in a civil war, life for civilians is as hazardous as for the soldier.

"In the eyes of colonels and generals, I wager, Thomas, I'm sure that victory is measured by how few of the enemy is left alive."

Flagrant smiting down of fit enemy after a battle had become commonplace. Every man killed here and now was one less danger to face tomorrow.

Royalists had, of late, in every battle, found themselves outnumbered.

Both the King and Prince Rupert had been paying mercenaries from Ireland and even Scotland to make up numbers, yet such were often the first to turn and flee. Scots, when finding themselves facing Scots, were just as likely to join their brethren and turn on the Royals who had been paying them.

It has certainly proved a war of fickle allegiances, George's memory summed up.

They spoke little when climbing the wall. The road was so far open to people migrating from east of the range, carrying whatever possessions salvaged from burned homes as their bodies could manage. Many realised they had been too optimistic, and many items were abandoned for others to pilfer or even exchange for something better.

Both lads had left sisters at home and had ever worried if they could have survived two years of frenzied war.

"And we both have older brothers, Thomas. Or had them when we left with such high ideals. Will we find they've been cashiered? Or murdered?"

"And parents? Can all have survived caring for families during such trials? Surely the Eden Valley will have seen Royalists battling with Scots on several occasions. Will they have been pillaging and burning like in the valley behind us?"

Both were concerned for George's twin sister.

"Bess is such a staunch Royalist, Tom. And such a firebrand. She'll as deliberately goad the Roundies if they came, rather than suffer their taunts."

Bess Fothergill was someone Thomas, too, had not only thought about but much talked about with George, particularly having lost his young wife in childbirth. George's twin sister was the girl he wanted to marry once home. He admired her outspokenness, a rare attribute for a woman in the time. He had even begun courting Bess when the war erupted. So he too was anxious on her account.

After they had run the last mile, the welcome sight of old John Adamthwait digging snow from the doors of his byre gave them extra impetus.

They arrived breathless, and he hugged both, tears pouring down the creases in his cheeks.

"Thank God ye both are safe, lads. And whole."

So considerable rejoicing ensued.

"And my family," George asked anxiously. "What know ye of them? Are all safe?"

"All that didn't follow'ee south, lad," old John told him. "Your brother left a week after'ee, and nobody's heard aught of any until this happy moment.

"Go, lad," old John added. "Scamper on now. Make your kin as delighted as you made me."

It was but a quarter mile to Tarn House and George was greeted with as much glee as received from the Adamthwaits. Yet the glee was quickly saddened.

His father Maythew had sickened with a fever and had been dead some six months.

"He worried frantically about you and William, George. We had had no word of either."

Beth couldn't stop the tears as she hugged him tightly.

George was shattered at having lost the opportunity of telling his father how much he loved him, how much he appreciated the care and learning the old man had heaped upon him.

"Neither Roundheads nor Cavaliers arrived this far north, George," Bess explained. "Even the Scots hardly tarried on their way south and haven't been back. Maybe they crossed to the eastern valley once south of the Pennines."

George explained how the Scots had indeed been recalled to Scotland, to travel up the eastern side of the range.

"It just proves, Bess, how fickle has been this war. The Scots all lined up at Marston Moor to do battle alongside the Roundheads got word that they were needed at home. Scotland needed but a few more men to drive out the last of the English guards. They just turned on their heels and scampered north up the Swale Valley."

Bess gave him their father's beloved old *meerschaum*.

"Maybe one of your brothers may like it," he had said when he knew he was going.

"And you are the first to return, dear George, so you have it."

She was also anxious for news of Thomas.

"He be safely home with his family, Bess."

"Shall I send a man over there? Tell them all to come here for a party tonight? We have so much to celebrate."

He agreed, and it was done. Bess organised the house-help to set a fire roasting a suckling pig as celebration of the boys being home. The combined families partied well into the night. And Bess was as happy to see Thomas as was he to see her.

The only sour note was having, still, no word of brother William.

"You say the Scots were not too much of a trouble here?"

"Damned little. Only one family in the entire valley got raided. Old Symon Busfeld's place. When lookouts on the scarp lit their fire signalling Scots on the prowl, Symon stationed himself by his cottage door, a white flag in his hand. Yet the Scots took no heed of it. They broke down a stone wall from the road into the sheep yard, randomly beheading sheep with sabres for following vassals to toss into carts. Others plundered fruit trees while soldiers swept on up to the house, firing muskets. Old Symon took a ball in his shoulder, but they let him be while they ransacked the house. They stole all his horses, cows for beef and dairy stock. Then when he swore at them, they torched his byre."

George wondered his father's attitude to all that.

He never did forget that false rumour old Symon spread, causing not only such hurt but dear Steven's death.

"That was the only action we saw during the entire war, George. The Roundheads won the north without even fighting. We all were forced to billet soldiers and had to sacrifice every morsel of grain and meat our farms could yield. But so long as we treated them fine, they treated us fine. The bigger towns didn't fare too well, however; we heard of much fighting and death. We rural people stayed destitute but lucky."

George rued the loss of his father.

But I shall not worry Bess now on what might have been decided before he died, re Tarn House. Surely it will have been willed to William. All that can wait until he comes home.

~ * ~

Bishop William Laud had been surprisingly and controversially created Archbishop of Canterbury by King Charles back in 1633. Several other bishops, seemingly worthy contenders, were passed over by both Charles and his trusted advisor, Duke of Buckingham.

From the very day of assuming his lifetime tenure, Laud remained not of merely faithful service to the King, but obsequious. He proved a major contender in developing the war of faiths within the Church of England into civil war. His fervour for High Church doctrine was at inflammatory odds with the growing Puritan doctrine, causing even deeper ravines within the Church. His and the King's policies on religion were so alike that fawning collusion was recognised by all.

When the King had declared in 1637 that the English Book of Common Prayer replace anything else being used by Puritan Presbyterians in Scotland, Scottish objections were so vehement that riots broke out. The Scottish Church revolted, spilling over to further inflame Puritan unrest in England. Laud took a tough stance, resorting to physical torture of clergy taking the Puritan path.

Puritans were violently anti-Roman Catholic and violent exponents of freedom of choice in observance to God; both significant reasons for swaying the Bray family's direction. Time was to prove the old story that once given power, adverse signs would begin to appear. Puritans began violently interrupting services conflicting with its ideals—the wearing of surplices and kneeling in prayer but two minor instances smacking of Catholic doctrine. On one occasion, a group of idealists broke into an Oxford chapel, stole all the surplices and thrust them into the dung-pit of a privy. On another, Puritan women broke into Lichfield Cathedral, desecrating the altar bunting and utensils with molten pitch.

An archbishop's duty was ensuring peace in all religious matters.

Laud had ever preached that all men were equal under God, so was it not too far a step to considering violence should repay violence. As Crown Prosecutor in actions against those defiling churches, he called for ultimate punishment. Those captured were beheaded.

Was the archbishop digging his own grave?

In 1640, just two years before the conflict broke out, Laud was charged with treason by a Puritan court and sent to the Tower. During the war, with London held by Parliament, he was left to languish in his cell for four years.

Now with Parliament all but ceded victory, the Archbishop of Canterbury, the country's leading church figure, was dragged from his cell and put on trial in a Puritan court. King Charles made an official Royal Plea for mercy, usually sufficient to free any prisoner.

England's leading Anglican was, however, hanged on Tower Hill, even without a sentence being reached. His remains were interred in St. John's College Chapel, Oxford.

Was this a warning of Puritan justice in Britain's future?

Thirty-four

"The King holds Market Harborough again."

After the Battle of Marston Moor and the fall of York, and believing the Royal army disintegrated, Cromwell retired south and permitted his army to take leave. All were to report to Cambridge by the first of next June.

King Charles retained the services of nephew Rupert and his army, every man in it happy at respite from fighting despite the Prince remained chafing at the bit for more action. Charles' exhausted troops had been driven from Scotland, so he had these men at hand, also resting. He had also been successful in convincing further Irish divisions that Cromwell intended a hard crackdown on the Catholic religion in Ireland, if winning the war.

"Isn't their execution of Archbishop Laud sufficient proof that they will make war on all other religious sects?" gloated Charles to the Irish.

After so many defeats, he was feeling somewhat buoyed by having his own troops under his control, and even some Irish, more frightened of Cromwell than they had ever been of Charles. Aware that Leicester was being held by only a small Roundhead force, he led his army there, to easily overwhelm it to again free that city. And again took the half-day march south to free Market Harborough before returning to Oxford.

Relieved that Cromwell had dispersed his army, he left but a token force to hold the re-acquisitions.

"The King obviously does not see the war over," I replied to Leyton Burgess's statement that peace had returned. "Especially when Soloman reports Cromwell's demand that all servicemen report back come June."

The families were gathered to celebrate his birthday and mine. They fell within days of each other.

"Why seem the particular towns of Leicester and Market Harborough so significant to his sense of security?" I posed. "With the war convincingly swinging Parliament's way, is the King using the same opening gambit to begin another? Or is this but an undeclared truce in the present?"

Only Soloman was convinced more was to come.

"Did Rupert take his contingent back to the Ruhr, do you know, Soloman?"

"I know not, Father. I would imagine he did. His force was sorely bruised. Surely they would have believed the Royalists soundly beaten."

Beatrix raised a finger.

"Are we all believing the war is over only because we hope so? Peace is what we have prayed for, and it has now arrived? Yet with the King taking our very neighbouring towns again, it affirms he sees the war still in progress. He refuted any truce by retaking Leicester and Market Harborough."

"He is simply making a statement, Mother. Surely the Royalist rout at Marston Moor was decisive. He cannot hope that starting again gives him a chance of winning. He is finished but refuses to admit it."

Dickie folded his arms as if to dot the 'i' of his statement.

"For all morning yesterday," he then continued, "Anne and I could hear the sound of cannon. Margaret Harborough is but six miles of Naseby Cottage, and with no clouds in the east, it could not have been thunder."

The two families had come directly from Sunday service where Vicar Torrens thanked God for returning the country to peace. He appealed to his flock to give succour to those bereaved and those suffering great loss like the Burgess family. Leyton had, once the billeting forces departed, hired workmen to get his house and farm back to order.

"I've no garden left, let alone orchards," he bemoaned.

His house was a shambles, and outbuildings were mostly burned as firewood to cook his livestock. And livestock yet uneaten disappeared with the departing army.

"They even stole my oxen and wagons to transport it," he further bemoaned.

I was able to donate to Leyton a milking cow, a hog with litter, an entire goat family of doe, buck and kids. I had also 'given him the key' to our vegetable garden and orchards. And promised regular donations of lambs for his table.

"Where is Cromwell, Soloman? Retired to Cambridge?"

Soloman smiled. Now he could discharge the volley he was saving.

"In Cambridge, Father, but hardly retired. He is training a new army."

"A new army?" All seemed aghast.

When deciding on the truce, Cromwell had moved his headquarters from Oxford back to Cambridge. There had been smiles all around the country at the King then making a feature of moving his own headquarters and family back into Oxford.

"Yes, another army, Father. He is calling it The New Army. It will be the cream of the Parliamentary forces. I was never a confidant of the general, Father. I met the man only three times and each time but briefly. It seems only that I had been well reported to him that he must have made the directive to see my family protected. But what he will do now, I have no idea. Discussions with others of 'junior' rank like mine have been wide and varied."

My interest in Cromwell was the note Soloman discovered when sorting files at the Cambridge office after returning from a stint at Hull. He had been assigned there during the Marston Moor battle. It was his duty to tidy up before taking leave. The note was the file copy of a directive that Bray House and its family were to be considered 'under my protection' and signed by Cromwell.

Only then did I realise why not only Abel Mason had been so co-operative, but how appreciated was Soloman's contribution to the Parliamentary cause.

"Wide and varied like what?" asked Leyton.

"Oh, that he may be training to take his New Army to Scotland or Ireland to crush the natives there. Or respond to any new war the King might start here. It is only conjecture that the war is not yet over. Is he training this army for action elsewhere once the King is fully defeated here in England? It is truce only opportunity to rearm, to rest his weary troops, to train new cavalry steeds? All personnel are under orders to report for duty the first of June. There must be a reason. Some say he will continue the war until the King is dead, then Cromwell will make himself King."

"Ah," gasped several of the assembly.

"The first of June?" asked Soloman's Mary. "Only yesterday you said you will be leaving for Cambridge next week? It is but April."

"Every staff member is still under orders. Henry and I must report early, me next week."

Mary broke into tears. Through sobs she mumbled, "Little Francis even now hardly recognises his own father. Can you give him another week before again departing, Soloman? Can you not tell the general you are ill?"

"I cannot do that. The man is a perfectionist. He will have his every day programmed for what is to be done."

"I am to report on the first of May," reported Henry. "Why cannot I report on your date, explaining that you are ill and I will undertake whatever duties he had for you?"

Mary grasped on it. She jumped up to kiss him, throwing her arms about Henry's shoulders.

"Oh, you are such a darling brother-in-law, Henry. I thank you on my behalf and that of little Francis."

"Oh, you are a darling vixen," said Soloman. "Have you been taking lessons from Mother?"

"Well said, lad," I said, jumping in. "Mary's plea had my dearest's stamp all over it."

Beatrix sat quietly with nowt but a smile to her face.

So it was decided by the women. Henry would ride to Cambridge on Monday next, reporting for work in Soloman's place.

"Thank you indeed, brother. However during the month, keep me informed of anything significant."

~ * ~

Unbeknown to all but maybe a few Royal spies, Cromwell and an exemplary young officer in the Parliamentary Army who had come to Cromwell's notice, by name Henry Ireton, were indeed planning Parliament's next campaigns.

The Earl of Essex after Marston Moor, ailing in health and having had enough of war, resigned his commission and retired. Cromwell was impressed by the battleground exploits of the young man beside him, hopeful that he might, within a short time, prove an excellent replacement. The 'Ironside' General was satisfied his New Army would, by midsummer, be ready for blooding. It wasn't known, of course, how many men would report in, but he was confident of at least half the number laid off. That would be enough to salt in amongst the New Army for a further month's intensive training.

"Those who had had their gutful will have deserted as we headed home from Marston Moor, Ireton. We know the numbers laid off, so my calculations should be close to the mark."

It was established that their major objective remain weakening Royalist forces.

"I little care, Ireton," Cromwell asserted, "beyond those with substantial manufacturing facilities like Oxford, what town and cities need be sacked. We shall fight only where we have confidence of inflicting considerable losses on the enemy. That must be our chief goal. So our spy network need be sound. We must have reliable information on the enemy's programme, on the enemy's weaknesses and strengths, and on the enemy's campaign plans."

"Rupert seems a predictable leader, sir," answered Ireton. "He is a professional soldier, and I hear that as a battle unfolds, he knows exactly when to spring his surprises. King Charles is entirely unpredictable. It is in Rupert's camp, then, that we need our most competent spies. We need intelligence on what 'surprises' he has in mind."

"My man's spies tell us, Ireton, that Charles has left but a token force guarding Market Harborough. I intend wiping it out to a man. My major goal is to strengthen our holdings Liverpool through Lancashire. To avoid the high country, we shall travel via Stafford. Both Market Harborough and Leicester are en-route. I want to prick the King's pride by retaking both."

~ * ~

What they couldn't know was that Prince Rupert was indeed still with the King in Oxford, plotting how to retake Lancashire off the Roundheads.

"We know, Uncle, that little of that countryside is left entirely in Parliament's hands. Also that Yorkshire is held by only a holding garrison. We should march north and free both. If we can do that, thousands of additional men will rise up to help. That happened for me when marching to Marston Moor."

"I agree, Rupert. Yet York is even more important that Lancashire. We can do both but it must be York first. It is the north's Royalist centre. If we are to win this war, we must retain the north—it is our major source of manpower. We should make directly for York through Market Harborough and Leicester, then straight up the east side of the Pennines. When York is relieved, we make for Lancashire. Your army and mine."

Prince Rupert sucked in a great breath.

A march through one hundred and fifty miles of Parliament supporters is lunacy! To travel via Lancashire is friendly territory— territory in which to enlist more men.

"Uncle. Because of my greater experience, you created me Commander in Chief of British Forces. My experience tells me we should march to York via Lancashire. It enables us to arrive with greater numbers."

The King didn't hesitate.

"Whatever your rank, Nephew, as King of this country, I outrank you. We shall travel the direct route. York is poorly defended, and if we leave within the month, we can be there before any alarm is raised. We can promote the ruse that we make for Lincoln."

Rufus concealed his anger but had no recourse but to accede—he was indeed outranked.

"However, before that," Charles continued, "I have a plan for Taunton. Our siege remains stagnant after a year. We should immediately direct a force there with the new sixty-pound cannon from our Oxford foundry. Once having secured Somerset, we have those seasoned forces to take north with us."

~ * ~

Soloman came to me with a message from Henry.

"This is interesting, Father. Cromwell and Ireton have decided to pull their troops out of Taunton. The master believes those seasoned troops would be better used laying siege to Oxford, disrupting whatever the King might be planning."

Soloman had the devilish smile on his face he invariably displayed on hearing snide news.

"The direct path from Cambridge to Taunton, of course, is directly through Oxford. Henry must ensure that his courier goes a long way around, to avoid being intercepted."

Only two days later, another missive arrived from Henry:

I have despatched a second message to Taunton. Our force there, after giving up the town, is not now to march for Oxford but head instead for Market Harborough. The master intends destroying the Royalist force there and Leicester when en-route for Lancashire, as a slight to the King.

"Cromwell is obviously piqued at the loss of Leicester and Market Harborough again, Father. He is intent on destroying morale—both the King's morale and his forces' morale."

~ * ~

Prince Rupert sent a message to his troops in Market Harborough and Leicester:

Prepare to join me on a march north. I leave within the week.

He sent another to his field commander at Somerset's Taunton:

Prepare to receive additional troops and armaments leaving Oxford within days. Taunton must be taken.

Oh, wasn't it ever a perverse war?

Thirty-five

7 June 1645

Beatrix wore a worried frown.

"Those poor people in Market Harborough, Richard. With all the to-ing and fro-ing, few homes, if any, can be left unscathed. Most will have been razed by this army or that. No-one can be protected from both. God help us if the Royals should come here. Look what happened at Burgess Manor—all by our own side. Should the Royals come here, Cromwell would only want to take it back again."

Suddenly a flurry of noise announced Henry arriving on the doorstep.

Not only was he out of breath, but his poor horse was thrashing her head trying to drive off the foam blowing up her nostrils.

Beatrix dropped the cushion she was restuffing to rush to him.

"Oh, my dear boy." She smothered him with kisses.

"What is it, lad?" I demanded. "Why in such a state?"

He struggled with his breath in gasping out the news.

"'Tis war again, Father," he gasped. "To arrive on our doorstep. The New Army is marching for Market Harborough under Henry

Ireton. It is already on the move, planning to bivouac at Pitsford Water. Cromwell himself will follow within days."

Beatrix gasped, grasping my arm as tightly as she had grasped Henry.

Then she rushed to the maid Hannah, who had brought water for Henry.

"Yes, give it to master Henry and then take that poor horse to stable and have the men see to it."

I took advantage of Henry's desperate swallowing to make my point.

"The road from Pitsford Water to Market Harborough is well east of the lake. It might well mean a dislocation of our routine, yet I do not see danger for Bray House. How much time before the army is at the Water?"

"The forward party, to begin raising of tents, preparing feed and raising stables for the cavalry, was right on my heels. They are there by now. The army will arrive two days from now and the hardware during the week."

I turned to Beatrix, who seemed to have grasped the urgency of the moment.

"Once the army arrives, my pet, the marketplace will turn into a madhouse. I suggest get Cook to take as many girls as she needs to right now buy up big."

I ran to the barn, where William was weighing onions.

"Boy, leave that and harness Thunder for the dray. Take your mother and Cook to the market. While they buy food, you stock up on livestock feed. Call in at Burgess Manor but do not tarry—just warn Squire Leyton. Tell him what you are about."

I hastened back to a Henry still gulping water.

"Did Soloman say if our protection remains in force?"

"Indeed it is in Soloman's mind. He will remind as many of the old staff as possible, also enlighten new staff. But there can be no guarantees."

The thought of a multitude of soldiers descending on us for sleep and nourishment, as had happened to Leyton, was ponderous.

I turned back to Beatrix. "Does Cook really need you at market? There is need for you here."

"I can instruct her. What can I do here?"

"Start packing up everything of value. Send a girl to the barley field to fetch Liam to me. I want him to assemble farm tools and equipment we cannot afford to have stolen. Meanwhile I will be opening the loft and letting down the ladder."

I turned to Henry. "Must you return immediately, or can you stay and help?"

"I rushed off, leaving only a note that I was coming to see if Soloman could join us. I must return immediately. I shall report that Solomon is still too ill."

"Your mare needs more rest. You have ridden her hard for how long?"

"Six hours, Father. I know she is exhausted."

"Take your old gelding. He might well be happy to give you good service again." We threw arms about each other, and he sped off.

My mind raced. It was trying to regather all that had come to mind when imagining us in such a predicament.

Oh, if only I had had Bea note it all down!

What Parliamentary forces had done to the Burgess property wouldn't leave my mind.

Our 'secret' loft was nowt more than a hidden attic. When Old Henry built the extension, it included an attic above Bea's and my suite. It had no staircase, simply a flap-door in the panelled ceiling and a long ladder secreted in the attic itself. The panel could be opened only by pushing a wardrobe beneath it and climbing atop. The objective was for women and children to hide in the event of just such a danger—a practice held over in large houses from Viking days.

Yes, same as Bea read to me recently about houses in the far north with secret attics or cellars to hide from Scottish marauders.

I clambered atop the wardrobe and pushed up the 'secret' panel, to pull down the ladder.

My seventy years of using brain, muscle and perseverance were beginning to tell on me. My heart was pounding like a millstone.

Oh, thank God for my many sons and the many skills my Bea has instilled into them.

~ * ~

The next several hours saw Bray House a hive of rushed industry.

Soloman, three fieldsmen and a maid were in the attic. Enough slate roofing had been removed to give them daylight that they could stow what had suddenly become treasures into various piles. Liam and other fieldsmen were passing the treasures up, and I was feeling like a conductor trying to keep all sections of our orchestra in tune.

Fortunately the weather remained fine, so all were able to work at top pace.

I hastened downstairs on hearing another horse race to the door.

It was Henry again.

"Just beyond Rushden, I encountered a fellow agent bringing me later news."

"Why? What?"

"There is a further problem, Father."

"Come to the parlour. I shall pour you wine, boy. Then tell me your news."

Henry grasped at the wine.

Beatrix hurried from bundling parcels of food in the cookhouse to join us.

For the next several frightening minutes, we listened to a revelation more ominous than the last. Prince Rupert's brother, Maurice, had arrived at Oxford from the Ruhr with his cavalry, bolstering Royal numbers.

"Spies told us he has been given maps to set out after Rupert's army en-route to Market Harborough. It must now be a massive army, Father. It should already be marching up the Cherwell Valley."

"Oh, dear God. So close?"

"Wait, Father. What this means is that the two armies are about to meet. The spy's report is that Rupert had designated Naseby Common as his bivouac for Sunday night."

My brain did a somersault. My Beatrix sat on a bed, hands cupped to cheeks.

"Today is Saturday?"

"Unfortunately yes, Father. Tomorrow night will see Parliament encamped at Pitsford Waters and the Royals at Naseby."

"Five miles apart, and us the meat in the sandwich?"

"But Naseby?" Beatrix exclaimed. "What for Dickie and Anne?"

~ * ~

"William!" I shouted. He was in the paddocks pulling foodstuffs. He came scuttling.

"Ride to Naseby, boy. Listen to what Henry has to tell you then go warn Dickie. He and John must move our flocks, or we could be ruined. If Naseby Common is to have an army bivouacked there, they must abandon the house. Bring Anne, little Richard and whoever of the servants he does not need helping shepherds move the flocks back here."

I left him sitting with Henry over goblets of wine.

Beatrix clung to me. "Oh my dearest, when is all this terror going to end? I know you have no answer, yet I depend on your strength to help me keep mine. I shall ever dread hearing again, horses galloping up to our door."

"War is a terrible thing, dearest. We have so often talked over the 'what ifs,' yet I guess always crossed fingers that it should never be us. Now it is. Brixworth could easily, now, become another Market Harborough. Every one of our boys has responded positively, which is a credit to you, my love, for tutoring them on values and practicalities."

I turned to Soloman.

"Soloman, lad, if you see that your responsibilities need you in Cambridge, we shall understand. Go if you must. You've brothers enough here, with Liam alongside them."

He took hurried leave of Anne and baby Francis. He and Henry galloped off together to meet up with Cromwell for instructions.

I felt as devastated at Naseby Cottage being in danger as I was about Bray House.

Early service Sunday morning at All Saints was packed.

The fear of war on our very doorstep had every Brixworth citizens on their knees, overflowing through the nave into the churchyard and even cemetery. All on our knees except, of course, the Puritan element, which loudly claimed kneeling to pray was a Catholic regimen.

Thirty-six

13 June 1645

"Naseby Village, sir," Soloman advised.

Lieutenant General Oliver Cromwell was eager to engage the enemy. He was holding a council of war, being updated on not only on the statistics of what his own force had assembled but estimates of the enemy's. And the lay of the land.

For local knowledge, he had the Bray brothers at his elbow.

"We have six thousand horse against their four thousand," he told his fellow generals and several colonels. "We have seven thousand men afoot against their three thousand, and we have a thousand dragoons as well."

"Not to mention our eleven cannon, when it seems the King has no heavy armament at all," added Ireton.

"But they have the better placement. We have difficult terrain to master on our left flank. Your flank, Ireton."

Cromwell instructed him to attack the Royalist outpost six miles south of its army's main body. He also ordered that during the night a force would skirt around Brixworth's east and occupy a ridge north of the main Royalist army. He questioned Soloman on the terrain to be expected. Solomon had no option but to recommend the approach taking in Naseby Cottage and Dickie's pastures.

I hope to God Dickie got Father's advice to drive his flocks west. If he is taking them east, he will be right in this contingent's overnight path.

"This will deter more Royal forces approaching from Market Harborough."

He ordered three field pieces established in that sector.

The morning of the fourteenth was foggy, each leader thankful for having so carefully surveyed the battlefield the previous evening. Both had to rely on the reports of spies to know what displacements were made overnight. Visibility was negligible. Action could be taken only once the fog lifted.

Royalists occupied a mile-and-a-half front. Their right wing consisted of cavalry under Rupert and Maurice. The centre comprised three infantry brigades with a regiment of horse in support. On the left was a cavalry division from northern counties, men who had escaped the Scots having overrun their homes, along with Prince Rupert's personal regiment of foot. Also left was the King, who had arrived the previous night with his personal guard of cavalry.

The Naseby Battlefield was large, yet even then its outlying edges were thick with hedgerows—hedgerows abutting Dickie Bray's acres.

Dickie, with Henry's warning, had had his shepherds drive his flocks to a neighbour's paddocks due west. His own lay right in the path of Royalist troops coming from Market Harborough in one direction and Roundhead troops from Pitsford Water in another.

Cromwell had arranged his army on the northern ridge. Ireton's wing comprised five regiments of cavalry on the left flank, five of infantry in the front line, with three in support. Three hundred musketeers were deployed in front, with two companies in reserve. In all, Roundheads occupied a front of two miles, outflanking the Royalist left. Some would be hidden by hedges, even when visibility cleared.

Dickie had by now already despatched in his dray to Brixworth, with one of his shepherds, his largely pregnant Anne along with his few treasures from the house.

"I'd reckon both sides will want our house as a field hospital," he had told her. "They'll no doubt make free with everything we leave."

"We shall lose our all," she wailed.

"We shall lose the house, my dear. But you should be safe in Bray House."

Dickie left to catch up with John, their four shepherds and dogs that had departed with his flocks in the waning hours of yesterday.

With the moon, they may still have two to three hours' start on the fog lifting.

Behind him, on the moor, the armies also waited for the fog to lift.

~ * ~

Rupert began advancing as the fog thinned.

Cromwell sent a regiment of dragoons into the right hedges where they could fire into the flank of Rupert's cavalry.

The Royalist centre advanced, Rupert keeping his own wing of cavalry in hand so that the horse and foot could hit the enemy simultaneously. The Roundhead infantry advanced over the crest to meet the Royalist foot. Time was against them, for only a single volley of musketry was sounded before it was fighting hand-to-hand, the veteran Royalists using swords and musket butts to make early gains in the bloody fighting.

Ireton's regiment repulsed its Royalist opposites, yet had to avert to rush to the aid of the beleaguered Parliament infantry. His troopers were driven off by Royal pikemen, and the general himself was unhorsed, wounded in the leg and taken prisoner.

At that same time, the second line of Royalist cavalry broke most of the Parliamentary horsemen. Some of Ireton's regiments were saved by dragoon fire whilst others broke and fled—some not stopping, according to later reports, until reaching Northampton City eight miles away. The Royalist right decimated Ireton's men, including reserves.

"Surely Rupert's cavalry is disobeying orders in galloping off the battlefield in pursuit of our fellows?" asked Soloman of brother Henry, the two perched high in a tree watching the fleeing Parliamentarians.

"How can I answer that? Yet one should expect so."

"Of course, dear brother. And I do think so. Yet if that was Ireton we saw being taken into custody, his cavalry is leaderless."

And as if on cue, the Royalist Northern Horse charged into Ireton's cavalry, sabres slashing.

"The master's men were magnificent," Henry told the family that night.

Solomon had recognised his duty to return to Cromwell's camp. Henry saw his duty as reporting home, that we were not left floundering as to what our safest course should be. Soloman had agreed and given him leave.

"We cashiered wandering horses to make our respective journeys," he told us.

"You did right, son. But did you sight Dickie?"

"Nae, Father. I imagine he was busy herding his flocks to safety."

"Did you see his house?" Beatrix asked.

"We were the other side of the common where the forest is thick, Mama. We were nowhere near Dickie's house. But it was right in Cromwell's path where he last night skirted the town to set up his northern attack posts. I fear it will have fared badly."

I dared not risk any of my family going near the battlefield so soon. I reckoned combatants seeking wounded to evacuate would, by now, have departed, but there would still be Gypsies going through pockets of the dead.

Henry told of Cavaliers, not only outflanked but outnumbered two to one, charging up a slope and into a rabbit warren.

"Many horses collapsed with broken legs while others simply panicked, throwing their riders. It was quite a rout. Our dragoons then swept through the hedges after the Royal infantry. Scores of Cavaliers began throwing down weapons and appealing for quarter."

"Any given?" I asked.

"None. Cromwell had given explicit instructions that no quarter be given. Reducing Royalist numbers is a major objective."

I recognised his intention to avoid going into gory details.

"We never did see the King flee, but did witness Sir Rupert galloping north. In a bid for Leicester, no doubt. He was followed by other horsemen and maybe a thousand or two afoot. Our cavalry was chasing them, slaying stragglers."

Before retiring for the night, Henry drew me aside.

"I left my horse saddled, Father. I shall leave quietly. I want to find Dickie to see how things went for him."

I knew he had had little sleep the previous night, let alone since. He and Soloman had led the army around the town. But I daren't deter him now. I too was anxious for Dickie.

"He was taking his flocks to the Carvell fields. Try there."

"It is the opposite direction from Naseby Cottage. But west I shall go."

I had primed both my pistols, in case we had unwelcome visitors during the fighting, and gave him one.

"A lone man creeping through the battlefield could face danger, boy. Put this in your belt."

I hugged him and saw him off.

He wasn't back for breakfast, so I told the rest of the family where he had gone.

"Let us hope the reason he is not back is that he found Dickie and all are on their way to check out Naseby Cottage."

Anne was nearly beside herself with worry on both fronts.

"I shall take horse and ride first to Naseby Cottage, then along the track the boys will be taking from Ed Carvell's house."

"No, dearest," said Bea. "Be reasonable. You are…"

Liam put a hand on Bea's arm yet addressed me. "I shall go, Father Bray. And shall take food and water for them. Who knows whether they might have eaten or not last night. And if they are en-route to the house, there will certainly be no food so close to the battlefield."

I gave him the other pistol, and he set off at a canter.

My Bea was pacifying Anne. "If Naseby Cottage is beyond restoring, my dear, we shall build it anew."

We were all relieved at Bray House having been spared. I understood Bea's magnanimous attitude.

At All Saints that afternoon, it was unanimous that the battle be considered a deserved victory to the Roundheads. Their foot soldiers had proved superior, although cavalry losses were substantial. The Roundheads had learned by now that both the King's personal cavalry units and Prince Rupert's were highly experienced and threats to be conscious of.

The service proved an extremely long one, with pleas from the pews as well as from the pulpit. Most sought God's help in sending angels to help clear Naseby Common of the blood and gore left upon it—every soul conscious that in the next pew were exponents of the other side. Who was courageous enough to call the other to task? All wanted only that something in their world was going to happen to make all things right again. Did yesterday's battle mean the war was over? Was there yet to be another?

Ignoring the Puritans who insisted on standing, I knelt to pray.

Wasn't yesterday decisive enough to mean the end? Don't the dead bodies strewn across the fields constitute decisive? Oh, dear God, why does honouring one side or the other have to make us suffer such hardship? Surrendering our loved ones to fight in your name? Be killed in your name? Where are forgiveness, understanding, brotherly love? Surely you have forsaken us!

Thirty-seven

"What ails thee, dearest?"

She threw herself into my arms. I had been absent most of the day, rounding up men in the district free enough of domestic hardship to help straighten out Dickie's problems. Beatrix hadn't slept through the night of the battle and then spent all next morning helping neighbours. Then the long church service. And was awake with nightmares most of last night.

"What ails me? Oh my dearest. Why seek a reason for all that has happened? The world has gone mad. What ails me is the stench of death wafting on the breeze—a minor ailment, of course, compared to what the poor dead suffered—their fear, anger and pain all scrambled into violent moments? And the worry of families waiting to see if their sons and brothers would come home? It ails me to realise the utter stupidity of all this horror because of religion. It is surely the most dreadful sickness."

I sat her down and squeezed in beside her, an arm embracing her. *Whatever can a man say at a time like this, to ease her pain?*

"There are so many things a person must vie for in the moment of imminent death. Does a man's mind turn to fear of the threatening weapon? The vision of hate on his assailant's face? His concern for his family? The utter helplessness of his situation? The utter uselessness of war? Each on its own must be a dreadful fear. There can be no answer."

"Oh, Richard. Could that dreadful moment include realizing God has also forsaken mankind? Conscious of the carnage, I cannot help thinking that. Even now I can hear the screams. Even hear the silence of the moment they die. Oh, Richard, can you feel in your heart that this battle might mean the dreadful war is over?"

I hugged as tightly as I dared.

"At least we have the consolation that our every child is safe. I am happy to let that compensate me for the heartache of these two yesterdays."

~ * ~

Two days later we heard Parliament had retaken Leicester, that Royalists were scattered far afield and hogs and foxes were still banqueting on Naseby Common. The King had lost his veteran infantry, his artillery and many arms. He simply now lacked resources to raise another army. Naseby indeed proved the last battle of the English Civil War.

Extract of a 1646 ballad, origin unknown:

To conclude, I'll tell you News that's Right,
Christmas was killed at the Naseby Fight:
Charity was slain at that same time,
Jack Telltruth too, a Friend of Mine,
Likewise then did die, Roast Beef and Shred
   Pie,
Pig, Goose and Capon no quarter found,
Yet let's be Content, and the Times lament,
You see the World turned upside down.

Thirty-eight

The Civil War was over.
So many took up the cry that everyone believed it.
The King had been thoroughly defeated at the war's biggest battle. Or had Marston Moor been as big?
Everyone seemed to have a different opinion—hard to assess when news was cast abroad by word of mouth.
"Does the war being really over mean all are brothers and sisters again? With but a single mind direction?"
"Only if you believe dissenters of Puritanism have all, overnight, discarded their faith."
"You mean the populace still remains divided on religious doctrine?"
The fighting might have been over, but mankind's dilemma remained.
It was time for Oliver Cromwell to spend many hours before his mirror, looking into his own and Britain's future.
Yet where would he draw lines between what he despised about Divine Right and his plans for a Puritan England? Would he seek retribution against Royal supporters? Would he take the King into custody and force him to abdicate?

No. I would then be accused of wanting to be King, which is furthest from any truth.

This land needs no King. It needs a body of God-fearing men to instruct the people on life. Leave the King hide wherever he has run to. Yet why does he hide? Out of guilt? Out of shame? Now there is opportunity for Parliament to rule. I will not arrest the King when he emerges. I need him whilst-ever the Constitution requires his approval on Parliamentary decisions. Parliament must be the power with the final say. That is what the war was about. My need, now, is to see Parliamentary Power absolutely entrenched.

King Henry was correct in wanting to free himself from the Pope's power. Yet he did it for the wrong reasons. He simply wanted an heir. And what happened? Five wives could between them give him only a weakly son, a son who hadn't even balls of his own before dying. But at least England was quit of the vile Roman shroud.

With Charles on the run, I can consolidate a power base with no space for kings. That is where I am heading. No king will ever again be head of the English Church. I will establish Parliamentary laws based on the Bible. They won't include Rome; they won't include putting Christian dogma in the hands of bishops. I will establish laws for religion as well as social order. I have been handed a broom, and I shall sweep from this land every religious dogma but Puritan ideals.

I am the country's housekeeper and shall not rest until Catholicism is dead and every social activity not supported by biblical scripture is dead. Elizabeth chose bipartisanship, James rewrote the Bible to his own interpretation and Charles tried forcing his father's Common Prayer dogma on not only Englanders but Scots. And likely had it in mind also for the Irish. No longer, under Puritans, can England suffer from Divine Right. I will change the structure of Parliament, enact laws for our entire United Kingdom, rewrite the Constitution.

Earliest need is to expunge the word 'Kingdom.'

What do I envision for this land? That it become a one-class society. A common creed. Yet more than just that. A land of common creed and common wealth.

Every man should enjoy common wealth. Commonwealth rather than Kingdom? So be it!

I shall declare it a Commonwealth of Powers enacted by an elected Parliament. Elected by the educated who have the ability to judge.

He gazed to heaven, put palms together, fingers to chin.

I will first establish a system built around Oliver Cromwell as leader. And my thanks, Lord, for helping young Ireton escape before the King's men could murder him. I have plans for him. Second plan is to convince the Irish that Catholicism is finished throughout the entire Commonwealth. I will take an army to Ireland. I shall crush the Irish as I crushed the English.

Parliament will suppress the Presbyterians and both High and Low Churches of England.

Within ten years, England shall rise as the world's icon of Purity.

~ * ~

King Charles knew that any hope he had of defeating Cromwell on the religion issue would be dashed should he fall into Cromwell's hands.

In disguise, he fled his Oxford enclave and surrendered to the Scots. He pleaded that as a legitimate Scottish Prince, they grant him asylum.

The Scots, realising that only the goodwill of Cromwell could now offer any hope of a Presbyterian future, on consideration of a forty-thousand-pound payment turned Charles over to Cromwell. A King's ransom? It surely was.

Cromwell at least paid him the courtesy of not choosing the Tower for incarceration. He was lodged under guard in Holdenby House, again a coincidence in respect of Brixworth. Holdenby House was but five miles southwest of Bray House. Prince Rupert had camped right by it en-route to Naseby.

Whilst Charles before the war had seen as many factions dividing the Church of England as divided Catholicism, Parliament, after the undeclared truce began, discovered just how many Parliamentary factions were emerging to divide it.

Divisive quarrels in both houses raged from the first day.

On the one hand was the Presbyterian element, on another, the Independents comprising several sub-groups including Cromwell's army. Another group was The Levellers, advocating freedom of worship along with the radical platform of giving the vote to all England's adult males. A fourth faction was the unpopular Puritan element, insisting on moral codes strict enough to rob the people of traditional freedoms in both social life and worship. Cromwell was its leader.

He lost no time in successfully having the "vote for all men" platform sent down. This was no time to be risking hard-won power.

Yet the King, ever the intriguer, encouraged by the general dissent in Parliament, managed to negotiate from his prison confines a secret alliance with the Scots. The Scots had a score to settle with Cromwell for his 'about-face' on the religion promise. He simply flatly refused to sanction their Presbyterian gospel.

Charles never believed that his chances of a victory over Parliament were dead.

So did all that add up to the war not yet being over?

Thirty-nine

22 September 1645

The war was certainly over in Westmorland.

The Fothergills, Adamthwaits, Busfelds and all others were thanking God for sparing St. Oswalds from the sacking suffered by so many northern churches and that the Scots had retired to their own side of the border. No longer were they raiding their southern neighbours.

Twins George and Elizabeth Fothergill of Tarn House knew why.

"It be because the vicar be Puritan. Pater always knew it."

It had become common knowledge since his death that old Maythew had persevered so long as churchwarden only to help foster private distrust in Puritanism, into all.

The one lapse in God's intervention in favour of the Fothergills, however, was the blanket of sorrow over brother William. Each day, month after month after George's arrival, they waited in vain for William to come home. They were never to discover if his sorry remains ended up in a mass grave on some battlefield. He had indeed been named the recipient of Tarn House in Maythew's will and testament, yet the family's solicitor in Kirkby Stephen filed a notation that until William's return, the next and only son in line would assume William's rights. The only other son was George, who did survive the war—he'd opted out after the Battle of Marston Moor.

Now a year later, sister Elizabeth, big of belly and dressed in white, married Thomas Adamthwait. Two months later, she gave him a son they named John.

Most in the village shared the celebration supper, the trend of conversation still on whether or not the war was yet really over.

"While the King lives, it can never be over," opined Royal die-hards.

"But surely with his armies so devastated, he cannot again raise a new one. Supply is exhaustible."

"He draws armies from Europe. Monarchies have always come to each others' aid."

"Even Prince Rupert's brother brought his army."

"Which was still insufficient to defeat Cromwell."

"The King has even the Irish on his side again. And the Scots. Didn't the vicar report last Sunday that Cromwell has rejected any notion of admitting Presbyterians into England? Or England permitting the rites to be practised even in Scotland?"

"Parliament has ever broken promises. Promises are made only to suit the moment's whim."

When one was brave enough to remind the rest of King Charles' many broken promises over taxes, he was promptly rounded on.

"King Charles never sacked churches."

"King Charles supports both High Church and Low Church gospels."

"King Charles permits Catholics in Ireland to have their own churches."

"Cromwell calls doing that simply keeping the Irish from rising in rebellion."

"King Charles supported Archbishop Laud."

That brought a moment's silence during which several blessed themselves.

"Does anyone else still offer private prayers for that man's soul?" asked one.

It was nine months since Cromwell triggered the archbishop's execution, and of course St. Oswald's vicar never mentioned the event. When questioned on it, he would reply only that it was not his congregation's place to enter into politics.

Many *ayes* were heard.

From all present were many opinions in favour of the King—and no dissenters.

~ * ~

Two years later

Walking home from Sunday Service at All Saints, Beatrix announced that despite 'only' fifty-eight years of age, she was finding walking home each Sunday, tiring.

"Patronising your body is not like you, dearest," Richard responded.

"You've ever complimented me, my dearest, on how straight I hold myself—the proud image I ever illustrate. The recent years, however, have tired me. Toting food into the town for war widows, helping lift wounded husbands and sons tending them, are all starting to tell. I'm ready to submit to driving the trap even to church."

"In future, dearest, when tending the sick, take Mops to do the lifting. We can't have you going lame on us."

She laughed. "I am not a horse in the stables, darling. And on matters of age and horses, I ask again that you stop riding astride. You are seventy-two, still sprightly for one so ancient…" She paused, looking up to let him see the twinkle in her eye. "…but bones are brittle. Should Twinkle-toes shy and unseat you, it could prove serious. Let us get another trap so we don't find ourselves arguing over timetables. You can teach Twinkle-toes to get used to shafts."

"Oh, he won't like that one bit. But, yes, I suppose I could persuade him—explain my problem. Yes, Dickie has a spare trap since John and Joyce bought their own. I'll requisition that. And a gentle horse for your gig. Dickie can afford to be generous. He's quickly recouping his losses incurred by the battle."

They discussed the sad news reported during the All Saints service.

Parliament had outlawed folk dancing and bear-baiting.

"Bear-baiting, yes, Richard. Yet folk dancing? All the enjoyment Morris Dancers have given me in life was a continuing joy. Me and many others."

"Yet another Olde English tradition banned by the Puritans."

He looked about, should anyone be close enough to overhear.

"I really am beginning to feel exasperated at the extent to which Cromwell is forcing extreme Puritanism on us. Many, I am sure, will never forgive his murder of the archbishop. Charles had his faults, yet Cromwell being confirmed King or overlord of the country is indeed a worry. Leyton feels the same. Parliament is not, to our minds, thinking of the people. Losing heritage traits is damaging everybody's morale."

"Oh, what a tirade, my dear. Unlike you to be so verbose. Yet I can but agree."

Ahead of them walked the younger generation still resident.

Soloman and his Mary had purchased a Brixworth house left derelict after the war. A purse from Richard made the purchase viable, despite cash reserves being near exhausted. They had a trap of their own to ride home. Soloman and his brothers all together bared chests and muscles to, over time, restore the run-down cottage to a liveable condition. Soloman was studying law.

Henry and William remained at Bray House, working on the farm, as had Jane and husband Liam with their young family. Richard and Beatrix remained fortunate in that all were Anglican High Church in creed. As common supporters of Parliament, however, all were beginning to waver. They regularly had Leyton Burgess to dinner on Sundays. His home, loosely referred to as The Manor, was slowly being restored. Whilst Brixworth Hall was rightfully the major home of the village, Bray House and Burgess Manor also shared the shoreline of the quiet Brixworth Lake, a feature of the area.

Leyton was widowed early in the war years and lived there with eldest son, James, and his young family. When it was realised that both Royal and Roundhead armies were heading their way and that a large battle was likely, they'd bundled all they could into their carriage and fled to wider family in nearby Spratton. Finding it empty, a mob within the troops forsook the war and made themselves comfortable in the manor, plundering Leyton's cellars. In obviously drunken sprees, they fed much of his furniture to cooking spits, stripped his larder of cheeses and smoked hams, denuded the walls of curtains and used tapestries for blankets.

James remained in Spratton while Leyton moved back to the manor, getting it back to liveable conditions.

"Meanwhile, you will sleep here," Beatrix had insisted. "Our resources are at your disposal, dear friend. Much fruit and produce we've already donated to other unfortunates, but there is enough left for you."

It had been made clear at church that morning how the aftermath of war still affected everyone for miles around. We had heard some grisly stories.

"Will Richardson told me, Leyton, that at Moulton by Pitsford Water after the battle every horse from every house was commandeered by Roundheads, while every house in Naseby was pillaged by both armies. I had already told you how they took everything from Dickie's place. It seems stripping villages has been considered 'fair game.' Even horses were taken, replacing steeds lost in the battle. Either that or sheer vandalism."

Leyton raised his beaker of wine by way of salute. "I'm glad they didn't raid your cellar too, dear friend."

"Maybe they sighted my appointed guards and didn't want to get even that close to fighting."

We tossed down the toast, and I refilled the glasses.

For a while we ruefully reminded each other of our boyhood memories of wishing for war—the real adventure of arquebusier versus cutlass?

"Oh, how perverse seems that memory now, my friend," he told me.

But we were soon back to the moment.

"Soloman told me that the King, despite a prisoner, still legally holds the right of sanctioning parliamentary bills. I asked why he sometimes approves bills that are extreme Puritan doctrine—banning folk dancing, for instance."

Leyton raised eyebrows, waiting for more.

"He suggests that maybe he chooses to approve some so he can deny what he considers the more destructive. Maybe even playing for time while he secretly tries to raise a new army?"

"Surely not."

I tried not to chuckle. "The fellow has never yet accepted all the defeats he had to stomach. He has bounced back from every one, scrounged men from gutters or foreign kings, to try again. Who is to say that he has finally given up? The fellow has pride. He wants his throne back. He is suffering imprisonment by maybe being somewhat patronising in approving Parliament's new bills. The blighter knows he now has both the Irish and Scots on his side."

And indeed, the imprisoned King went on to actually approve abolishment of all Christian holidays including Christmas and Easter! The Bible gave no mention of Christmas, nor of celebrations for Easter nor other Christian anniversaries—enough for the Puritans to declare them abolished.

Layton was highly incensed. "Parliament is turning itself into a body of absolute rogues. Absolute idiots. I cannot but believe that the Parliament we supported during the war was simply duping us until the war was won. It confounds every Englishman by interfering with his very social life. A rumour in town, Richard, is that it has on its agenda that every English man and woman must wear only black and white raiments. Coloured clothing is to be banned."

"Well, that certainly isn't in the Bible. It is difficult to know, these days, Layton, what is fact and what is malicious rumour."

"The King could be the one guilty of malicious rumour, of course. Can you really imagine the Scots suddenly turning on Parliament? One of the reasons they sided with it during the war was that Charles was trying to force Anglicanism on them and banning Presbyterian."

"Well, I don't know. Many Englishmen are quite disoriented by war experiences. Most had never ventured from their home parish until the King on one hand and Cromwell on the other had them marching all over the country. Discovering that Englishmen elsewhere speak entirely different dialects has likely upset their senses of security just as much as the see-sawing fortunes of war. How can any man today have faith in a future?"

Forty

The summer of 1647 saw many things getting back to normal. Travelling tinkers were again abroad hawking everything from bonnet ribbons to iron cooking pots.

Brixworth Lake teemed with carp, gudgeon, freshwater shrimp and eels to delight every taste. Beatrix persisted with both her painting of trees and flowering shrubs and textile weaving. As sexton at All Saints, I most enjoyed participating in weddings because they were happy times for families. I tried to avoid the gloom of funerals.

Our family was not so scattered that we didn't see all regularly, although only Henry, William, Jane and Liam still resided with us. We enjoyed summer days, outdoors and evenings indoors. Highwaymen frequented traffic lanes at night, summer and winter. It was still not a time to be abroad on lonely roads.

Cotswold Lions had really proved their worth for Bray & Sons Grazing. They were indeed hardier than any breed Father Henry and I had used for experimenting. I signed the entire grazing business over to Dickie once he was resettled in Naseby, and he paid me a comfortable living wage. I no longer worked. Our Brixworth fields and orchards fell on Henry's shoulders. It seemed he and William were the sons to continue the Bray House farm.

Bea and I luxuriated in what we termed a retired life.

"I only wish, Bea, that dear old England could be as content. Cromwell may have proven a competent general on the field of battle, yet the nation remains divided."

Soloman still worked under the Cromwell banner because he was well paid and it was an excellent office while studying law at Trinity College. He hoped to succeed to his law degree next year.

"Not that I find it easy still working for such a man, Father. He is by far a changed man from he I so idolised. He was then a man endeavouring to thwart the King's excesses and bring order to the laws of the land. Yet having achieved, he leads his Puritan Party in the House in a most dogmatic fashion. His religious ideals allow no popular suffrage, no equity for the people—ideals I had thought were his goals. I now realise how many were misled."

"Is he angling to take the throne?"

"Oh, no. He is opposed to royal powers. He came upon us at a time when we had a bad king. We saw Cromwell as a saviour. Yet now we have helped him achieve mastery over the King, he uses the power to solely further Puritan ideals. My fear is that he will resort to military force to achieve it, exactly as King Charles was attempting with the Scots and Irish. His hatred for the Catholic Church borders on revulsion. He is intent on sweeping Catholicism from our entire kingdom. Yet, Father, you and I know the Irish love for Catholicism is as intense as our love for Protestantism. He has undertaken to destroy it, and the destruction will be utter. I am greatly afeared there is to be as ruthless a bloodshed in Ireland as here."

"Do you realise what you are saying, son? If anyone outside this house heard you say those words, it would be treason. You will lose your head."

"That, Father, is his goal. I see it in so many of the enquiries he makes. Many pass across my desk. I am one of his legal advisers. He is angling to change laws that will help achieve his goal. His Puritan Party is the fastest growing party in the Lower House, and even now, some are among the Lords in the Upper, let alone the bishops."

"You put great fear into me, lad."

The next week a cavalry detachment led by Puritan Cornet George Joyce marched into Holdenby House and took the King. He was taken to Hampton Court Palace and imprisoned under close scrutiny.

"Puritan spies intercepted messages from King Charles to the Scots, Father, detrimental to Cromwell ideals. He is now under severe intimidation."

On 22 July, following the New Model Army publishing a declaration denouncing leaders of the Presbyterian faction in Parliament, a group of army apprentices invaded the House of Commons, threatening Independent MPs.

Late in July, fifty-eight members of Parliament, including the speakers of both houses and a handful of Lords, fled their homes and hid.

On 2 August, Parliament set out a series of proposals to which the King must conform. They included:

Royalists could not run for office for yet another five years.

The Book of Common Prayer was allowed to be read but not mandatory, and no penalties should be made for not going to church or attending other acts of worship.

The sitting Parliament was to set a date for its own termination. Thereafter, biennial Parliaments were to be called, sitting a minimum of one hundred twenty days and a maximum of two hundred forty days. Constituencies were to be reorganized.

Episcopacy would be retained in church government, but the power of the bishops would be substantially reduced.

Parliament would control the appointment of state officials and officers in the army and navy for a period of ten years.

The King rejected them out of hand. He had been getting good responses from not only the Scots and Irish, but also several Royal armies of Europe who had again promised to come to his aid should war renew.

On 7 August, the New Model Army marched on London and reinstalled the captured MPs, several having been 'coerced' into supporting Parliament. Cromwell's New Army was in effective control of the entire country, including both Houses of Parliament.

On 20 August, Oliver Cromwell marched into Parliament with an escort, passing a bill annulling all proceedings since the raid on Parliament in July. Most had favoured the Presbyterian and other non-Puritan groups.

~ * ~

It was a bitterly cold morning. A pinching frost was hardening the hoar on leaves, and the wind howled through forests. Late frosts and heavy rains during the summer had resulted in poor harvests, so by winter people were hungry.

Beatrix had her eyes glued to *The Gazette*. "It says here, dearest, that in the south-east, even parliamentary supporters are complaining of the increasing taxes to maintain the army. They want it disbanded."

I was working numbers on our fiscal shortcomings. I eased the monocle out of my eye and turned to her. "It was but a month ago people were lauding the fact the army was about to put down the riots over hunger."

"It is the old story, darling. They tell us what they want us to hear. Either that, or they invent stories."

"I would like to see one on the reason for appointing our new vicar. We know it, but no sane man dare put his name to it."

Beatrix plucked off her pince-nez. "Fear has become part of everyday life, dear. When I came to Brixworth, Leyton told us of the murders of parishioners who were Puritans. Today the fear is face-about. Puritans putting the fear into us if we speak against them."

The popular Vicar Anthony Torrens had been replaced following the appointment of a Puritan bishop in Northampton City. It was happening all over the country. We had expected it, yet it was still a shock when it happened. We were so incensed that we joined the scores of dissenters. We ceased going to church. We performed prayer services at home.

We missed the weekly gossip sessions of course, so now had only the weekly *Gazette* and Soloman's visits to inform us of news.

"Why don't we drive to the town square and see what is the latest on the bulletin board?"

"Indeed, my dear. I shall change into something warmer. Will you ask William to harness Twinkle-toes?"

"And I shall bring a blanket along with umbrellas."

We left Twinkle-toes at the livery. I gave the fellow tuppence to hook a feedbag of oats over his head. Beatrix mingled in the market square while I called into the Kings Arms, a questionable name for the times to be sure, yet where much news could be gleaned.

The King versus Parliament was always a regular topic.

"The King escaped Holdenby House and sought refuge with friends on the Isle of Wight. But 'the friend,' afeared for his own life, turned him over to Parliament. He is rumoured to now be in the Tower."

"The prison of no return?"

It certainly seemed King Charles was signing his own death warrant.

The topic soon changed to the price of wheat having soared to the point that the village baker could not bake bread.

In the square I stood back and watched my dearest involve herself with a man with his ankles in the stocks. I knew her well enough to know this was something she would want to do on her own—part of her independent nature. I could see she was managing perfectly. The fellow could but sit on the cobbles with nowt to support his back except his arms. Children as ragged as the fellow himself were gathering lumps of horse-dung from the street and shying them at him. His only self-defence was using his arms and hands to shield his face, which forced him to lay flat on his back with his eyes closed. I could see nothing on the notice-board to suggest his crime.

My Bea shooed the children off. She took a cloth from her creel to clean his hands and then gave him an apple. She stood behind, her legs supporting his back while he ate it, at the same time, keeping the children at bay.

"May the good Lord bless, ye, woman," he croaked, once having chewed core and all.

"Would ye like a drink of water?" she asked.

"Aye, I would that, ma'am."

She walked but the several yards to the town pump and filled a wooden pannikin. Several hung alongside. Walking back with it, she noticed the children standing back, watching. Her bearing and attire stamped her, in their eyes, gentry. The younger had fingers in mouths, just staring. When he'd finished, she replace the pannikin on its hook, nodded a 'good-day' to the fellow, who put his palms together as if in prayer.

"Treat the poor gentleman kindly," she said to the children, with the hint of a smile.

I joined her then. We sauntered through the market, buying a flitch of bacon from the swine-stall, and then went about our mingling, ears probing.

Just as the town clock chimed two, a courier pasted a new news-sheet on the notice-board.

"It says, dearest, that the navy has mutinied. Ten warships have deserted from the King's service, declaring allegiance to Prince Charles, son of the imprisoned King."

"Good heavens," I exclaimed. "Cromwell cannot ignore this. It must surely be the outbreak of a new war."

Beatrix quickly reached up and clapped a hand over my mouth. "Darling, be careful. Ears are everywhere."

A second notice displayed reported Royalist bands had marched in force into Wales, occupying the significant Pembroke Castle. Cromwell despatched his army to begin a siege.

It seemed England's second Civil War was under way, the King having had nowt to do with it. It was revolution.

~ * ~

Weather permitting, Beatrix and I began daily visits to the Bulletin Board.

It took almost two months before Pembroke Castle surrendered. Cromwell's army never did best the twenty-foot-thick walls, but its engineers found the conduit delivering drinking water to the castle and severed it. That ended the siege. Cromwell ordered the castle 'slighted,' destroyed to the stage of never again being of use in military defence.

From Kent, a ten-thousand-strong army under the King's colours marched to Wales. They sacked three other castles, restoring them to Royalist strongholds. Bea and I were distraught that day, walking back to livery where we'd parked the trap.

"We thought the war was well and truly over."

We drove home with dashed spirits.

"If Cromwell wins this second war, Bea, oh how distressed I am at what terror he will enact on Royal supporters. He will drive this country back into one of hate even greater than religious wars of the past."

Her mind reeled.

"Oh, how it seems, my Richard, that you are changing your spots? And I cannot but agree. Our future looks dour, whatever the outcome of this war. I think I have seen the change coming. When Soloman was called back to Cambridge, I began dreading the possibility of the family splitting asunder. Is it too much to hope that all can now suddenly want to return to Royal power rather than Parliamentary?

"Can there ever be a return to a peaceful sharing?

"And is Soloman now in danger? Will they call Henry back also?"

Forty-one

George Fothergill couldn't believe the war had started again. "How can it start with the King imprisoned?"

Thomas Adamthwait had not even an opinion. "All we are told is that there is fighting again. We are warned the Scots may invade again—this time helping England against Parliament?"

"What? Where did you hear that?"

"At Lodge rehearsal last night."

"From whom?"

"A cousin visiting from Brownber. He read it in a Bulletin at Appleby."

"Thank you for telling me."

"I was getting around to it. I needed to first say that the war seemed starting again,"

George put his hand on his friend's shoulder. "John, dear fellow, sorry for doubting you, yet your news astounded me. But the Scots? They were totally in disarray after the end of the war. Surely they haven't built a new army in such short a time? Why should they anyway? They may well just sit back this time and watch. And what of the King, anyway? Surely, now, Cromwell will execute him."

"We don't know. But there has been fighting in Wales. The Royals were beaten again."

"Oh, that we have this fear starting all over. If the Scots are to build an army, they may well come to purloin our men. And rape our women?"

"Our children are too young to be targets, George. And Elizabeth is noticeably pregnant again, so she is doubly lucky."

What they were unaware of was that right then, the Scots were indeed invading. Yet it wasn't in the Ravenstonedale direction. They were making for Lancashire's Preston.

What they also didn't know was that George had been right. The old Scottish army was quite dissolved. The new army was with yet untrained troops and with untried leaders. Cromwell arrived to find the Scots already spread about the Lancashire countryside. The battle proved a massacre.

The Scots lost two thousand killed and nine thousand captured.

Cromwell, according to *The Gazette*, lost 'upwards of a hundred.'

~ * ~

When the bulletin board in Brixworth Square reported that Parliament's Fairfax had taken Colchester in Essex and that England's second Civil War was over, we couldn't believe it.

Cromwell must surely have decided to alienate the Scots, for a troop of soldiers marched into Parliament and arrested all forty-five Presbyterian members. All were sent to the Tower. All remaining members not declaring for Puritanism were suspended. Of the original four-hundred-fifty-member Lower House, only fifty Puritans remained.

"A Rump Parliament, if ever a description was apt," I muttered when Bea read it to me. "The House of Lords, my dear, which has the right of veto, is daily numbering but three or four members. Not even a quorum. It seems the Lords of England are too afeared to attend."

"This is what Cromwell has reduced our country to? It is a shambles. A joke."

But we had a serious problem right in our home. We hadn't heard from Soloman for three months.

"Should we be sending Henry to find out the situation?"

"If Soloman is in any sort of danger, then Henry too could be compromised. But what danger could Soloman be in? Surely you are not suggesting they have found him guilty of some malpractice? Imprisoned him?"

"We cannot know. It's the not knowing that is so worrying."

"It certainly is strange that he doesn't write. If anyone is to go, I should. And I will."

She clasped my arm and pulled herself to me.

"Oh, darling, you are seventy-three. Be sensible. It is fifty miles. I worry about you even driving the trap to Naseby. You cannot drive to Cambridge. We shall both go, and I shall drive. You may relieve me if I tire."

She has that look about her that tells me I have no choice.

"When do we leave, dearest?"

When the rest of the family heard what we were embarking on, they were horrified.

"What? You aged pair travelling alone? The roads have highwaymen. You will be fair game for them."

Mary suggested that as Soloman's wife, she should go.

"If you go, young Francis will be distressed."

William stood. "Mother, Father and I shall go. Fifty miles and back is a long distance. A hundred miles is too much for a single horse and trap. And who knows if Soloman is ill and needs to come home? We shall travel by hired hack. That way we change horse and even carriage as often as we like."

"Well said, boy. We shall do it as you suggest."

It was early autumn, and leaves were yellowing, some red and already falling. Prettiest time of year to be travelling, yet we were on a journey of worry.

"It is a road Soloman and Henry could cover in six hours."

"The livery man told us there is an inn at Huntingdon on the Ouse. We shall sleep there, dearest."

"You have that ring in your voice, again, that tells me I dare not argue, dearest."

She leaned over and kissed me.

William, squeezed in beside us, smirked.

I had a loaded pistol tucked in my belt, and William nestled a musket in his arms. Neither of us knew how to use the musket. It mattered not, because we had neither balls nor powder. It was merely for show to deter highwaymen. It was Leyton's. We recalled our argument on the arquebusier. He wanted to send a fellow with us, but I assured him we had our own fellow.

"We are simply on a family errand, Leyton. We will handle it."

He knew me well enough to know argument was useless.

We hired a carriage with an easy fold-down roof and a filly old enough to be easily controllable. We had to accept that Twinkle-toes was not up to a hundred-mile journey.

We talked about all and sundry as the hours passed, having little trouble other than several fords to cross, not knowing how deep they might be. We left it for Gentle to judge them. Gentle proved up to her name and was quite reliable.

Even in front of William, we rubbished Cromwell. We already had him a guilty man, he whom we had championed for so long but who had let us down. Us and hundreds of thousands other Englishmen. Certainly we had wanted an end to the King's excesses, yet it became a war of religious factions. Oh, how deceitful of all!

And now was our Soloman in some way a victim of it all? He who in the best of intentions saw Cromwell a Godsend? To be so thwarted?

The three of us talked unguardedly of each of our children, the course their lives had taken in domestic, social and political genres, how they had reacted in each.

"Every decision made, my love," she told me, "illustrated so much of the character each has acquired. And surprisingly, each at different stages of their life."

When we got to William, the youngest, I said to him, "William, lad. You helped established opinions on all your brothers and sisters, so why don't you begin on your own good points and bad?"

He had to think hard, of course, yet the seventeen-year-old made quite a presentable job of self-assessment, albeit with hints from his mother.

After it, we agreed that assessing all had been a worthwhile exercise. We as well agreed that having had the Naseby battle on our doorstep had been a major point in developing the characters of all.

We made Huntingdon after a more comfortable journey than expected, with no mishaps.

"Had there been one, I am sure Gentle would have come to our aid."

"Even against highwaymen?" William asked.

"Quite likely she would have kicked the life out of the man," Beatrix replied. "Gentle obviously recognises us for people who appreciate her."

~ * ~

We deposited William in a room of his own for the night, so we could make frantic love.

Whether it was the strange environment or celebration of our joint efforts in raising our family, indicated by the day's discussions, neither could know. Yet it was a journey to our more youthful years. The uniqueness of it being in a strange environment added to the allure. It brought us even closer.

Our second day proved as delightful.

Gentle made the decision as to whether or not she was up to another day like yesterday, for she greeted us most enthusiastically. So we kept her on.

We could not follow the Ouse, unfortunately, it being the biggest river any of us had ever seen, but the road to Cambridge proved a well-used and busy track. Not the series of country lanes we had witnessed yesterday, but considerable traffic that Gentle met with blasé confidence.

Cambridge was the busiest city any of us had seen. It took many stops and questions to find the headquarters of General Cromwell.

We both hoped he would not be there. Neither wanted to be embarrassed should we find ourselves confronting him. Belligerence might be difficult to hide. Whilst he was the man who had orchestrated protection of our home during the great war, his behaviour since declared the man a rogue.

We left William with Gentle while we entered and enquired for Soloman Bray.

"Oh, he has not been here for quite some time," the clerk told us, setting both our nerves on a knife-edge.

"We are his parents. Do you know where we can find him?"

He consulted with others. "He is in the army hospital, sir."

I held on to Beatrix. If he had been in a hospital for months, he must be extremely ill. "Can you direct us to it?"

"Of course, sir." He pulled out a sheet of parchment and drew a map, marking names. I pushed Beatrix to the fore.

She asked him several questions, explaining we were strangers in the city.

Finally she turned to me with a forced smile. "I know where to go and where to enquire along the way."

Then suddenly, for no reason, she burst into tears.

I cuddled her to me. "What is it, tell me, for God's sake."

"The hospital he is in... is for mad people."

Forty-two

I had never seen Beatrix so angry.

William, on seeing us coming, lifted the reins and held them taut so Gentle would stand fast while we boarded.

She let me help her climb aboard, to hurriedly then push poor William into his corner.

No "Please let me drive, William," not a word—simply an ungracious shove as she snatched the reins from him even before sitting. Then she waited until I was seated. She then waved a ripple of reins along Gentle's back, so hard that the poor creature threw her head up in surprise. I was sure that had I not been sitting between her and where the whip was lodged, she would have used it.

"Soloman mad? My Soloman?" was all she said.

It was neither question nor statement. She seemed simply expressing thoughts aloud.

I felt it best to say nowt. She knew the directions we should take, so I just let things rest. The fact William also said nowt indicated he too believed just letting it ride was best. I couldn't see him, for Beatrix was between us, sitting erect.

This was my gentle wife, his gentle mother who had taught all our children the value of patience and self-control. She was certainly exercising self-control, if not patience.

Yet she hadn't forsaken them in her pique. She made no sudden "Giddup" order nor rushed pull on a rein to bring Gentle out into the busy traffic. She seemed under excellent control, easing the mare to the right-hand side of the street, ready to make a turn.

It was a long, quiet ride to the outskirts of town. We came to a great six or seven-foot-high wooden palisade reaching fifty or more yards in each of the two directions we could see. A pair of wooden gates broad enough and high enough for a coach and four was all that broke the expanse.

A large sign by the gate had some long words in a frame.

"Hospital for the Army Disabled," I heard William almost whisper for my benefit.

Disabled? Army? That doesn't sound like a mad-house. Yet I guess 'disabled' covers a broad range of handicaps?

My heart pounded with dread fear. We could see the roofs of a number of buildings inside the palisade, all of two stories, some with windows, some with iron grills.

Beatrix pulled up to the gates.

"William, please ring the bell," were the first words she'd uttered since her "My Soloman" outburst. He jumped down and tugged at the bell. We heard it ring some distance away.

An attendant came.

"We have come to enquire after Soloman Bray," William informed him.

The fellow opened the gates wide enough for us to drive into the courtyard.

"Do you have a pass?" he brusquely asked.

William had not come into the office with us back at Army Headquarters. He turned to us.

I alighted.

"When asking the whereabouts of our son at Army Headquarters, we were told to come here. We were given no paper."

"Follow me," he said, just as brusquely.

"I will leave my lad here to water the horse and then follow. Which office should he ask for?" I asked.

"Administration."

No 'sir' nor any sort of civility. I am not at all impressed with this place.

I turned to William. "Lead Gentle to the drinking trough, lad, then take her to the stable and rent a feed bag to leave on her. Ask your way to Administration."

"Aye, sir," he said with almost a smile, giving me a knuckle salute.

Beatrix even smiled. She hooked her arm in mine as we followed the pertinent pup.

Once indoors, it was surprisingly untidy. Even dirty. At Army Headquarters in the city, everything was spick-and-span and the staff courteous. Not so in their hospital.

I repeated our mission, and without a word, the clerk moved to one of the voluminous books on his table, opening it.

"What name is the patient?"

"Bray. Soloman Bray."

"Admitted when?"

"We are not sure. Maybe some months ago."

He let out a long sigh and began flicking pages, running a finger down columns. He found it after not too long.

"His mind is gone. Is that the one?"

I was shattered. I needed to swallow deeply before I could even reply. Beatrix's arm tightened in mine, and I heard a gasp escape her lips.

I squeezed her arm in turn.

"Maybe. May we visit him? Then we will know."

Surely they wouldn't have two Soloman Brays in the hospital.

He called a young man to him. "Soloman Bray, Asylum Ward Sixteen," he instructed.

I felt Beatrix begin to fall. I had to grab at her, just as she righted herself.

"Oh, dear God," she whispered.

We were led outdoors and across a yard to another building of stone. William joined us as we arrived there. It was single story and with iron bar grills over the windows. Just the sight of such a building sent shivers up all our spines, I reckoned.

As soon as the fellow opened the office door, the stink of unwashed bodies mixed with that of vinegar stung in my nostrils. Again I felt my Bea shudder.

I reached behind and touched William, illustrating with the same finger that he should go to his mother's other side and take her arm.

We were led down a corridor that had green damp mould making random patterns over its walls. Cell-like rooms lined each side of the hallway, all doors wide open. The squalid stench here was worse. The only light and fresh air inside the building came from small barred windows in each cell. Only some were open.

At the end of the hallway beyond us was an open door, beyond it, an outdoors. The view beyond extended to the high palisade that had faced the street. Men in the yard were walking or standing, some alone, some in groups.

Room number sixteen held four cots, the blankets filthy. They had no other furniture except a single small table with drawers. Only one man was there, asleep. We could see that it was not Soloman.

Our guide led us outdoors, where we immediately recognised our boy. He was sitting on a bench with two other patients, all clad in dirty jerkins and knee-length breeches, bare legs and leather shoes. All were bareheaded, although our boy's head was swathed in a dirty bandage.

Beatrix had one hand to her mouth, the other pointing to Soloman. She was all choked up.

"Hold your mother here, William," I whispered loud enough for her to hear and made for Soloman. All three fellows turned, seemingly curious at being confronted by visitors.

I held out my arms as I approached, but Soloman sat as bemused as his friends.

What? He doesn't recognise me?

I turned to our guide. "This is my son. He doesn't seem to know me."

"He don't know no-one, sir. He don't speak to no-one, either."

I felt my heart pounding again. This fellow had called me 'sir.' *He seems our best choice so far of getting near the facts.* "And his head bandaged?"

"He was shot, sir. Not in the war. He was with General Cromwell, sir, when an assassin fired a pistol. Tryin' ter kill the general, 'e was, sir. Mr. Bray got hit instead. That is the record what come with him. He must 'ave an'ard'ead, sir—the ball just bounced right off. But'e just don't remember anyone, sir."

I turned to Beatrix and William. "You heard?"

They nodded.

I walked up to Soloman. "Do you know me, lad? Your father, Richard Bray?"

His body didn't move, but his eyes did. They smiled. I'd swear they smiled.

But he slowly shook his head, just kept staring at me. He made no attempt to look past me although he must have noticed I wasn't alone.

I took his elbow, conscious of his body odour, and led him to his mother. He walked ever so slowly, not like the Soloman we knew, always walking briskly and with purpose.

"Do you recognise your mother, Beatrix? And your brother, William?"

I looked into his eyes as he appraised each face, his eyes seeming to say *yes*, but he did not nod his head. He kept appraising them as if trying to make up his mind.

"Oh, you dear boy," said his mother. She started to embrace him but pulled back.

She turned to me. "I don't want to frighten him. Can we take him home?"

"I'm sure we can." I turned back to him.

"Would you like to come home with us? To Brixworth?"

I tried illustrating a beaming, welcoming smile.

He didn't speak but gave a half smile. Now he nodded. And without even turning to farewell his friends, began walking slowly, more round-shouldered than we remembered him, towards the door to the cells.

I could see Beatrix was holding back tears, yet the determined look was back in her eyes. "Do you think he will come with us?"

"He seems pretty much inclined."

I turned to William. "Come, lad. You gently take his left arm, I'll take his right."

As we approached the door of Cell 16, I deliberately began talking with him again. "We have a nice house in Brixworth. Maybe you will recall it when seeing it. And a lake with great carp abounding. And brothers Dickie, John and Henry. And sisters Frances and Jane. Do you remember those names?"

By this time we had walked straight past Cell 16 without him even hesitating and were in the Asylum Office.

"We are taking him home."

I didn't ask permission. Putting it this way placed the onus on them. I wanted them to see my mind was made up.

"You will have to sign him out, Mr. Bray. With your address, please."

Wow. Now I am 'Mr. Bray', and he actually said 'please.'

I made my mark, then asked William to write in our address.

He wrote me a pass to present at the Administration Office.

We walked him through there, had the gate opened for us, and all four squeezed into the dray.

Was that a glare of disapproval in Gentle's eyes at seeing four of us?

"We shall upgrade to a light carriage for our return trip," I told them.

But Beatrix's mind was fixed on Soloman. "First, we must bathe him and dress his bandage. Let us return to the inn and have them bring a tub and warm water to our room. You, darling, and William, can bathe him while I shop for clean garments."

She looked at his shoes.

"They seem good enough for getting back to Brixworth. Do you have a crown in your fob, darling? That should cover his raiments. You will find bath soap and *eau de cologne* amongst my things in the bureau. I shall have a boy walk me from the store to the inn."

Forty-three

Two years later...

Oh what a blear day! Is it a sign of more bad tidings? I've never been so harried. Time seems to just linger beyond the moment's pale. Oh, for a secretary! But I am paid so little for my services that I cannot afford one.

George Fothergill had married Julian, daughter of Richard Skelton of Armathwaite Castle on the west bank of the Eden, near Carlisle. For the very purpose of protecting the area from Scottish invaders, it was built in the fourteenth century over the rubble of the old that dated back to Norman times. Julian had been able to garner for George, through her father's offices, a local post in the widowed Queen's service. He reported to her what he considered information of the Eden Valley communities she would likely want to know. He collected on her behalf the Royal Taxes applying.

It was not an enviable job. He disliked pressuring friends and neighbours feeling the pinch of poor agricultural seasons. Such a task weighed heavily on his conscience.

"Of course I realise Julian thought it a favour she was doing me," he bewailed to Thomas. "But it is most time consuming as well as personally unpleasant at times."

"At least, George, it gives the Queen opportunity to read how difficult the Puritan push is proving so detrimental in people's lives. What she can do about it, other than store it away in some archival cupboard, I simply cannot imagine."

The King had been tried, yet even before the judges had reached a verdict, Cromwell had King Charles executed. The spilling of Royal blood inflamed a huge proportion of the population.

"Regicide is an immoral outrage," the people cried. Many diehard supporters of Cromwell during the war had, by then, deserted him. Englanders found the thought of republicanism repulsive.

"We had a bad King," seemed the only credence given. "We wanted more power in Parliament than in his hands, but that doesn't excuse regicide. Cromwell will never be forgiven this," they whispered to friends.

It was particularly felt in the Royal north.

Cromwell had declared England a Commonwealth, his preferred term over Republic.

"Or is it that it is a weak appeal to the already disgruntled?" friends asked of each other in quiet tones. It had become dangerous, in many parts, to be overheard.

A new fear reached into people's hearts.

"Wasn't the war fearful enough?" they also queried while realising none could answer.

The republic was to last eleven years, during which Puritan pressure rampaged.

Cromwell, created Lord General of Army, having purged dissenters from Parliament, took his New Army to Ireland to subdue forever sporadic uprisings against its anti-Catholic rulers.

"But to exact such ruthless reprisals, Thomas. Hardly Christian, is all I can say."

For near a twelve-month, Cromwell burned, pillaged and murdered Irish Catholics with as ruthless a hatred as was his beheading of King Charles.

"A third of the entire population massacred, sold into slavery or died of famine and plague, some reports say, Thomas."

"Surely hardly credible for a churchman, George?"

"He has reverted to burnings at the stake, Thomas. And to drawing, quartering and beheading corpses after hangings. He is a fiend, leads his thugs into churches holding masses, massacres the entire congregation to then burn not only the churches but commit the further Catholic blasphemy of burning the bodies in it."

"He is a mad fiend gone berserk!"

Cromwell had indeed shipped thousands of prisoners of war and political activists to West Indies labour camps. His scorched-earth policy throughout Ireland contributed to lack of food throughout the country, plague the result. Catholic landowners were dispossessed with the stroke of a quill, their lands given to New Army retirees.

With another stroke of the quill, Roman Catholicism was banned, churches either stripped of their Catholic trappings and replaced by Puritan Anglican or razed to rubble.

On return to London, he initiated a bill on Ireland that passed through both Houses. It included

No Catholic permitted to own land.
No Catholic permitted to vote
No Catholic permitted to hold public office
No Catholic permitted to work in Civil Service
No Catholic permitted to own a weapon
No Catholic permitted to own properties valued at more than five pounds
No Catholic permitted to be educated in or out of Ireland
No Catholic permitted to earn more than one-third the value of his crops
No Catholic permitted to practise as a lawyer
No Catholic facility permitted for training new priests
No foreign priests permitted to enter Ireland
Every Catholic must pay a tithe to the Anglican Church

From that day, priests entering Ireland from the Continent were hunted down, hanged, drawn and quartered in town squares.

~ * ~

Cromwell proved the new 'British Intent' was not only to occupy, govern and exploit Ireland but to eradicate the Celtic culture and superimpose Anglican culture upon the people totally alien to it. By guile, gun, coercion and quasi-legal manipulation, the British have attempted to divest the native Irishman of his language, his religion, his lore, his literature, his traditions and his customs. The ultimate goal, therefore, to first sterilize the Irish people, then rebuild them into Anglicans...

—from a pamphlet *The Ultimate Tyranny*, Brendan Sean Barrett, written in his prison cell in Manchester's Strangeways Prison, 1880.

~ * ~

Inflamed that Scotland had declared for Prince Charles, even declaring him King Charles II, Cromwell took an army to Scotland, trouncing its twenty-six-thousand-strong army. He left a resident army there. With both Ireland and Scotland now firmly in his grasp, he approved a handful of selected Scots to take places in the 'Rump' Parliament.

Returning with his army to England, he worked his way through Westmorland, sacking churches that had disobeyed the law in respect of practising any doctrine but extreme Puritan.

Churches reduced to rubble included Ravenstonedale's St. Oswalds.

In London, he was proclaimed Lord Protector of England, Scotland and Ireland.

Forty-four

The last two years had been trying times for the Brays.

Every effort had been made to assume normal routine and family camaraderie. Neither proved easy.

Soloman's memory lapse on most influences in his life continued shutting out most things.

He had spoken not a word, yet was slowly responding to other family members.

We had moved Mary and young Francis from their little home in the village, renting it out to a group of widows establishing a needlework service. In our 'new' wing of Bray House, we returned the various pieces of furniture used when Soloman and Mary occupied it after their marriage, hoping that something amongst it might jog some memory.

It had been extremely difficult for Mary, of course, trying to play the wifely part when he didn't remember her.

"Especially at bedtime," she at first needed to explain. "He accepts being told we are husband and wife, yet feels strange sharing a bed with me. He dares not touch me."

She was often in tears over the monstrous hurdle in their relationship.

"Should I fall asleep before him, he will leave the bed, lift Francis from his cot to cuddle down with him on the sofa. At least he has immediately taken to Francis."

He spent countless hours both indoors and out, staring at things like pieces of furniture, drapes and portraits, the many outbuildings, even the people—yardsmen, servants and all the family. His wife and mother were the two he would spend most time on, fingering their hair, their faces and hands, the rings, broaches, pendants and clothes they wore. Yet never spoke.

I had to quite retrain him to bathe frequently, pluck at his teeth with fishbones, tend his hair. He would spend hours watching the womenfolk do their own, and it was obvious he learned, for he would exactly copy their hairstyles with his own.

Many things he needed no instruction on. He remembered how to dress, to eat our various foods. He could quite remember how to read and write. We all were ever intrigued at the some things he found strange, yet others familiar.

However, happily for all was that he withdrew from none of us—even illustrating a need to accept our word on advice and directions.

Yet we all longed to hear him speak. We never made attempt to disguise conversations at mealtime. We included him when verbally or illustrating with hands any matter. I would ask him simple questions in the hope of one day getting a reply.

Fortunately the occasions he looked confused or frightened were rare. These mostly when abroad, shopping excursions or visiting friends.

He was coming around gradually. Francis was an immense help as he grew, forever asking questions as tots do, waiting for an answer.

"I get the feel it is going to be one of those occasions that we hear him speak," said Mary. "It is with Francis that he has most rapport. A blessing from God, I am sure."

Yet it wasn't to be.

It was during tea in the afternoon, basking in July sunshine, that something cropped up about the war. Liam had recalled how lucky we had been to have the lake persistently yielding up fish and eels. We all were so startled when Soloman grinned and announced, slowly but clearly, "Abel Mason certainly liked your eel pasties, Mother."

Oh, what a moment to remember!

~ * ~

From there, he came on marvellously. Not necessarily remembering incidents like that as much as the ease he was feeling with each of us.

"He is becoming our son again," I told Bea. "He is again beginning to think of us in our true relationship. And his relationship with Mary, for instance. He understands about Liam not being a brother but a brother-in-law. And understands, without it being explained, how and why Dickie and John are at Naseby rather than here."

"Yet he has never mentioned his work, do you notice?" Beatrix asked. "And chooses not to enter any conversation we are having about Oliver Cromwell, despite we get highly agitated at times. I wonder does he understand and deliberately hides the fact?"

We had agreed never to ask him if he remembered his accident.

"He certainly is aware of the scar, the bald patch he keeps fingering his hair over. Yet it is something he hasn't yet raised. I continue to feel we should leave it to him. He has enough to do just slotting things he does remember into their proper crannies."

Time from then moved more quickly. Our sadness at our boy's inability was no longer hovering like a cloud over our lives. We instead were imbued with a new gift of life. We felt him reborn, again needing our care to ensure he progressed along the right paths.

Inside, I yearned, however, to know what was in his mind on the political turmoil we faced. He had known Cromwell so well. I felt it hard to believe that all our dinner conversations about the fellow's actions in Ireland wouldn't have sparked some memory. Our comments were never guarded. He must have wondered why we were so vehemently castigating of Oliver Cromwell.

Beatrix grabbed me as I came in from spreading oats for old Twinkle-toes to forage for and began jigging around in a reel. She was laughing happily.

"Whatever has got into you, my dear?"

She looked over a shoulder, and then whispered, "Mary just told me she thinks she is pregnant again."

Oh, what wonderful news that was, on our boy's progress.

~ * ~

The year 1652 was a good one for us. In February, Mary delivered a daughter to Soloman. In June, Henry married. In November, John married.

Whilst many remained only irregular parishioners of All Saints, all realised that with only Puritan churches in the entire country, one had no option when it came to weddings, baptisms and funerals.

We were simply having to put up with what Cromwell wanted.

"Has the war really ended?" people would well keep asking.

"He is now at war with everyone but Puritans."

He had again marched his army into Parliament, arresting all who were not Puritans. The most recalcitrant of them he hanged. By the end of next year, he had us at war with the Dutch over trade differences.

Then he declared war on witchcraft. The Bible declared, in Exodus 22:18, *Thou shalt not suffer a witch to live.*

Cromwell's thugs were on constantly arresting any woman with a craving for lust, who were by habit spiteful or ill-natured, reported with healing powers, with warts or brown moles on their bodies— these supposedly where Satan had sucked them. And many more such categories. Those accused were tortured into admission and hanged if not burned. Women throughout the land were afeared for their lives.

In 1655, Cromwell, by now untouchable, dissolved Parliament and declared he would rule without it. Could anyone not believe these were the very actions Cromwell declared unconstitutional about King Charles? Yet nobody dare affront him.

Did he secretively believe himself there by God's right?

Forty-five

My world fell apart when my dearest Bea suffered a heart attack.

It was all so sudden. One minute she was arranging flowers she had brought from the garden in her creel, and next she fell to the floor.

I heard Anny, Beatrix's personal handmaiden who had been with us seemingly a hundred years, scream. I hurried, best I could, for I, too, was these days somewhat failing. There she was, crumpled in an untidy pile on the carpet.

I collapsed alongside her and hugged her to me before Anny helped me lay her supine.

"Water, Anny. Quickly, bring water."

I hurried to remove her shoes. I had heard tight shoes sometimes caused the heart to flutter.

Anny didn't move other than to pull a kerchief from her belt and wipe her sobbing eyes. "She is gone, sir. Already gone."

Mary came running. Then Jane. All the men were out on the fields.

My gut ached. It was tied in knots. The dryness of my tongue near choked me.

When the men were brought, they lifted her on to a settle. I got on my knees beside her and felt for her heart. I dreaded the confirmation yet needed convincing.

Yet hope had failed to linger.

Jane had fingers to my dearest's inside wrist.

Anny reached her fingers down and closed the eyes.

I stayed her hand.

I need one last look into those wonderful eyes before they too disappear forever.

Forever?

I suddenly realised I didn't want there to be a forever. My heart had also just died.

It didn't, although I desperately wanted it to.

But I was glad I was here and not having to be told it by others. I was with her to her very end.

Into my mind first flew a strange realisation. Before even thinking of getting word to my other children, my mind flew to letting the Calfes know. Was it fate bringing them to my mind? Fate reminding me that the Calfes were my beginning with her? That they should also be with her at the end?

I must have my dearest write them and…

"Oh," I said aloud. "She has really gone?"

Jane cuddled me.

I heard Mary say, "I'll get word to the others."

~ * ~

My Beatrix was laid to rest 29 April in our Lord's year of 1657.

I rued the fact Anthony Torrens was not at All Saints still, to recite the litany in our High Church ritual. But fate cannot always work in our favour.

"I will have a mausoleum erected in her honour," I told the children. "She earned it."

Meanwhile, she was interred in All Saints' earth. We filled her creel with daffodils and spring's rhododendron in a variety of colours, and I laid it on her coffin.

Through tears I watched my sons lower it, then cover it with earth.

Near every soul in Brixworth came. They loved her as did I.

~ * ~

The very next day, I made my last will and testament. Dearest had many times suggested I should.

"I shall have enough distress hovering over me without knowing the taxman will take more than his share. Nor facing the risk that our many sons might fall to bickering."

The very evening after the funeral, I called all together, telling Dickie to send his Anne and children home without him.

"I want to address all my sons."

I told them I would tomorrow venture to the town of Walgrave, where my lawyer resided, and make a will.

"Dickie, you already have title to the Naseby property, purchased solely at my expense. You have already contracted with John that he is an equal partner in Bray Grazing. So, John, that also is my contribution to you.

"Soloman, you already have title to your town estate, again purchased solely at my expense. You have your barrister's degree, paid for at my expense.

"Henry, for your diligent work at poor pay here, you will have Bray House. You will have opportunity to share the yet unused part of the Judkin property with Dickie.

"William, I will be naming you Executor of my estate and all my appurtenances on its land. There will provision for you and Henry to liaise on sharing."

As I rose to my feet, I felt every joint creak. Having buried my dearest, I'd spent the rest of the day planning my death.

Was I suddenly beginning to feel my age? Maybe I was. I had been conscious of late that not only my toes but fingertips seemed to be playing tricks on me. Toes had acquired a habit of getting cramps. Fingertips were becoming less sensitive. Yet I should expect it. I had enjoyed considerable health during my many years.

Leyton didn't last so long—I at least bested him.

~ * ~

Cromwell set about what he called the 'cleansing of England.' All religious trappings not conforming to his strict Puritanical code were to be destroyed.

"Another Reformation?" clamoured the people.

The north particularly suffered, as did all areas to support the Royals in the war. He alienated half the land by imposing a ten-percent tax on assets of all who had supported the King. The Puritanism that Cromwell imposed would change the lifestyle of all. It banned the few traditional pastimes people had left. Dancing of any description became totally illegal in all countries of the nation. Games of chance, including the playing of cards and dice games, were banned on the pain of death. Any sign of sexual interest publicly displayed could land either party in the stocks. Fornication became a whipping offence.

"One can find all the pleasure needed in life by walking the paths of righteousness," he proclaimed.

His "walking the paths of righteousness" included the smashing of not only church windows that contained hint of fleshly desire in their etchings but even the most magnificently crafted engravings in metal and stone. Gold and silver cups and altar embellishments designed in any but Spartan austerity were confiscated, precious metals melted down and altars reduced to rubble or kindling. In some cases, loved churches considered unduly 'frivolous,' those carrying carvings or etchings in any way ornate, were firstly torched and the standing masonry reduced to building blocks which the villagers were invited to use for building a church of austere lines. Masons who for all their lives had striven to carve the most ornate flowers, cherubs and aesthetically pleasing designs wept. Gravestones carved as such were smashed. Ancestral paintings in many a lordly mansion displaying even a hint of bosom despite this may well have been the height of fashion and grace in their time, even valuable paintings of the great masters, were confiscated and burned.

Cranmer's book of Common Prayer was declared too Papist and banned, supplanted by a less imaginative regimen. Traditional burial rites were replaced by a totally impersonal service, and marriage rites were banned in favour of a colourless exchange of vows. Musical instruments were confiscated and burned; the singing of other than Psalms was banned as was listening to music other than Psalms.

"Life under Puritans is proving more restrictive than Popery," the people bemoaned. "They have gone too far. They rob us of our very culture."

~ * ~

On 13 October 1657, not even six months after her mother's demise, Jane, sister of all the Brays and wife of Liam Penn, died after having suffered for many months a wasting disease.

"At but thirty-five years of age? Dear God, but you have made the world unfair. Why not take me too so I can be with my Beatrix?"

Did God hear?

Maybe so, because two weeks later, he took Yeoman Richard Bray.

Epilogue

The nation witnessed, on 3 September 1658, a dramatic end to the Civil War period. Cromwell died.

The country celebrated with bonfires, dancing, music and laughter.

The Commonwealth fell apart, and Charles II returned from exile to begin the next Restoration, unravelling the tangle of new, restrictive laws that so burdened the people. He had his father canonised—*Saint Charles Stuart and King Charles the Martyr*.

England's people, Royal supporters from day one, those who chose to consider it now best to 'go with the mob,' those who wished only to be on the winning side, the pragmatic who accepted that change meant adapting to new regimen, all over-reacted in a public sense, a peaceful and joyous over-reaction. They adopted a glaring rebuttal of Puritanism—necklines plunged and sexual freedom rampaged in streets and pubs.

The new King over-reacted as dramatically. On 12 January 1661, twelve years from the day Charles I was found guilty at the instigation of Oliver Cromwell, his son took revenge.

On that day, Cromwell's body was unceremoniously exhumed from its repose in Westminster Abbey, along with those of his son-in-law Henry Ireton and the President of the Regicide Court, John Bradshaw. The three corpses were dragged by their ankles to Tyburn and hanged on scaffolds, to swing to taunts and jibes of the crowd of thousands. At sunset, they were taken down and ceremonially beheaded. The bodies were drawn and quartered and then buried in Tyburn's common grave for criminals, the heads conveyed to Westminster Hall, where the King had been tried, and mounted on pikes.

Charles II then exacted a ruthless search-and-destroy mission of Parliamentary 'renegades' of the war years: dozens of Cromwell enthusiasts responsible for the execution of King Charles were hunted down with ruthless efficiency, and Tyburn's beheading block flowed red with blood for weeks.

~ * ~

'Dickie' Bray married three times, siring six children. He died at sixty-eight.

Soloman Bray married twice, siring three children. He died at seventy-nine.

John Bray sired ten children to two wives, all but three dying in infancy. He died at eighty-three.

It was a John Bray descendant who eventually married a descendant of Elizabeth Fothergill-Adamthwait.

Henry Bray married but once, siring two children, Solomon and William.

William Bray also had an only wife, bearing two daughters. He died at forty-seven.

Several generations down the line saw a Bray-Burgess daughter marry a Brixworth Richardson. They migrated to Australia in 1856. *An Epic Life* (Wings-Press ISBN978-1-59705-514-7) tells their story.

~ * ~

At Ravenstonedale in the temporary new church of St. Oswalds in 1682, George Fothergill's children placed a marble tablet:

Here lyeth the body of George Fothergill of Tarn House. Esquire of the Queen's Majesty's Receiver for Westmorland, Lancashire and Cumberland, who departed this life April 26, 1681.

Faith and Frenzy

In 1685, a Fothergill cousin was burned at the stake in Tyburn.

When St. Oswalds was rebuilt on the rubble of the old in 1744, a stained glass window incorporated this memorial:

To the glory of God and in memory of Mrs Gaunt, daughter of Anthony Fothergill of Brownber. She was the last female martyr burnt at Tyburn for the cause of the Protestant Religion, Oct 4, 1685.

She was Issaybell Fothergill, cousin to George of Tarn House. She had been arrested by agents of the "Iniquitous Judge Jeffries of the 'Bloody Assizes.' Her involvement and trial are reported in detail pp14-16 of *The Fothergills of Ravenstonedale* (see acknowledgements).

~ * ~

TRANSCRIPT of the WILL of Richard Bray... 1 May 1657

IN THE NAME OF GOD AMEN:

I Richard Bray of Brixworth, in the County of Northton yeoman I meane Richard Bray thelder calling to my remembrance the uncertaine state and Condicon of this transitory life, and considering withal that like as death is most certaine and assured to all creatures then soe is the time and place thereof most uncertaine and unknowne, willing therefore and minding by gods grace and assistance before my departure out of this life soe to dispose of that little which god of his great goodness and mercy has lent mee in this life, that the same may bee first pleasing to almighty god of heaven and earth to the reliefe and comfort of my children and Issue wich god of his infinite mercy hath blessed me withal and satisfaction to all men, being now in whole and perfect memory Both of mind and Body (thankes Bee to god therefore) doe this first day of May In the yeare of our Lord god one thousand six hundred fiftey and seaven make ordaine and declare this my last will and Testament in manner and forme following **ffirst**. I give and willingly bequeath my soule into the hands of almighty god my Creator hopeing through the death and passion of Jesus Christ His only sonne and my Saviour to obtaine pardon and foregiveness of all my sinnes and my body to the earth from whence it was made and to bee buried at the discretion of my Executor herein hereafter named and declared.

And for touching and concerning All my Landes Ten'ts and hereditum(ts) whatsoever in Brixworth aforesd and all the singular my goods and Chattles Cattles household goods cropps and all thinges else whatsoever that god of his mercy hath lent me or wich I have within the Realme of England I dispose and bequeath them as followeth.

I give and bequeath unto Richard Bray my eldest sonne one shilling. I give and Bequeath unto Soloman Bray my second sonne one shilling. I give and bequeath unto John Bray my third sonne one shilling I give unto Henry Bray my fourth sonne one shilling I give and bequeath unto Wm. Bray my fifth and youngest sonne one shilling. I give and bequeath unto ffrances Gunnell the wife of Edward Gunnell my daughter one shilling I give and bequeath unto Jane Pen my Daughter the now wife of Wm Pen one shilling all Lawfull money And I will that all and evry the sed legacy Bee payd to each prty to whom the same belong when hee shee or they shall demaund the same Lawfully or within one day after such Lawfull demaund made

I give and bequeath unto my beforename sonne Henry Bray and to his heires and Assignes forever that prte of the howse and homsted with the appurtnnce whatsoe thereunto belonging and appertaining now or late in the Tenure or accupacon of mee the sed Richd Bray thelder or my Assignes in Brixworth aforesd and wich I heretofore purch.... to mee and my heires for ever of my before named sonne Richd Bray by deede appear .... I alsoe give and bequeath unto my sd sonne Henry Bray and to his heires and Assignes (for)ever all that one halfe yard land with the appurtnance whatsoever thereunto belonging .... and being in the feildes and Boundaryes of Brixworth aforesd and wich I heretofore purchasd of Vallantine Judkin sonne and heire of Clement Judkin deceased wich sed half yard Land now in the Tenure of the sd Henry Bray wth the appurtnces PROVIDED yat nevertheless and my will and meaing is that the sd Henry Bray his heires or Assignes shall pay or cause to bee payd unto my sd sonne Wm Bray fforty powndes of Lawfull money of England within the time & space of three years to Bee accounted from the day of the date of this my Will and Testamt. And if Henry fails of the payment of the sed fforty pounds then I will and Bequeath the sd howse and Land before mentioned to Wm, and his heires for ever but if Henry pay the sd fforty Poundes to Wm according to the time Permitted aforesd then my will is that Wm. shall have nothing to doe with the pr misses but shall disclaime to Henry all his right or title wich hee shall or may have in or to the same according as my true intent and meaning is and live lovingly like friends and brothers. All the rest of my goods unbequeathed my debts and legacies being payd my funerell rites and ceremonyes ended I give and bequeath them solely and only unto my beforenamed sonne Willm Bray who I doe make and ordaine my sole and only EXECUTOR of this my will Desiring and intreating Mr Paterick our minister and John Lucas of our town to see that this my present last will & Testament bee really and truly prformed as my trust is it shall and I give each of them one shilling to Buy either of them a paire of gloves and I doe hereby disclaime and annihilate all former and other wills and Testms . By me made in IN WITNCE whereof to this my present last will and testamen the sd Richard Bray thelder have sett and putt my hand and seal the very day and yeare (first) above written In the presence of these witnesses whose names are under written signed & S ....

    Thomas [xxxx])   the marke of
    the mark of   ) all of Walgrave   Richard Bray
    Richard Mabbutt)   thelder
    Gme Ro. Langley)

Author's Note:
1) The above transcript is as true a literal copy of the original handwriting as is diligently possible. There is considerable time-worn damage to the parchment. The symbol '....' illustrates missing areas, and 'xxxx' indicates indecipherable words.

2) The references to pairs of white gloves in the will, I am told by English researchers, dates back to the fifteenth century. It was common for the deceased to leave funds for the purchase of white gloves by those officiating in the ceremony (clergy, pallbearers, etc), that his body pass, by courtesy of the gloves, unsullied by the trappings of human frailties.

3) Whilst later records affirm that his children were literate, Richard's mark on the will was of two vertical quill strokes. Each witness also signed with marks.

Meet Kev Richardson

A retired journalist, Kev Richardson continues writing. His several novels on the founding of white Australia's convict history are legendary. He spent many years touring the world writing travel articles for airline magazines, his experiences now the basis of his *Brogan* series of action/adventures, and more recently his *Beresford Branson* series. These are interwoven with biographies of significant people—results of his extensive family history research.

Kev has the distinction of having all his fifteen novels published to date awarded 5 stars or 5+, 5++ and even his latest, **My Red Cross**, a 10 star (first 10 star in the history of *Conger Book Reviews, USA*) All his books are available in both eBook and Paperback. He is twice married yet now enjoys a single life, relaxing in the Himalayan foothills of exotic Thailand. Two more titles are in the publishing pipeline and three more in work in progress.

Other Works From The Pen Of Kev Richardson

Letitia Munro (October 2008) - A true tale of Australia's first white settlement. In witless ignorance, convicts transform the world's biggest prison into a land of free enterprise and pride.

To Plough Van Diemen's Land (June 2009) - Children of convicts spawn a new ethos. Titia's descendants learn by surviving hard knocks and bad luck. Some fail, yet many convert empty pockets into acres of sheep. Social taboos become interwoven in the nation's spawning culture.

The Terrible Truths (December 2009) - Third in the *Letitia Munro* trilogy finds children and grandchildren swept up in the traumas of having to hide the truths of their heritage as societal values change. Australia emerges as a veritable beehive of mines as minerals of every description begin showering riches on the land.

Brogan (May 2007) - Life on Australia's desert edge. Brogan, born in the drifting sands of the far outback, exemplifies the blood-and-guts characteristics by which Aussies are recognised, even today.

Brogan's Bust (November 2007) - lying a courier service in the Amazonian jungles where graft and corruption make mockery of the law, Brogan finds backstabbing amongst cartel middlemen turns a hiccup into a stumble that generates into a fall to begin a slide that snowballs into an avalanche.

Brogan's Bella (March 2008)
Isabella and Brogan are victims in a deadly hijack. A carefree journey becomes a nightmare of death and terror. A year of incarceration and intimidation finds them facing the cutting of their very throats for even knowing the truths behind the hijack.

Brogan Abroad (February 2010) - A modern Brogan is embroiled in three simultaneous adventures. He plans none yet finds each destines him to having his throat slit in some dark alley. *Yet what can a man do,* he laments, *when to accomplish one I must fail at another?*

Misadventure (March 2011) - Brogan is off on a spine-tingling adventure in South America. He and his Becky hadn't counted on FARC taking hostages, military coups and drug-smuggling. This tale will really keep you turning pages.

Gerard Rawes (November 2010) - Gerard's life is transformed from rags to riches. In England's eighteenth century, the emerging industrial revolution catapults him out of his world of serfdom into London's elite.

An Epic Life (August 2010) - True tale of reaching across the world to fulfill dreams—a major achievement in the nineteenth century. Two couples whisk their very lives into a froth-and-bubble existence to create, on the far side of the world, a dynasty.

A Welcome War (May 2010) - Finalist in the EPIC Awards 2011 WW2 was the most welcome and alluring war of all time. A ten-year-old lad becomes influenced more by military strategy, political power, and bathos than by parents or mentors. "It beats schoolwork, hands down!"

Pacific Paradox (March 2012) - A British son is banished to the South Pacific to learn responsibility. Suffering hunger and kidnap, he is working in Guadalcanal when Japan invades.

My Red Cross (February 2013) - First 10-Star Award from Conger Book Reviews A Red Cross agent in France during German occupation faces intimidation, fear, love, hate and pleas for help. He is trying to be Father Christmas, Jesus Christ and everybody's parent, yet has little to give but hope.

Letter to Our Readers

Enjoy this book?

You can make a difference

As an independent publisher, Wings ePress, Inc. does not have the financial clout of the large New York Publishers. We can't afford large magazine spreads or subway posters to tell people about our quality books.

But, we do have something much more effective and powerful than ads. We have a large base of loyal readers.

Honest Reviews help bring the attention of new readers to our books.

If you enjoyed this book, we would appreciate it if you would spend a few minutes posting a review on the site where you purchased this book or on the Wings ePress, Inc. webpages at: https://wingsepress.com/

Visit Our Website
For The Full Inventory
Of Quality Books:

Wings ePress.Inc
https://wingsepress.com/

Quality trade paperbacks and downloads
in multiple formats,
in genres ranging from light romantic comedy
to general fiction and horror.
Wings has something for every reader's taste.
Visit the website, then bookmark it.
We add new titles each month!

Wings ePress Inc.
3000 N. Rock Road
Newton, KS 67114

www.ingramcontent.com/pod-product-compliance
Lightning Source LLC
Chambersburg PA
CBHW071152070526
44584CB00019B/2757